Master Musicians of India

Hereditary Sarangi
Players Speak

Regula Burckhardt Qureshi

University of Alberta, Canada

Routledge
Taylor & Francis Group
New York   London

Routledge
Taylor & Francis Group
270 Madison Avenue
New York, NY 10016

Routledge
Taylor & Francis Group
2 Park Square
Milton Park, Abingdon
Oxon OX14 4RN

Printed in the United States of America on acid-free paper
10 9 8 7 6 5 4 3 2 1

International Standard Book Number-10: 0-415-97202-7 (Softcover) 0-415-97201-9 (Hardcover)
International Standard Book Number-13: 978-0-415-97202-4 (Softcover) 978-0-415-97201-7 (Hardcover)

Library of Congress Cataloging-in-Publication Data

Qureshi, Regula Burckhardt.
   Master musicians of India : hereditary sarangi players speak / Regula Burckhardt
Qureshi.
      p. cm.
      Includes bibliographical references (p.   ) and index.
      ISBN 0-415-97201-9 -- ISBN 0-415-97202-7
      1. Sarangi players--India--Interviews. 2. Sarangi players--Education--India. I.
Title.

ML398.Q74 2007
787.6'1690954--dc22   2006031356

Visit the Taylor & Francis Web site at
http://www.taylorandfrancis.com

and the Routledge Web site at
http://www.routledge-ny.com

Contents

List of Plates

Acknowledgments

The Study

Many people have contributed to making this book a reality. First and foremost I thank the master musicians themselves for their personal interest and continuing support in helping me learn their music by including me into their world, accommodating my short time lines and deficient memory, and permitting my use of tape and video recording. My special thanks go to their families for their background support and hospitality, above all to the late Mrs. Sabri Khan, daughters Farzana and Babli, and their four brothers: Ghulam Sarvar, Jamal, Kamal, and Gulfam; Ram Narayan's daughter-in-law; Dhruba Ghosh's mother and his late father, Nikhil Ghosh; and Archana Singh's late mother Mrs. Adhar.

Next, I want to extend my gratitude to my Indian family and friends who, from 1965 onwards, enabled me to connect and study with sarangi masters and, on subsequent visits, to reactivate permanent bonds of familiarity and extend them to my teachers. In Lucknow, my heartfelt thanks go to my parents-in-law Saeed Ahmed Qureshi and Siddiqa Khatoon (Bajia), and to our most dedicated friend Khalique Ahmad, as well as to the late Mahmud Raza, Parveen Talha, and above all Muhammad Rehan "Tuti," who assisted me with documentation and video recording in both Lucknow and Delhi. In Karachi, I gratefully acknowledge the late Husna Bano Jamil (Ammi), Haseena Sheriff, and Sheriff Enayatullah who organized my study with Hamid Husain, as well as singer and patron Muhammad Iqbal, a close disciple of Hamid Husain from Bombay.

My father-in-law also introduced me to my first music institution, Lucknow's Bhatkhande Music College, where I was fortunate to meet and learn from principals Pandit Ratanjankar and S.S. Awasthi and later observed many classes. Also to be recognized are V.V. Shrikhande, principal, and Ashok Banerjee, research officer of the Uttar Pradesh Sangeet Natak Akademi, who shared the academy's interviews with musicians with me. In Delhi, I owe a huge debt of gratitude to Shabi Ahmad of the Indian Council for Historical Research, who has been an invaluable friend and research associate since 1975. Thanks are due as well to my friend and colleague Dr. Shubha Chaudhury, director of the Archive and Research Centre for Ethnomusicology, one of several music institutions that expanded my horizon on music research in India. I also wish to acknowledge the good fortune to have known, and learned from, three great musical figures in Delhi; Acharya Bhrashpati, Naina Devi, and Dr. Kapila Vatsyayan. In Bombay I was fortunate to benefit from two major Indian music institutions and their leaders: the National Center for Performing Arts and its then director Ashok Ranade (where I taught ethnomusicology in 1988), and Sangeet Research Academy West, through excellent seminars regularly organized by Arvind Parikh, himself a leading musician taught in the hereditary milieu.

Finally, I want to thank my fellow Western sarangi players and researchers who have generously shared experiences and advice, particularly Joep Bor, Nicholas Magriel, and most of all Daniel Neuman, who has shown me how a Western disciple can take care of his teacher and fellow disciples. It remains for me to acknowledge funding for this field project from the Social Science and Humanities Research Council as well as from the Shastri Indo-Canadian Institute.

The Book

In creating the English from spoken Urdu/Hindi, I gratefully acknowledge the expert assistance of Mridula Nath Chakrabarty in translating the conversations in Hindi (Chapter 10, Hanuman Prasad; Chapter 9, Bhagvan Das and Santosh Kumar; and portions of Chapter 5, Dhruba Ghosh). Sincere thanks are also due to Vinod Bhardwaj and Robina Virk for translating from Hariyanavi (song by Shabbir Husain in Chapter 2), and to Shyam Pandit and Srishti Nigam for Hindi bhajans (Santosh Kumar in Chapter 9). Since all translations were made from audio recordings (including the written memoirs of Hamid Husain, which are only extant in my recorded reading), translation also required transcriptions from the original Hindi or Urdu in the appropriate scripts. Words were often unclear or unfamiliar to all but musical insiders, requiring extensive and intensive reviews, checks, and consultation with the authors as well as with music specialists and linguistic-cultural insiders. My sincere thanks go to colleagues, family, and friends for this help, but most of all to Saleem Qureshi, whose superb linguistic competence and cultural insight continues to inform and improve my understanding of texts and their contexts.

Preparing the book itself was a major journey requiring research assistance at various stages, most ably provided by Jonathan Dueck, Allison Fairbairn, Karim Gillani, Veronica Pacheco, Niyati Dhokai, and Nicole Vickers. I thank them all. And I particularly wish to acknowledge Michelle Kennedy's excellent editorial feedback and suggestions for each chapter, as well as Amelia Maciszewsky's thorough drafting of the glossary. Above all, I appreciate Kaley Mason's impeccable and always thoughtful editorial review and care of manuscript preparation in all its aspects. My colleagues Daniel Neuman, Harold Powers, Martha Feldman and Bonnie C. Wade, were most helpful in providing reading reports to the publisher. I was fortunate to get Bonnie Wade's always insightful as well as useful advice on this project and manuscript at various stages. At Routledge, I much appreciated working with editors Constance Ditzel, Devon Sherman, and Jennifer Genetti, as well as former editor Richard Carlin. The final kudos go as with all my Indian work, to Saleem Qureshi and to a transcultural partnership that has enriched my research, because it is my life.

Note on Transliteration and Musical Notation

Transliteration is a simplified adaptation of Platt's *A Dictionary of Urdu, Classical Hindi and English* (1977), using his integrated scheme for both Urdu and Hindi, but with minimal diacritics marking long vowels for the sake of easy reading. Urdu and Hindi terms are italicized at first occurrence. Italics are also used in the chapters to set off introductory and descriptive passages from the main text.

Musical notation is in the form of the Indian solfa system, accompanied in parentheses by numbers identifying the scale degrees which correspond to the Western major scale:

sa	re	ga	ma	pa	dha	ni	sa
1	2	3	4	5	6	7	8

For ease of reading altered scale degrees are not marked in the notation, but they are identified for each raga in the Glossary at the end of this book.

As is standard in Indian notation, a dash (-) represents one durational count, usually executed as a prolongation of the previous note rather than a pause.

Fonts are used to distinguish different modalities within speech utterances as well as between speech and action. The default setting for the musicians' texts is a non-italicized font, while my introductory paragraphs are in italics, as are my descriptions and annotations conveying the relevant actions that accompany the conversations. Within the text, words in Urdu/Hindi are set off by italics, while in the introductory sections—which are already italicized—Urdu/Hindi words are not italicized to create the same distinction. Words delivered with special emphasis are italicized.

Quotation marks in the form of standard double quotes denote direct speech quoted within the text. Single quotes are used to identify English expressions used by the speaker while speaking Urdu/Hindi, in order to give the reader a sense of the spoken language. For the same reason uniquely expressive or pithy Urdu/Hindi terms are highlighted by inclusion in the text along with their English translation.

Figure 1 Map of South Asia with locations relevant to this book.

Preface

This book is a labor of love—love for Indian music; love for its glorious bowed instrument, the sarangi; and above all, love and gratitude for the hereditary musicians who have been my teachers. They have generously agreed to present themselves and their oral knowledge on these pages. The book is a homage to these masters; it celebrates their central role as the living source of Indian music.

There are compelling reasons why the words of these artists should reach the minds and hearts of music lovers outside the traditional world of Indian musical communities. First and foremost, they are my teachers; they have welcomed me into their world and included me into their lives. The words in this book are part of what they have taught me as their disciple and as a student of their instrument, the sarangi. I owe them a debt of gratitude, and a commitment to promote their remarkable art and knowledge.

Second, these artists are the direct bearers of the Indian musical heritage, an essentially oral tradition. Both their collective knowledge and their individual experience shed important new light on the life of Indian music. But these musicians speak; they don't write. Their words and their wisdom remain integrated into their teaching of the oral practice that is their music. Their performances may be recorded, but their words are rarely heard in the wider discourse of music, which is framed by bourgeois elites and situated within modern institutions of musical learning. The few exceptions are found embedded in writings by (mostly) foreign disciples (Bor 1986–1987; Kippen 1988; Neuman 1990; Rai 1983; Sorrell and Narayan 1980). Disseminating their knowledge has been a challenge.

Unlike sitar and tabla, the sarangi remains little known outside the music community, despite the wide appeal of its rich sonority. And until today, its unique practice and rich palette of idioms can only be learned from its own hereditary experts.

Third, and most immediately crucial, sarangi playing has become a vanishing art. Sarangi players may be a uniquely intact hereditary community, but their patronage has dwindled. Several of my teachers have taken their knowledge to the grave. And poor survival prospects have forced entire hereditary sarangi communities to stop teaching the instrument to their children while the sarangi has remained an outsider to the booming amateur and school music movement in India.

At the same time, the horizon of the sarangi is expanding. International exposure and recordings are offering new opportunities to some players. Support from Indian cultural institutions, including two groundbreaking conferences on the sarangi, is generating new awareness and patronage (Uttar Pradesh Sangeet Natak Akademi, Lucknow; Bharat Bhavan 1989; Rai 1983). My book joins these initiatives.

The fact is that Indian music has become a world music, and even the sarangi is becoming part of Western music curricula (Rotterdam Conservatory; University of Alberta). Globalization, however, is sustained through living local practice and by what they call tradition: the way it comes down (*chala a raha hai*). This book speaks of local practice by musicians who literally embody tradition. It does so through the voices of individuals, outstanding artists and teachers, each of whom makes his own history in a changing world. Unmediated by scholarly discourse, they offer their words spoken in lively interactive situations of teaching and learning, argument and laughter. Through their words I want to draw the reader into the special magic of their music room, where making music, making performers, and making music history is a family affair.

But the world of the music room and its conversations are entirely oral and personal; they remain elusive for those not related through ties of family or discipleship—and for those not conversant in Urdu and Hindi. I was fortunate to be able to record my teachers' words while they taught me as their disciple and as a student of their oral tradition. My interactions with these teachers was especially fortuitous because today's new generation of musicians can no longer sustain the close-knit hereditary milieu of their fathers.

Discovering Orality: An Indian Experience

Two paths joined together to make my entry into this musical world possible: one is my own musical formation; the other, more elusive, has to do with my Indian enculturation. As a musician focused professionally on a bowed string instrument (cello), I brought to India an abiding urge to make sense of this music and what it means, both to players and listeners, but above all to me. Music had to become my personal connective with India.

But that was after I had tasted life in India and in Pakistan, the twin homes of one with familial ties across their borders, and after intensive study of Urdu. In truth, my enculturation started with Urdu poetry, with verses informally recalled and recited to say something special, to capture a moment of shared conversation and make it memorable. This spontaneous poetic conversing introduced and then bonded me to Indian ways of being—and to one of oral poetry's outstanding practitioners and interpreters, Saleem Qureshi. As a Western musician raised on the solitary literacy of print culture, I was instantly attracted to this Indian sonic practice, where poetry is at the same time deeply personal and actively social, literary and oral, and philosophical as well as convivial.

The jump from words to music followed naturally, for both were intimately connected within the milieu of postfeudal connoisseurship to which Saleem belonged. Music making, too, was spontaneously interactive and social, even when deliberately learned and abstractly structured. But unlike a verse, this improvised music defied verbal interpretation. How to enter the inner circle of musical speakers, of musicians, became an ongoing pursuit through cycles and spheres of learning. In the process, my focus gradually and inevitably expanded from sonic competence to the dynamic of musical performance, and then to music makers as cultural agents confronting social and historical forces.

My search for connecting with musical otherness in India began well before the Beatles, when Indian music was little known in the West. The sounds of Saleem's Indian recordings had remained irritatingly contrary to my musical aesthetic. But during our first summer in his city, Lucknow, a visit to the famous Bhatkhande Music College showed me another way into the music: learning an instrument.

I discovered the sarangi in the hands of Mirza Mahmud Ali, a striking old man clearly at sea within the classrooms of Lucknow's famous Bhatkhande Music College and their orderly lessons. I immediately saw the sarangi as a successor to my cello that had bonded me in Switzerland with the intense Hungarian émigré Paul Szabo and then in the U.S. with the affective mastery of Leonard Rose. My first lesson with the old man's son, Mirza Maqsud Ali, began a young musician's journey into Indian music and into discipleship. A second visit enabled me to learn briefly from the already renowned Pandit Ram Narayan in Bombay. But it was Ustad Hamid Husain in Karachi who accepted and taught me as a ritually sanctioned disciple. I humbly entered my teachers' worlds on their terms, for my goal was personal formation, not ethnography, and my music was not for scholarly scrutiny.

Their teaching of music was inevitably also a teaching of culture and of society. When, two graduate degrees later, I returned for an intensive reconnecting with sarangi training—perhaps a second chance at becoming a real sarangi player—it was as an ethnomusicologist with an ethnographic goal. Since my beloved ustad had died, I sought out the renowned Ustad Sabri Khan who, as a distant relative, could provide musical continuity. Studying in his Delhi home, surrounded by his family and disciples, was real participation in hereditary training.

At the same time, a project to explore "the musical and social life of the sarangi" led me to Hanuman Prasad Mishra in Benares, and in Lucknow to Bhagvan Das Mishra, (with his son Santosh Mishra and his female student Archana Yadav), as well as to Bahadur Khan and to Yaqub Husain and Munawwar, both relatives of my very first teacher. In Bombay I returned to Pandit Ram Narayan and later connected with Dhruba Ghosh and Sultan Khan. My deep personal thanks go to all these artists for the gift of their music and knowledge. Most of all, I owe thanks to my Ustad Sabri Khan and his whole family, and especially his disciples, foremost his son Kamal Sarvar Sabri, as well as his nephews Nasir Khan and Ghulam Sabir, and the late Shabbir Husain.

I also received much help from sarangi players who could not be included in this book: Ghulam Sabir Qadri and Inder Nath Dhandra in Delhi; Altaf Husain, Jai Narayan Mishra, Kanhayya Lal Mishra, and Rameshwar Prasad Mishra in Lucknow; Baijnath Mishra in Benares; Masit Khan in Bombay; Buland Iqbal, Umrao Bundu Khan, and Zahid Husain in Karachi; and Nabi Bakhsh, Nathu Khan, and Nazim Ali Khan in Lahore. My sincere thanks go to all of them.

The 1990s, finally, enabled me to bring the two worlds together, literally. Both our worlds had expanded: my teachers and even their children were now touring, teaching, and even living abroad. Sabri Khan's sons were touring abroad; he himself had been a visiting professor in the U.S.; Sultan Khan had joined his old partner instrument, the tabla, in a world success with Zakir Husain; and Ram Narayan's daughter had moved to Canada. On my end, I was establishing Indian music and ethnomusicology in my university; and both my teachers and I attended conferences on the survival of the sarangi across northern India.

My commitments of an academic appointment and the challenge of institutionalizing Indian music turned the vision back on itself: Indian musicians, including sarangi players, have entered a world of Indian music in the West, breaking the fence of their Indian culture garden, and our worlds have converged in a global ethnoscape of music. Voice, subjectivity, strategy, and agency were theirs as much as mine, whether we sat in my house or theirs. From an ethnographic present in which they enacted their traditions to an outsider in India, our interactions had become part of a global expansion of Indian music.

The conversations in this book, then, offer uniquely personal encounters with individual agents of this history. This is not to deny the broader goal of writing a historical study of hereditary music making and its transformations. But how could I subject my beloved teachers to the harsh gaze of poststructuralist theorizing? How could I turn affect and shared aesthetic experience into anthropological data? This dilemma had me put interpretation on hold for a different priority: honoring my commitment to the individuals who make interpretation possible in the first place, to let them be heard on their own authority, not as representatives of a collectivity or as quotations in a scholarly argument.

I am grateful for my teachers' assent to presenting their oral wisdom in print. May this book convey a sense of their enthusiasm, their wisdom, and their art as they create and transmit the life of their music. May it also help support that life.

Introduction

Hereditary Oral Knowledge: A Global Perspective

Indian music has two distinct musical systems: Hindustani and Karnatak, or North and South Indian music. Of the two, Hindustani music is regionally dominant, extending across Pakistan, Bangladesh, Nepal, and, to an extent, even Afghanistan. This classical musical heritage has for centuries been a hereditary specialization among communities of musicians serving landed patrons, including princes and royalty. Children are born into an environment of musical immersion and taught to become professionals by their father or a family elder.[1] In a process of transmission that has been entirely oral, they learn the musical system like a language and later teach it to their children[2]—rarely also to a dedicated student from outside the community. Today hereditary musicians continue to prevail at the top of musical competence, but under conditions of reduced or fundamentally altered public patronage by the Indian state that has attracted a vast contingent of middle-class performers, many of whom have themselves become disciples of hereditary masters, recognizing the inimitable qualities of the oral hereditary milieu even as its existence is threatened with extinction.[3] At the same time, Hindustani musicians have had increasing access to patronage abroad, extending their reach across continents into the expanding sphere of world music.

This preamble draws a global frame around a very local story by and of hereditary Indian musicians. The story is about the private life of a music that today inhabits the world. Indian art music has joined its Western counterpart as a second language of art music circulating in the global sphere of public culture.[4] Its audiences, students, and patrons are a multisited constituency that includes universities, art communities, and the global ethnoscape (Appadurai 1996) of South Asian diasporas with its dynamic connections to the homeland.

What does Hindustani music bring to the world of art music? In an intriguing way this music is both ancient, conservative to the extreme, and governed by the strictest rules; at the same time it is totally contemporary, created at the moment of performance as an expression of individual creativity. The global success of Hindustani music clearly lies in this combination of a highly elaborated, aestheticized, theorized, and professionalized musical language of melodic (*raga*), rhythmic (*tala*), and compositional (*bandish*) repertoires with equally elaborated but highly flexible procedures for generating musical structures in performance (i.e., improvisation). This improvisational capability is based on total retention and recall of all aspects of musical knowledge; it's all in the head, as Ustad Sabri Khan says, and so concentrated that it could fit into a small cup—nothing is written down, and nothing else is needed.[5]

What further distinguishes Hindustani music is its uncompromising, self-consciously Indian sonic and semantic identity. A crucial part of this identity is conveyed in improvisational dialogue between musicians and, most important, between musicians and listeners, where musicians both speak and respond to their listeners. This flexible enactment of an art music system is rooted in the integrity and creativity of its oral transmission, so that in a Canadian discussion on Indian music and culture, the outstanding young hereditary sitarist Shujaat Husain could simply point to himself and say: I am Indian culture.

Globalization is a Western-dominated enticement to join the gallery of "world music" artists on the terms of what is marketable according to the parameters of the global concert stage and record bin. Hereditarily trained Hindustani musicians, from Ali Akbar Khan and Ravi Shankar onwards, have been masters at responding to world audiences and patrons, thanks to their improvising skills (read: compositional versatility). At the same time they have been shaping these audiences, using the same skills to expand their listeners' earscapes and time sense from brisk, brief, and modally simple "pieces" to slow, hour-long raga elaborations. They have created a following for their instruments in the West, including the sarangi—despite its low status in India.[6] And some have increasingly taken control of their own music in cross-musical collaborations that go under the name of "fusion" but are becoming bimusical conversations among equals.

In the face of this successful expansion, why present a most intimately localized and personal account of hereditary musicians now? Because it is exactly when they are at their most global that Indian musicians need to tell us who they are and what their music means. How has this core identity of Hindustani music been passed down; what is that milieu; and how did, and do, individuals emerge from it as finished artists equipped to take on the world? In other words, what history of their music do they bring to the global musical mix? Where are the historical sources for the processes of oral transmission of this improvisatory music?

There is a considerable literature on Indian music and its history, generated by formally educated scholars and performers from outside the hereditary milieu who have drawn from discipleship with hereditary masters and adapted that knowledge to the needs of the national cultural establishment and its educated middle-class constituency.[7] But individual discipleship remains the way to professional excellence, and the hereditary milieu remains the acknowledged source of the Hindustani oral tradition/ heritage. I know no better validation of this claim than the publication of an invaluable book, entitled *Musicians of India, Past and Present*, which contains nothing but annotated genealogical tables of musical lineages, including their proliferating nonhereditary disciples (Dasasarma 1993).

The history of this orally transmitted music as a global music begins at home, literally, in conversations with the tradition's practitioners. To bring their hereditary milieu to life, however, requires a different history, one that presents the discipular and familial interaction in their context, in which musicians themselves do the talking, interactively and, yes, improvisationally.

What makes knowing their stories particularly important is that it connects the present world expansion and the translocality between home and work sites that Hindustani hereditary musicians have practiced within India for well over a century, under feudal rule. Does this mean that their family networks could be adapted globally? Or will the impact of global expansion further strain musical family ties, and with what effect on musical transmission and execution?

In order to include these processes within a global horizon of musical thinking, the still Western-dominated idea of music history as a linear textual chain of antecedents needs to be opened up to the possibility of a history of music as embedded within a family group and repertoire being stored not in a library with a text, but in a brain with a context; being learned not from books, but from orally transmitted words that are being generated not declaratively but interactively. In other words, it is a history that is based on ethnography, in the vein of initiatives to bring ethnomusicology and musicology, or anthropology and history, into dialogue.[8] This kind of history demands its own, different set of premises, where the social is not separate from the musical, where continuity is not a time line, but a network expanding in both time and place, linking many sites where each site is an intimate local family universe.

This book makes a beginning toward such a history for Hindustani music, based on an extended study of four decades (mid-1960s to 1990s) that is itself transnational, but is focused on the local hereditary anchoring of this oral music and on the local strength from which its musicians have made the history they have shared with me in their own words and interactions. To become a primary historical source that is readable cross-culturally requires translating this knowledge into a text that conveys their agency with both comprehensibility and ethnographic integrity, while acknowledging the challenges to musical understanding and presentation that come with entering a milieu of study where all learning is always personal. The global frame has emerged naturally from my teachers themselves, through their easy acceptance of the global expansion of their music, and also through their concern for a global understanding of its integrity. This makes local foundations all the more crucial to record and support—which is what this book is all about.

Looking for a Dialogic Ethnomusicology

To realize the goals of this project in an accessible way, they first of all need to be gathered into a genre appropriate to presenting outstanding performers and teachers, individuals who embody one of the world's great musical cultures. *Master Musicians of India: Hereditary Sarangi Players Speak* is a book that combines—as well as struggles between—three quite different genres of writing that target musical/cultural protagonists: biography, interviews, and that special genre of ethnomusicology: discipular ethnography.

First, this is a book about individual musicians, or, more accurately, composer-performers. Thus it fits the traditional musicological genre of biography or "life and works" studies—here not of one individual, but a group of related artists (the Bach family, the Russian school) who themselves acknowledge strong musical and social bonds with their artistic group. Their creative and professional lives are showcased for both information and inspiration, based on an assumption not only of individual competence but of inherent cultural, musical value. But here the biographical will to chronology is sidelined by the central presence of the musicians' words about themselves, presented in direct speech. This makes the musicians themselves the authoritative voice while marginalizing, if not eliminating, the writer's interpretive preeminence, or at least reducing her verbiage.

Books of interviews with musicians and artists most commonly take the shape of verbal portraits painted by individual artists of themselves with due guidance by the interviewer. Interviews can also be turned into a collage of primary source information on an artistic practice, as envisioned by the author who does the mosaic (Berliner 1993; Gitler 1985). Either way, artists' interviews tend to be a reified and unproblematized genre (oriented to culture-historical consensus, artistic image, and audience preferences). What is rarely addressed—or is taken for granted—is the (cross-) cultural and social context that surrounds and informs individuals' words and actions, not excluding the guiding hand of an interviewer and a compiler's topical agenda.

The musicians' words are more than interviews elicited for the purpose of appropriate representation for a book. They are conversations, lessons, life situations negotiated through verbal interaction. All these "speech acts" are exchanges between individual musical protagonists and their interlocutor, me, their student, a term that here covers personal discipleship, informal studentship, and research inquiry; it also covers a relationship marked by the acquired insidership of a quasi-"halfie" (Abu-Lughod 1991) [9]. These, then, are personal conversations taking place in very specific contexts; at the same time, their effects are suprapersonal in that they engender the very milieu in which their music lives. More than words about music and musicians, they are the stuff of musical action itself, warts and all.

Ethnographic access to this musical world is mediated by discipleship, a central practice in ethnomusicology that is foundational to numerous important studies, especially in India (Brown 1965; Kippen 1988; Neuman 1990; Powers 1959; Slawek 2000). If not the primary reason for field research, learning to sing or play has contributed to the formation of authors as disciples who pursue capitalized and lower-case "culture" in tandem, compromising the observational and relativist stance of anthropology with the cultural idealism of humanists and the shop talk of fellow musical practitioners. We absorb our teachers' words to learn their music, we capture them as an authentic manifestation of their lifeways, and we hold them up as interpretive truth of cultural experts. In the process, we become the master's voice.

Discipular ethnographies are less explicit about the process by which their words became ours. The starting point is clearly recording technology; after all, we are after the sounds people make and how we make those sounds ourselves. Capturing music lessons on tape has long been standard procedure for reproducing our teachers' words no less than their music. More generally, recording what our "informants" tell us in the field has long been the crucial ethnographic tool of learning about others; in Clifford Geertz's words, "We can but listen to what … they say about their lives" (1986: 373).

But sharing their words with our readers is another matter. Conversations or interviews, even of celebrities, have at most a marginal existence in ethnographic literature. "We don't publish transcribed field recordings," was a normal reaction to my proposal for this book. Behind it is a prevailing consensus that to record streams of directly given cultural materials amounts to what Geertz terms "a text-positivism that won't do." For this quintessential interpreter of culture, "the burden of ... telling the reader what it is others are saying" is not so easily shed (1986: 374).

The burden of textualizing others has been lightened considerably by the received mandate for ethnomusicologists as well as anthropologists to produce, for Western consumption, the generalizations about (social and racial) "others" that are subsumed within the term "culture." Such "ethnographic authority" comes at a price, however. James Clifford points to the fundamental dilemma of textualizaton: it subsumes individuals encountered in the field within typifications and inevitably banishes dialogical and situational aspects that lie at the core of any ethnographic encounter (Clifford 1983). How can these be recovered? That situations of interlocution should themselves be textually represented amounts ultimately to a call for ethnographers to relinquish a power position and to unravel the typifications of "culture" altogether (Abu-Lughod 1991).

The subsequent debate over agency and appropriate representation has been strongly focused on individuals, which is in line with the individually located sense of Western subjectivity (Crapanzano 1980; Dumont 1978; Rabinow 1977). To counter the quasi-scientific practice that considers informants as "a case of the general," ethnographers have been moving toward respectful portrayals, calling for new forms of writing to convey the particulars of individuals' lives (Abu-Lughod 1991). The most direct response to the concern for agency has been a search for new strategies toward having research partners speak for themselves.

How Can the Informant Speak?

Ethnographers have long elicited and recorded oral texts as primary sources of normative cultural information (Boas 1966). To convey authoritative documentation, these texts were made subject to a wide range of representational tactics. Informants' words have been turned into topically arranged summaries or edited into coherent statements in answer to the ethnographer's (often omitted/ unrecorded) questions (Griaule 1965). More contextualized ways of including informants' voices are found in works that embed conversational passages within ethnographic accounts, whether they pursue a theme or the portrayal of that very individual (Dumont 1978; Lortat-Jacob 1995). A number of remarkable "portraits" of individuals (Crapanzano 1980; Shostak 1983) nevertheless lack clarity as to the ethnographer's control over topics of conversation, not to mention the (in most cases necessary) presence of a translator, turning the dialogue into an unacknowledged ménage à trois.

A significant shift initiated by sociolinguists has been the textual representation of what informants say to ethnographers as speech events (Bauman and Sherzer 1989) rather than as depersonalized and timeless cultural materials. Exploring language performance, the "ethnography of speaking" is focused on shared more than on individually unique verbal features, but it introduced local, temporal contexts into speech documents, thereby opening a vista of dialogue as ethnographic process involving all participants, scholars included (Darnell 1989).

Dennis Tedlock extends this concern with textual integrity to the general domain of ethnography and its excess of interpretation. His concept of "dialogic anthropology" includes full published dialogues that occurred face to face between ethnographers and informants so as give readers uncompromised access to the texts that form the basis of authorial interpretation in the first place (Tedlock and Mannheim 1995: 262). Such access will enable readers to focus reinterpretation on the words of the ethnographic subjects rather than their interpretation by the ethnographer whose words tend to dominate by their mass and coherence (Tedlock and Mannheim 1995: 257). Recorded dialogues offer the best opportunity to let informants speak for and about themselves with more words than the ethnographer; that alone is a bonus. Dialogues also expose the ethnographer's actual role in conversations and helps reveal what she is prepared to observe (Dumont 1978) in the "field," so that the reader can identify the consciousness that has shaped the fieldwork in the first place.

All this being said, first-person texts by informants are not necessarily monuments of agency. To begin with, their very existence in recorded form conjures up questions of ownership. Easily produced with or without participants' consent, recorded conversations, like musical performances, are a special kind of cultural property that impose serious responsibilities as regards conditions of use, even if permission has been granted. What should be selected, and by whom, in turning living speech into ethnographic information addressed now to a culture-external scholarly reader on whose approval the possibility of a publication will depend? In most cases, the ethnographer ends up in charge of creating the publication, even when the text is mostly, or at least jointly, authored by her informants. No matter how dialogic the representation, the representor is its agent, since creating an ethnographic text is the very raison d'être of her ethnographic work.

In preparing such a text, can the ethnographer serve two masters: her research partners and her academic constituency? Can she provide textual integrity for informants while also crowding the text with explanatory interlocution and editorial interference, not to mention translation from the original language—all in pursuit of "cultural translation" for the outside reader?

I believe that this is ultimately not an issue of textualization. The crux is the ethnographic relationship itself, especially given differentials of power as well as of culture. Michael Asch (2001), who draws on his work with Native Canadians as well as on Buber (1958) and *Levinas* (Hand 1989), posits a "relational I" that stands always in a "face-to-face" relationship with "other" through respect and dignity even while also accepting irreducible differences between each other, and even after leaving the "field." Above all, our relationship must be just. Thus respect for cultural otherness is important if that otherness is part of what I see as the other's equivalent humanity to my own. But "reliance on cultural difference does not necessarily promote a just relationship" (Asch 2001). Indeed, acknowledging, even respecting difference can also serve to essentialize cultural others in their "culture gardens" (Fabian 1983). Enabled by a position of power, an ethnographer's violence of difference can be as objectifying as the violence of the same (Agawu 1995).

The notion of a relational self posits self-affirmation through relations with another who sets limits to my capacity for free action. Interestingly, this happens to be the dominant concept governing Indian musical teaching and learning. The master-disciple bond is sanctified through the ritual of "tying the thread"; it makes this mutual commitment explicit by invoking metaphoric family ties. And how to reciprocate the teacher's generosity is an ongoing part of the hereditary training process in Indian music. As an ethnomusicologist, I need only to continue to stand in the place of a disciple facing her Indian teachers and factor those conditions of our relationship into my subsequent professional relationships, a triangulation in which I must mediate between the demands of two relational roles. The text of this book represents such an attempt at mediation, along with the restraint that responsibility toward others entails.

Refamiliarizing Ethnographic Representation

Ethnography is centrally a product of verbal encounters in which statements are made with a purpose to a specific listener (or more than one) who is also an actor in the encounter. Hence my textual presentation must factor in conversational and lesson partners and set the context for their statements. The primary listener and conversation partner is myself, situated in two, often overlapping learning contexts, one focused directly on the instrument and its music, the other one focused on the world of the musician, his music and instrument.

In a sense, then, this book is—*pace* Geertz—inevitably a fieldwork account focused on one or more individual research partners through the text of our conversations. Ethnomusicologists have produced a variety of such accounts (Frisbie and McAllester 1978; Rice 1994; Vander 1988). Here I want to steer the genre toward a more explicitly dialogic presentation by attending to two major structural concerns regarding both ethnographer and her others (Tedlock and Mannheim 1995). The first is to make the ethnographer's practice transparent by disclosing the realities of her actual contact with the authors and with mediators dealing with language and translation. The second concern is to de-essentialize cultural particulars of the other, and instead situate them within the personal dynamic of the person as an agent.

By invoking our personal encounters with the living sources of ethnographic knowledge, we refamiliarize that knowledge. As an anthropologist, I see this as completing a process that began with defamiliarization, a deliberate move away from personally and intuitively based interaction with cultural others by suspending judgement, a distancing that creates space for otherness to reveal itself on its own terms. Put in another way, this is a journey from the commonsense familiarity based on my own intuitive sense of the other, to a familiarity attentive to difference and predicated on learning where the other situates himself (Asch 2001; Abu-Lughod 1991). Refamiliarizing ethnography is also the fieldworker's "owning up" to being the beneficiary of those personal relationships within which all ethnographic "research" is embedded.

Acknowledging the familiar is in fact following what is a quasi-standard practice in discipular ethnography. Ethnomusicologists, especially as disciples, have tended to maintain the familiarizing stance, unwilling to take a defamiliarizing stance in the first place, but also thereby neglecting the opportunity to engage with the broader cultural and social issues within which individuals are inevitably enmeshed. I consider such an engagement as crucial for many reasons and will address this issue in a subsequent interpretive project where individuals will not be at the center. My first priority, therefore, is to create this book for and about the teachers to whom I owe my insights—and my Indian musical life to boot.

My first step toward respectful collaboration turned into a lesson in "I" and "thou" reciprocity. When consulting with my teachers about their priorities for the book, I found that I was projecting my and my discipline's concerns with voice and agency onto priorities that were reciprocal and pragmatic rather than individual and theoretical: "I gave you my knowledge so that you could learn. Now you do with it what needs to be done," meaning "I have my expertise, you have yours." Simply put, they expected me to use my assets in their favor, just as they had used theirs in mine.

Thus concerns of voice and interpretation are my concern, while theirs is the pragmatic priority to have their art be known in the world, to have their qualities showcased, to be accorded the respect they deserve as artists.

I propose to integrate the pursuit of their goals with mine in a combination of ways. One is to make the text accessible and profile the individual artists in addition to embodying their unique message. In addition, each artist must be showcased and profiled separately. Finally, the artist's world and words have to be made accessible in order to sustain a readership.

Textualizing Oral Interaction: Text and Language

Seen from a relational standpoint, ethnographic writing is itself an act of reciprocation; it is a return action in response to receiving knowledge. The form of the text, as Margaret Somerville observes, emerges from the relationship (Somerville 1991). The key here is integrity, of the textual choices, of the translation, and of the mediations. Textualizing their oral knowledge is showcasing them personally through their oral world and its riches. Rather than by their proxy, the conversational text positions me as the seeker and recipient involved in a complex, dynamic interaction. What makes this textualized interaction further compelling is the possibility of participation, even for a distanced reader. To convey this participatory dynamic is a major goal for me, since I see in it the very uniqueness of this oral culture.

A significant aspect of oral participation is its flow in real time, the shared experience of a present that Fabian terms "coeval" (Fabian 1983). I have largely retained the actual dialogue in script form, to entice the reader into experiencing the dynamic process of speaking and listening in real time, even though—or rather, exactly because—it slows down the reading process and prevents the reader from quickly scanning the text for information.

The original language of these conversations is Urdu and, in some cases, Hindi, although Hindi-speaking musicians often included Urdu expressions when speaking with me. With few exceptions I have translated their words myself, struggling with all the issues entailed in the process. Few of these artists spoke in English, hardly any of them fluently. More important, they did not operate musically in English except in the rare case of teaching foreigners, and in that process a wealth of nuance and meaning simply disappears.

Professional communities have their own way of speaking about their specialization. Among Hindustani musicians, this is reinforced by their socialization within an endogamous hereditary community. In fact, some *bradri*s (brotherhood or community of hereditary musicians) use a special way of pronouncing words that makes them incomprehensible to outsiders, when that is desired. At the same time, their patronage links variably expose them to sophisticated literate speech, which they emulate when talking with patrons. The result is a conversational language rich with diverse reference, but also capable of highly specialized shop talk.

To convey this richness in translation without cumbersome explanations poses a dual challenge of veracity and readability. My priority was to capture something of the flavor of the conversational style and to render it into a comfortable English that is inspired if not actually informed by the special Indian sensibility for English as a long-established Indian language. Indian writings on musicians, generally authored by educated patrons and disciples, have also offered a model of straightforward amiability that well conveys discipular respect and informational accessibility.

The texts I have chosen for each of my teachers are meant to offer coherent and salient sets of conversation that, to my best understanding, convey each artist's personal and artistic qualities through the flavor of the unique interaction between us. To capture that flavor I translated complete conversations directly from the recording as well as using transcriptions from Urdu or Hindi script. Despite a commitment to maintain this textual integrity, some editorial interventions were inevitable, first of all to leave out what the speakers did not mean to be for public consumption. The dialogue structure was left intact—including some rather coercive questioning from me—but in the interest of readability I reduced my excessive affirmative responses and even questions, and generally eliminated off-topic insertions caused by interruptions.

What posed a special challenge is repetition. Far from being what Western ideation considers redundancy, repetition, in my experience, is a central part of living orally and aurally. Not only is repetition the way to implant a message of knowledge or of musical sound in a student's memory, it is more generally the means of reiterating what is salient for living life. Saying things over again is to remind oneself, and to assure remembrance among those close; it is as much a means to impart new information to juniors as to recall what is already known and from whom it was received, whether it be professional highlights or principles of living life. But repetition does not translate well into the limited space of a book whose purpose is informational as well as experiential. For this reason, I have also reluctantly curtailed occurrences of the same statements by different musicians and instead focused on profiling each artist vis-à-vis his colleagues.

Finally, there is the challenge of providing necessary explanations without unnecessary interference. I do identify salient Urdu and Hindi terms for reference while setting off annotations visually or keeping them out of the text itself (in a glossary and in endnotes, where needed). To minimize explanations in the text, information on background and context are offered in this introduction.

Artists and Access: Bringing the Peacock's Dance in View[10]

Master Musicians of India: Hereditary Sarangi Players Speak is punctuated with interpretive initiatives that serve three mediational purposes, each auxiliary to my teachers' conversations. Interpretation here is a flexible tool of mediation in a dialectic involving ethnographic subjects, interpretants, and audiences. This is conventional ethnography reversed. The musicians' words are the message; mine are the trope added to facilitate their comprehension. The first purpose is to facilitate access to the oral musical and social milieu and social-cultural milieu of the musicians. These include, above all, contexts of time, place, and professional community. My background sketches of these contexts (in this chapter) represent consensual information drawn directly from musicians and patrons, from my own experience, as well as from other ethnographic and historical sources. At a local, particular level, an introductory sketch is added to each conversation as well as explanatory comments on aspects of content, where useful. A glossary of salient Urdu/Hindi terms and concepts is also appended (Chapter 13).

The second and central purpose is to facilitate culturally and personally appropriate encounters with the artists and their art. Each artist is personally introduced and showcased in an introductory section to the chapter bearing his name. This presentational as well as informational text is deliberately shaped in the image of the "official presenter" who plays the culturally sanctioned role of respectful mediator. Now usually called "compere" or "master of ceremonies ("MC")," her task is to appropriately introduce an artist or important personage to the assembled audience, whether at court or in the concert hall.

Like the compere, I include in these introductions the place from which I relate to the artist, thereby facilitating transparency between our voices. Since I wish to enable the reader to factor in the ethnographer's role as well as to factor it out, so as to encounter the artists directly, I have endeavored to insert myself in the text with as light a hand as my writing skills permit. Photos and recordings, finally, serve to showcase the artists as well as to document the ethnographic present of our encounters.

Situating Hereditary Musicians: Background

Why Sarangi Players?

Along with the sitar and the tabla, sarangi playing has been central to the practice of Hindustani or North Indian (and Pakistani) classical (*klassiki*) music. Sarangi music is deeply expressive as well as highly virtuosic, and distinctively enhanced by ornamentation. The only bowed instrument in

Hindustani art/classical music, the sarangi is played upright (like a cello) with a heavy, arched bow while the fingernails of the left hand slide along the sides of strings made of gut. Its sound resembles the human voice, enhanced by the shimmering resonance of numerous resonating wire strings. By musicians' consensus, sarangi playing is technically and musically demanding: from the absence of frets and the wear and tear on the player's fingernails to the solo mastery of ragas and styles, as well as the ability to provide a singer with instant melodic accompaniment and tabla players with a rhythmic timeline.

Sarangi players have been perhaps the most numerous among hereditary instrumentalists, at least since the beginning of the 20th century. As accompanists and teachers of voice as well as sarangi, they were found wherever Hindustani music has been practiced, across the entire Indo-Gangetic plain and the width of the Indian subcontinent, from West Punjab (Pakistan) in the west to Calcutta in the east, and including major centers in Maharashtra. Sarangi players are quintessential hereditary musicians and make up one of the most distinctive groups among them, along with tabla players, who generally belong to the same musical families. More than any other instrumentalists, sarangi players are highly versatile musicians. They create their own exposition of the classical raga repertoire while also replicating instantly the styles and melodies of singers whom they accompany. They have traditionally taught singers and enhanced their performances. And they are the source of rhythmic melodies for tabla and dance.

Today the sarangi is evoking special interest in India as well as in the West as a sonically compelling instrument that adds a uniquely Indian counterpart to the Western predilection for bowed string playing. At the same time, the instrument has become marginalized and is seen as a threatened aspect of India's musical heritage. In response, several "sarangi conferences"—government- and industry-sponsored affirmative-action events—have brought together sarangi players from across India and the world (Bhopal, Lucknow, Bombay). After being relatively unknown outside India, an increasing number of sarangi players have achieved international status.

The question of the sarangi's survival remains, however. Among younger musicians, there are only a handful of sarangi players. Fifty years ago, sarangi players were likely the most numerous group among hereditary instrumentalists/musicians, but today their number has diminished drastically, especially in contrast with players of other instruments. The crucial difference is that the sarangi was left out of the huge constituency of middle-class music lovers, amateurs, and professionals. Unlike tabla, sitar, flute and harmonium, the sarangi is not a standard subject at schools and colleges.[11] Among the many guidebooks on playing musical instruments, the sarangi is entirely absent, and so is any modern or institutional adaptation of the instrument and its pedagogy. In other words, the sarangi remains ensconced in its hereditary oral milieu.

Changing Patronage and Musical Institutions

The root of the problem lies in the sarangi's unique place in India's recent musical and social history. Until the early 20th century, hereditary musicians were the only guardians and exponents of Hindustani music; it was their exclusive privilege and duty to deliver music to patrons in a feudally based economy, most prominently at the courts of numerous princely states and major landholders across northern India and what is now Pakistan. At court, sarangi players had a dual role as solo players and as accompanists for all singers, from high classical to "light" vocal genres.

A related counterpart to feudal patronage were the salons of courtesan performers who were sustained by the nobles and the rich in urban centers across northern India. Sarangi players acted as the principal teachers, composers, and accompanists for these singers; they also accompanied their dance. The *kotha* (salon) in fact was the first secular public venue for art music, but one that was unacceptable to the Victorian morality of the educated Indian elites who would lead the country to independence.

The Nationalist movement, starting in 1906, supported the reform of classical music to make it a centerpiece of Indian national culture. Spearheaded by educated reformers in Madras, Calcutta, and Bombay, a remarkable infrastructure of bourgeois musical institutions was gradually established, opening up musical literacy, training, and performance to a broad middle-class public. By the time of independence in 1947, music colleges and schools, state and central music academies, public concerts, and music conferences (i.e., festivals) began to provide new patronage and employment for musicians across the major cities of India.

But the greatest new patron—as well as musical arbiter—was All India Radio. Designed to maintain and disseminate classical music, the radio created a graded audition system for performers, a hierarchy of educated music administrators, and a cadre of "staff artists" for accompaniment and for membership in the new national orchestra. Sarangi players gained some prominence once the radio had banned the competing harmonium as a musically inadequate accompaniment. In general, All India Radio provided a new authority structure for musical value, gradually replacing traditional connoisseurship.

This replacement was sealed with the abolition of princely states and landed estates (by 1952), effectively terminating court patronage. Sarangi players were hit even harder by the police closure of courtesan salons (by the mid-1960s) and the public stigmatization of courtesan singers. Given the few patronage options, staff positions at radio stations became the prized goal of the most competent players, especially in major cities that also offered freelance opportunities. Some outstanding sarangi players were also able to move into the light-music production of recording studio and film music, mainly in Bombay.

In the last decades of the 20th century, the international expansion of Indian music has created new performance, recording, and even teaching opportunities for instrumental music, especially for musicians with some Western-style education. Lacking middle-class performers, the sarangi still has an image problem, but it also benefits from the high valuation of bowed string instruments in the West, as well as from the Western success of the tabla, traditional partner of the sarangi in vocal accompaniment.

The problem has been a lack of livelihood at home. Especially with the steady devaluation of sarangi accompaniment by singers, the instrument has increasingly lost ground across South Asia, going from a situation of continuing patronage in the 1950s to circumstances that have put into question the hereditary profession itself. Some accomplished sarangi players have taken up singing or learned a different instrument; some have left music altogether. Inevitably, many parents have chosen not to teach their sarangi inheritance to their children. Others direct them to the tabla, which has traditionally been taught in the same families. And some find the resources to send their children to school and even college. Only a few have made sure that even with school and college education, their children's hereditary calling is not neglected.

Within this context of historical transformation, sarangi players have been making choices that have to be understood in relation to their particular circumstances of time and place. In terms of time, my teachers speak from within three historical moments within the first 50 years of Indian (and Pakistani) independence. Each "moment" represents a generational and musical phase within that period, as well as different stages in each musician's career. As for place, their careers are of course inexorably linked with the major musical centers in which their lives and work literally take place. I shall attempt to present both dimensions as intersecting contexts, making reference to my teachers where their individual lives embody these contexts.

Five Centers and Three Historical Moments

Five major cities, all centers of Hindustani music, of hereditary musicians, and of sarangi playing are the locus of my teachers' lives, and of my study with them: Delhi, Lucknow, Benares, and Bombay in India, and Karachi in Pakistan. All five are cultural centers of Urdu and/or Hindi; the first three belong to the heartland of both languages. Apart from Karachi, each city has offered patronage feudal courts and courtesan salons where hereditary musicians—and sarangi players in particular—thrived. After independence in 1947, each city has continued to offer varying combinations of institutional and private patronage, including, of course, a major local station of All India Radio (AIR) and later of Doordarshan television, both government monopolies until the late 1980s. At the same time, the five cities are also very distinct from each other in their local elite culture and economy, their mix and level of patronage, and the professional opportunities they offer musicians, especially sarangi players.

Delhi   As the imperial and national capital, Delhi records a strong illustrious presence of musicians in official roles linked to the high culture of display of political power. Special residential areas and government patronage continue in the form of excellent housing, stipends, and national awards. Elite patronage is considerable, but government patronage is paramount because cultural policies in support of music are most directly realized and most extensively institutionalized in the nation's capital. This has most directly enhanced the scope of All India Radio's Delhi station and its musicians (Sabri Khan, Shabbir Husain). Conversely, political upheavals in the capital have repeatedly caused musicians to find secure patronage elsewhere.

Lucknow   Lucknow has been a center of Muslim feudal culture, Urdu literature, and music, first under its own king and even under the British-supported landed elites. The city's preeminence in music, including dance, became enshrined institutionally in one of India's premier music colleges (founded 1927) and later in state academies for both music and dance. The college has uniquely employed sarangi players to accompany and even teach rudiments (Mirza Mahmud and Maqsud Ali), attracting fine performers from other cities (Bahadur Khan and Santosh Kumar Mishra). Meanwhile, feudal-style engagements from landed patrons and courtesan salons continued until the early 1960s, and some wealthy patrons still engage musicians as performers and teachers. The complete erasure of courtesan salons along with a change in elite composition has caused considerable attrition of hereditary families in Lucknow. Now the most prominent position for a sarangi player is that of staff artist at AIR (Bhagvan Das Mishra).

Benares   Culturally and musically a counterpart to Lucknow, Benares has been a center of Hindu feudal culture and remains, of course, the prime North Indian religious center of temple and pilgrim patronage, especially of devotional songs and scriptural dance representations, but also of classical raga music. Benares is the home of the Brahman Mishra (also spelled Misra) community of hereditary musicians, many of whom have benefited from this patronage privately and institutionally (Hanuman Prasad Mishra). Among sarangi players, however, many have had to go elsewhere to find such employment, leaving their joint families behind (Bhagvan Das Mishra). Like in Lucknow, salon patronage in Benares was terminated around 1960. In addition to Lucknow, Calcutta has continued to provide performance and teaching opportunities for sarangi players (Bhagvan Das Mishra). Most recently, Benares Hindu University has finally created a post for a sarangi player in its music department as accompanist, providing institutional recognition to the instrument (Santosh Kumar Mishra).

Bombay Different from feudally based urban economies, Bombay is above all a commercial center of India. The city has for decades been the metropolis of Hindustani music, attracting hereditary musicians from all over northwestern India, thanks to a convergence of the Maharashtrian-led reform movement and its remarkable success among the large educated middle class as well as the traditional patronage of wealthy benefactors. For over a century, patrons from different communities have built a public concert scene and teaching institutions (Dhruba Ghosh), including the National Centre for Performing Arts (Ram Narayan), offering hereditary musicians patronage and connections to a wide range of career opportunities. In addition, both recording and film industries became consolidated in Bombay by the late 1940s, making it the studio capital of India. The thriving Hindi film industry paid well for sarangi players' traditional composing and performing skills while offering anonymity for work that did not enhance their classical music standing (Ram Narayan, Sultan Khan). However, the recent opening to global trends of Western popular music and technologies puts the demand for the offering of traditional Indian musicians in question.

Karachi Resulting from the enormous population dispersal at India's partition, Karachi became the hub of a huge Muslim immigration from urban centers in India that included many hereditary musicians. Dominated by an educated Urdu-speaking elite, the city offered immigrant musicians powerful patrons, especially while it was the capital city of Pakistan until 1969. An intense drive to transplant Muslim high culture saw music patronized but hardly institutionalized beyond the Indian radio model (Hamid Husain). Additional support for building an art music scene came from foreign cultural centers and from the Westernized Parsi community, but this amalgam did not survive the first generation, nor the subsequent radical puritanism of the Islamist movement.

The Sixties (1965, 1968/1969) Within the first two decades of Independence/Partition, major nation building in India—according to the founding vision of the Independence movement—had been accomplished in the economic and industrial as well as social and cultural domains. A comprehensive grid of governmental institutions managed a largely state-controlled economy and a quasi-socialist social and cultural policy. Cultural policies were proactive, synthesizing a national culture for the nation as a whole. Thanks to a new cadre of music scholars, art music with its ancient and spiritual foundation in Sanskrit treatises stood as a centerpiece of national culture, sustained by a grid of central and state academies, concert organizations, teaching institutions, and of course All India Radio. A very large number of hereditary musicians, especially sarangi and tabla accompanists, had found permanent employment as "staff artists" at radio stations across the nation. Others were affiliated as occasional performers on the basis of the juried grading system of radio auditions. At the same time, private elite patronage continued, though on a more limited scale. I encountered my teachers in Lucknow, Bombay, and Karachi. In each city, hereditary musicians faced the challenge of adapting to middle-class reformers now in charge of ensconcing music in bourgeois institutions and replacing those musicians from middle-class ranks. On the other side, my teachers, with a few exceptions, were the first generation to establish careers after Independence, benefiting from new opportunities. They were also the last generation to be trained under pre-Independence conditions.

The standard arrangement for middle-class students was "tuitions," at the student's home that included some hospitality for the teacher and of course financial remuneration. Only Pandit Ram Narayan, who lived in a middle-class apartment, taught me at his home. At that time, none of my teachers knew more than a few words of English; all verbal teaching was in Urdu or, in Ram Narayan's case, in Hindi. My study and immersion enabled me to follow my teachers and make myself understood; furthermore, cultural expertise was always close at hand, thanks to personal connections, but in an overall sense I was a novice.

The Eighties (1983, 1984, 1985/1986)   Indian democracy had revived after the dictatorial excesses of the mid-1970s; Indira Gandhi was assassinated. Intellectual and artistic excellence was well established, and a generation of young and highly educated musicians was emerging from the culturally mobilized middle class. Internationalization of Indian music was beginning to have notable effects on the music scene, especially through concertizing abroad, leading to new patronage and a trickle of foreign students. Western appreciation of the sarangi as a quasi violin (and the tabla as an instrument of unimagined virtuosity) enhanced the solo demand for the sarangi, even in India. Sarangi players were recorded for the Uttar Pradesh Music and Dance Academy, and the first ever sarangi *mela* (festival-conference) brought together 189 sarangi players from across India, including a few foreigners and, for the first time, two young women (both represented in this book along with their gurus, Ram Narayan [Chapter 4] and Bhagvan Das [Chapter 9]) (Bor 1994).[12] In Pakistan, on the other hand, Islamization had diminished the public legitimacy of music, further reducing prospects of patronage for a coming generation of musicians (Qureshi 2000).

The 1980s (1983–1985) became the axis of my most intense involvement with the sarangi/sarangi players, both as an aspiring performer on the sarangi, and also as a scholar exploring the wider world of hereditary sarangi players in the region. Along with Lucknow, Delhi became my major hub of study, with expansion to Benares. Most musicians I connected with were from the same first post-independence generation and now at the peak of their professional and personal lives, enjoying the weight of seniority, authority within their community, and reputations as performers and successful teachers, above all of their own sons (Sabri Khan, Bhagvan Das, Ram Narayan). Concerts and teaching abroad were beginning to happen, and in tourist destinations, foreign students were more common (Sabri Khan, Hanuman Prasad, Ram Narayan). However, I also connected with some sarangi players who found too little scope as musicians and stopped teaching their children music (Bahadur Khan).

In addition to these facilitating facts, my own acculturation and musical as well as linguistic competence enabled me to experience musical life in this period more broadly as well as more deeply. In particular, language had now become a means for me to fully join the ongoing conversation that oral transmission consists of. And I was now free from the constraints of being a young female in an exclusively male social environment.

The Nineties (1992, 1997) The 1990s are above all marked by the introduction of a new market-oriented economic policy and the growth and consolidation of prosperous Indian settler-diaspora communities in North America. Their patronage was increasingly shaping the reception of Indian music in the West both culturally and economically. Hindustani music had become a global mediascape as well as a global ethnoscape, with room even for freelance solo sarangi players like Dhruba Ghosh, Sabri Khan, and Sultan Khan, who followed Pandit Ram Narayan with tours and teaching appointments in the West. In the world musical marketplace, the best musical and performance skills of hereditary musicians are valued even in the absence of "education," thus giving new opportunities to outstanding hereditary artists. On the other hand, radio employment was being reduced, and the cultural hold of state media diminished. These developments have made Bombay and Delhi the prime international take-off points to establish personal patronage links in Western cities. With their bowed-string appeal, some sarangi players become global strategists, banking foreign experience as cultural capital at home, or even moving to the West. But a modern education and English fluency are crucial assets to career building, since the competition from young, educated, middle-class musicians is fierce, in India as well as the diaspora.

Clearly, the 1990s are seeing a generational shift from my teachers to their musical offspring. My teachers' students are few, nurtured by their excellence but also by their families' support and financial sufficiency. With one exception, my teachers trained their students without the help of senior relatives. Of their children, only a few are sarangi players; more play the other family instrument, the tabla, since it offers greater opportunities for a starting musician.

In theory, sarangi players could turn the disadvantage of the sarangi's scarcity around and benefit from the fact that the niche of their instrument is not crowded with nonhereditary musicians and remains essentially a "birthright" instrument. But the very absence of demand from outside makes that a difficult prospect. The crucial question is: can these few young players keep themselves, and thus the sarangi, alive until it gains a status equivalent to that of other instruments, so that sarangi players can share in the expanding patronage of Hindustani music at home and abroad? Time will tell.

Meanwhile, an epoch of sarangi mastery is coming to an end. But hereditary oral knowledge continues as long as it is passed on *sina-ba-sina*, "from heart to heart," and as long as there is that most crucial of contexts: a self-reproducing social network for musical transmission.

Kinship, Musical and Familial

The core relationship of Indian musical transmission is that of master and disciple, a personal bond that has spiritual and musical dimensions as well as social ones, particularly of recruitment and reproduction for the discipular chain. Among hereditary musicians of Northern India, the social network for musical transmission is a kinship-based universe of actual and potential relatives. Collectively, that network is called *bradri*, the "brotherhood" or community of musicians, as they are identified by people of other professional networks or social status. Bradri is the broadest concept of a Hindustani musician's social identity (Neuman 1990). The term is used by both Muslims and Hindus, though set within different larger social concepts, the *jati* or "subcaste" for Hindus and the *zat* or social class for Muslims. Both serve to situate musicians' bradris within the category of professional specialists or artisans.[13]

Within this collective identification, what makes hereditary *musical* identity possible for an individual artist? The first answer that my experience has generated is: family, in the immediate sense of household, and in the broader sense of kinship. Bradri itself is, in practice, a continuing extension of kinship.

The immediate and primary sense of family is patrilineal: a hereditary line of musical succession from fathers to sons (and perhaps daughters) based on a commitment to invest their musical heritage in their own lineage first and foremost. In my experience, the core of being a hereditary professional is the generational succession of the master's music. The intermeshing of musical and filial succession is simply a given. As a concept, master-disciple equals father-son. But the relationship includes a variety of equivalences: "father" can include father's brother(s) (Santosh Kumar Mishra, Bahadur Khan), paternal grandfather and his brother (Bahadur Khan, Sabri Khan), maternal uncle (Yaqub Husain), and even a maternal grandfather can become a "father" cum teacher (Hamid Husain).[14] This broader concept is *gharana*, a mostly music-specific term that refers to a household or extended family but is also used in the general sense of family or household identity.

In India I learned that kinship is a universe extending far beyond the immediate family into community itself. Within a stratified social order, distinct caste/class groups are identified by patrilineal descent and their boundaries maintained by a tradition of in-group, or endogamous, marriage. Hereditary professional communities of musicians are ancestral to this Indian social organization and enshrined in the Hindu caste system as well as the class structure of Muslims in South Asia. Marrying within the group creates both close-knit families and widely cast networks of relatives who are linked to each other by marriage ties. For Muslims, unlike (North Indian) Hindus, endogamy includes marrying paternal or maternal cousins; this results in a highly flexible and often bilaterally oriented family structure, where the mother's lineage can be as important as the fathers.

In terms of managing the musical heritage, marrying within the family permits keeping its immediate musical heritage intact, while the wide marriage universe of the bradri permits accessing the desirable musical heritage of other families through either a son's or a daughter's marriage. Musical expertise is collectively preserved in the family. It is also informally legitimized by senior master musicians and ancestors. In a formal sense, senior members representing the bradri may be called in to monitor teaching results in a guildlike manner. Assuring the level of expertise is important for disciples who will carry forward the heritage and use it to support the master/father and family in turn. Discipleship in the formal, ritual sense (*shagirdi*) cements this musical filiation and its mutual obligation between teacher and student. Masters do not enter this lifelong commitment lightly.

This is particularly the case with students who come from outside the bradri and whose long-term commitment may be difficult to assess.

Bradri Identity: Networks and Hometowns

A named bradri traditionally populated a delimited region within which prerailway traveling was possible. Probably originating in Punjab, there are at least three such regional groups with home locations across Punjab and into central Uttar Pradesh. Those bradris are traditionally sarangi and tabla players, and recently have also introduced other instruments as well as singing in their families.

The sarangi players in this book belong to four major regional bradri locations and identify themselves with a major hometown within each (see Figure 1); Ustads Sabri Khan and Hamid Husain are both "Muradabad people" near Delhi, in the most prominent and numerous bradri of sarangi players that is also identified with the dominant hereditary musical community of Mirasi ("inheritors"). Because Ustad Hamid Husain grew up at the court of nearby Rampur, he added that town and its glamour to his name. Sultan Khan belongs to the "Sikhar people," a princely state in Rajasthan, and also identifies with the hereditary community of Dhari ("praise singers") in the same region. Bahadur Khan belongs to Banda, a principality in the south of the region; he identifies with the hereditary community of Kalavant ("artists") that was originally brought to Banda by its nawab. Both Hanuman Prasad and Bhagvan Das belong to Benares, where they identify with the large Mishra Brahman community of musicians, though their families originally came from nearby villages and were identified as Kathak ("dancer–musicians," literally "storytellers"). Likewise, Mahmud Ali's lineage belongs to and identifies with Lucknow, where they have resided for well over a century. Ram Narayan and Dhruba Ghosh identify their region of origin (Rajasthan, Bengal), but do not use a professional group identity; instead, each identifies his father as his primary teacher. Ram Narayan and his family are from Udaipur in Rajasthan, and he identifies his father as his primary teacher, while Dhruba Ghosh uses no local affiliation beyond Bombay, but he identifies himself with the professional stature of his Bengali father, Nikhil Ghosh.

It makes sense that musicians' definitions of their own identities have often been composite and variable, representing profession, hometown, as well as place of patronage. What remains constant is membership in the "brotherhood" that provides its members with a professional and personal network of relatives, often traced through complex marriage links, wherever they may reside. Even living away from the bradri's hometown or region, musicians can expect family and bradri members to provide a major network of support. Those who lack such kin group affiliation, like

Ram Narayan and Dhruba Ghosh, miss this support network, but they both have strong links with middle-class supporters in Bombay.

Since the 19th century and the presence of railways, musicians have increasingly moved between their home ground and often far-flung places of work. For at least a century before that, musicians were settled (as a professional group) in particular towns and locations allocated to them most often by local rulers in accordance with their accessibility to places of patronage. Individual musicians either worked locally or fanned out to seek professional opportunities, leaving their families in the common hometown or neighborhood and their sons training in the charge of senior relatives, with visits during holidays. Today, when employment requires continuous attendance on the job, it has become increasingly common for the family of the musician to follow him to his place of work, but even in the large cities, neighborhoods of musicians are common, and bradri members will make room to accommodate incoming "brothers." Even living away from the bradri's home, family and bradri members provide the major support network in a strange city. On the other hand, living within a bradri can also be confining, given its collective tradition of social control and rules of seniority.

Modernity and Hereditary Oral Transmission

Like all musicians, sarangi players have adapted to the new social institutions of music making. The major change has been from freelance work to wage employment in educational and governmental institutions, and from the continuity of extended families living in ancestral towns and unaffected by their star musicians' mobile careers, to individual families settling in diverse places of employment, mainly in larger centers, where they experience the milieu of modernity and partake of its opportunities for alternatives of education, training, or wage labor. Those who stayed with music have had to confront the disciplining demands of institutional employment and patronage, starting with time, and with situationality. This is so well exemplified in that famous clash between a great ustad's gradually evolving performance and the strict studio timing for what was to be his first—and last—radio broadcast (Luthra 1986). Such external changes gradually encroach on the way time is spent at home as well, hence affecting musical training, and ultimately the music itself. Most recently, the economic opening—and with it the open market of new media and global access—is creating a new set of options whose effect is yet to be assessed.

On the level of teaching and transmission, the exclusion of the sarangi from institutionalized teaching has kept alive and viable the in-home teaching of family members, even to total outsiders. Western students have been attracted to the bowed sarangi since before the Beatles; several became disciples of the masters in this volume (Sabri Khan [Chapters 1–3], Ram Narayan [Chapter 4], Hanuman Mishra [Chapter 10], and Hamid Husain [Chapter 11]) and later published books on the topic (Sorrell 1980, Neuman 1990, Bor 1986–1987). The impact of these teaching relationships has yet to be assessed, also in relation to the gender barrier that traditionally defined this exclusively male instrument.

Perhaps not accidentally, it was soon after my first visit with Pandit Ram Narayan in 1969 that he started teaching sarangi to his daughter Aruna and, remarkably, made her the inheritor of his art. Much later, Bhagvan Das Mishra started teaching a female student, Archana Yadav, soon after working with me in 1984. Both broke the instrument's premodern gender barrier: Aruna as the first female solo artist on the Indian and global stage, Archana as the first female sarangi player in a government dance academy. Significantly, both masters and female students are Hindu. Especially among Muslim bradris, musical heredity remains a male domain that can be countered only when or until the sarangi joins other instruments taught in music schools and colleges.

Sublime or Subaltern? An Afterthought

Hereditary musicians have long had a dual identity. Seen from a historical as well as an ethnographic perspective, hereditary musicians have long been revered for their art, even though they have been assigned low social status for practicing it.[15] Artistically, they are the indispensable creators and preservers of the sublime oral musical heritage of India. But socially, they have occupied a clearly subaltern position as providers of specialized professional services, even as their noble patrons formerly recognized and rewarded their greatness as performers. Ethnographers have implicitly embraced the concept of service provider in the spirit of the "Little Tradition" of earlier scholars, who distinguish between the shared high culture of urban cosmopolitan elites and local and rural versions of that high culture. More recently, Indian scholars have done much to historicize and document the condition of subalternity, problematizing this concept in several directions. Subalternity thus subsumes the subject of the Little Tradition (Singer 1980/1972), but extends far beyond its occupational class confines embracing urban communities marginal constituencies, and reaching across caste and professional boundaries and beyond. Still, the powerful challenge remains: "Can the subaltern speak?" (Spivak 1988). Historically, musicians were subalterns who could sing (and play) but hardly speak; their patrons did that. Even today, most public discourse about music and musicians tend to come from music "specialists" of the educated middle class.

In practice, subalternity is not only structural, it is relational, as the term itself denotes. As their listener and as their student, I, in fact, become their subaltern. They, as artists, assume hegemony over their listeners and students, their "clients," even as they accept their patronage. This duality offers to nonmusicians a special space for making a tactical shift toward acknowledging the musicians' agency that transcends the confines of their class. At the same time, subalternity among hereditary musicians has persisted in the face of a new class of nonhereditary middle-class musicians endowed with the social and educational assets of the new national elites.

Seen in this context, making the "artist interview" the representational choice for this book becomes a move toward redressing the social situation hereditary musicians have collectively been confronting. More than a genre of convention, these artists' interviews articulate how art—and in particular the performative, interactive art of music—can be enlisted as a public site for asserting both their artistic and social authority. All that is required is to listen: to their words as well as to their music.

Delhi: Center of Power

CHAPTER 1

Sabri Khan

My Guru, a Complete Musician

Introducing Ustad Sabri Khan

Ustad (master teacher) Sabri Khan is above all a very fine and very knowledgeable musician and a master teacher of his art. In addition, or rather, in conjunction with these two areas of competence, Sabri Khan is also a builder: of relationships and of improvements in music as well as in living. He acts as an advisor and facilitator to students and family as well as to community members, but most of all, Sabri Khan is indefatigable, always ready to undertake a task and to do what it takes to see it through.

As a result, Ustad Sabri Khan has the loyalty and attachment of his students and the respect of his peers. From an early age he helped support his elders while raising eight children. He trained and educated four sons, three as musicians and one as a commerce graduate. For his daughters he arranged marriages, three to musicians within his bradri or hereditary community, and he also looked after less-well-off relatives and bradri members. Thanks to the support of his wife and daughters, Ustad Sabri Khan has had an open and hospitable house where visitors were always welcome and tea or a meal was served any time he requested it.

While Sabri Khan worked very successfully within the classical musical milieu of Delhi and All India Radio, he was always open to change and new challenges. Starting with his first employment in the Tamil unit of All India Radio, he successfully used opportunities to learn new music and techniques, to teach foreign students, to perform for foreign audiences, and even to play foreign music with artists like Yehudi Menuhin. Living and working in the capital of the country was a crucial reason for the access Sabri Khan had to such opportunities. The fact that he could use them to his advantage over other colleagues was due to his remarkable musical competence, versatility, and intelligence. Added to this is his untiring hard work combined with an unusual flexibility and alertness to the need for helpful connections. Sabri Khan learned how to cultivate such connections not only for his own and his family's benefit, but also for his students and others who often came to ask for his help while I was staying at his house.

Ustad Sabri Khan began his childhood and early training in Muradabad, center of his bradri (brotherhood or community of hereditary musicians). At only 14 years of age, he passed the audition at All India Radio and permanently moved to Delhi, where he built his career and his family. For many years his house in the old city was a center of music and musicians until, in 1989, the government allotted him and other eminent artists a house in the fine residential complex built for the 1988 Asiad Games. Now retired from the radio, Sabri Khan continues to perform, teach, and work on the careers of his two youngest sons, one of them a sarangi player.

For me, Sabri Khan was the ideal ustad when, in 1984, I was ready for a summer of intensive training on the sarangi. As a distant nephew of my first ustad, the late Hamid Husain Khan, he could provide continuity of style and technique, since both ustads were trained in the same local hereditary tradition centered in the town of Muradabad, not far from Delhi. Also ideal was the fact that Sabri Khan was already familiar with visiting Western students and their need for intensive, short-term attention. Despite an extremely busy professional and personal life, he generously included me in the musical life of his home and made me his disciple in both principle and practice.

After getting over a bit of initial awkwardness caused by the presence of a woman in an all-male musical environment, Sabri Khan related to me with ease; he (and I) also appreciated my husband Saleem's culturally honed, patronlike presence at crucial junctures, especially our first meeting and, of course, the discipleship ceremony, as well as our later, more familial visits to his new house in Delhi.

In retrospect I was extremely fortunate to experience discipleship with Sabri Khan while he was still living the traditional lifestyle of Old Delhi: being surrounded by neighbors of the same professional community, starting a young son, Kamal, on the sarangi, and accepting a nephew as live-in disciple, stepping out to pray at the neighborhood mosque or getting the tea man to bring up a tray for visitors. My recordings have captured that life and its vitality when Sabri Khan was at the height of his career and achievements. On my return in 1992, I found that the family's move to the Artist's Complex in New Delhi led to a more modernized lifestyle adapted to a new

Figure 2 Sabri Khan, portrait, Delhi, 1951.

generation of hereditary musicians with whom Sabri Khan does not hesitate to keep pace. This is best reflected in the careers of his three musician sons and of course in the progress of his many disciples that includes their finding salaried positions, the most coveted employer being All India Radio. Of his sons, the eldest, tabla player Ghulam Sarvar, had established himself as a musician in England; the teenager, Gulfam Sabri, also a tabla player, was touring in South Africa; while the young sarangi player Kamal Sarvar was making a name for himself in Delhi. And his nephew Nasir Khan had found employment in the premier Indian dance academy and became his teacher's son-in-law. Sabri Khan's most recent artistic initiative took him to England, where he performed the father-to-son legacy with his three sons in concerts as well as on CD.

Along with tradition, I also need to contextualize my discipleship vis-à-vis his already established record of teaching "foreign" students, most outstanding among them Daniel Neuman, thanks to whom he experienced being a visiting professor at the University of Washington, though that took place only after 1984. Even before I knew him, Sabri Khan had learned to manage basic communication with foreign students in English.

My own approach was different. I deliberately bypassed English because it was a medium through which Sabri Khan would try to enter my conversation and I would miss out on his, including that of relatives, other musicians, and students. Instead, I strove simply to join in his speech world with the result that the language between us was quite naturally Urdu. Our mostly prosaic, if occasionally poetic, conversations, and my cultural and social familiarity with Muslim Indian milieus did create a bond of understanding and social interaction between us that was remarkably special, because it was so natural.[1] My abiding gratitude goes to Ustad Sabri Khan, a remarkable teacher, artist, and human being, for all his gifts—musical and simply human.

Family Training: A Tough Foundation[2]

Sabri Khan introduced himself most expansively during my final visit to his house after a summer of learning from him, perhaps because only then did I feel confident that he would really want to share his personal life and his advice for mine. For the last time I had arrived at the Ajmeri Gate and hailed a bicycle riksha, the only transport small enough to negotiate the narrow lanes inside the walled city of Old Delhi. Ustad Sabri Khan's house was located in Mohalla (neighborhood) Nyariyan. Walking past the bustle of a busy water pump, a tea stall (from where strong milky tea was often ordered for visitors), and a few goats and chickens, I headed for the dark staircase to be surprised, once more, by the sudden brightness of a freshly washed terrace in the sun and the promising sound of plucked strings filtering through the open door at the right. Inside, Ustad Sabri Khan was tuning a sarangi while smoking a cigarette. As always, white sheets were spread on the floor and bolsters lined the walls, offering flexible and comfortably informal seating.

The inviting smells of a fine midday meal wafted across the terrace from the family's living area. On this day, Ustad Sabri Khan invited me for a farewell lunch served in the music room, which also is the living room for receiving male visitors; the place for women visitors is the family area. Students and relatives were invited as well, and I felt part of the family now. After lunch, Mrs. Sabri Khan and her daughters joined us, especially me, for their own farewell.

Later in the afternoon, Ustad Sabri Khan and I had our last conversation. The master made sure to impart necessary points of knowledge to me, and to give me a chance to clarify matters of my special concern. In the process, he told me about his own training and career and the lessons they contain for me, his student. Still present was Sabri Khan's younger brother Ghulam Raza Khan, who adds an occasional comment, but the women and children of the family only come in for a brief visit.

Figure 3 Sabri Khan, recipient of Padma Shri and Padma Bhushan Awards, his home, New Delhi, 1997.

My Grandfather Taught All of Us

Sabri Khan: My grandfather was my very first teacher. From my childhood he made me practice a lot. In the morning, when people went to say their *Fajr* prayer at 5 A.M., he called, "Get up and get going, get up and get going." That's how. He had his stick in his hand, ready to go. It was to ward off any stray cat or dog that was around at this early hour, since the way to the mosque was long.

That was in Muradabad. Our house was on the edge of the river Ram Ganga. There were few people around that area. That's where I learned to play. So, after waking me he went to pray. Now I should be sitting there practicing. If I took off, I would get beaten. If I played something wrong, he snatched the bow out of my hand and hit me, on that very hand, he hit my fingers, or whatever he wanted to hit, any part of my body. *He points to different parts.* You know, that's what our elders did. And he was my father's father. My mother used to see it with sorrow, but she couldn't say anything.

My grandfather put in a lot of work with me. My father too was trained by my grandfather. He also taught my father's brothers (chacha). And my paternal uncle Raza Husain, my grandfather taught him too—he is the one who was here in the morning—now he left for a job, he got a 'casual booking.' What I meant to tell you is that my grandfather beat me, and those beatings—the teacher's beatings—are good for the student, this I have to say.

Regula: Everyone says so, all those with good training.

Sabri Khan: Yes, Bade Ghulam Ali Khan got beaten a lot, by his uncle Kale Khan Sahib—a lot! I got beaten a lot. I mean, a lot—the most among all of us who played sarangi in our neighborhood. One boy was Ghulam Sabir Qadri, he also practiced there; his house was just across from ours. Ahmad Raza's house too, it was right beside ours, very close. It is still there, that house. And my father's elder brother (*taya*) lived in front of us (*hamare samne*), and a bit to the side, also in front, lived Ghulam Sabir Qadri. He also had his father make him practice.

I was more than naughty! I would leave the sarangi and run off, to play around with other children outside. I was small, seven to eight years old. Now when my grandfather returned from the mosque, he came to look for me: "Where are you!" But I was playing by the river, running all around. So he had me captured by other boys: "Catch him and bring him here." I did not go on my own; I was too afraid.

The sarangi he made me play on is still in Muradabad, a really small instrument. And he made me practice in front of him while he was sitting and smoking his waterpipe. I was also the one who brought him new fire bowls (*chilam*). I had to fill them with coals, and keep the fire burning; sometimes I got my fingers burned. You know what I mean? They got burned when I filled the bowl and put it down on the pipe stand. But my grandfather did not go anywhere. He never got up from there. He stayed in our front sitting room, while the family (women and children) were in the inside rooms. From there a door led to the sitting room, a large room with a sitting platform (*chauki*). When someone came, he was invited to sit there: "Brother, do sit on the platform." Everyone who came to visit sat on it. I was in a corner with my sarangi, practicing. They had put a small platform there for me.

And there was no fan in those times. In the summer I was bathed in perspiration.

Regula: Did anyone play tabla with you?

Sabri Khan: No one, not with me, though my paternal uncle played the tabla, Nasir's grandfather. Muhammad Yusuf, he was a very good-looking man—*very* good-looking. You've seen the build of his son, Yasin, Nasir's father. But Yasin is nothing in comparison to his father; what a huge, broad chest he had. He played sarangi and also tabla, and he sang. And he had great strength, he was a wrestler.[3] He used to leave his house wearing a sarong of silk and a long silk shirt; he looked just splendid. His name was Muhammad Yusuf and he was my father's brother. He was very handsome and he also played the sarangi very well.

But these uncles did not stay at home much. They had finished their training and now went out to do performances in different places; one went to Bombay, another to Calcutta, another to the court at Indore. They stayed in Indore quite a bit.

At home it was I and my grandfather, and my grandmother, and my mother. My father stayed away from home. Actually, my grandfather played sarangi extremely well, and he was also very family-minded (*kasbi*). It was he who taught everyone, my father, my father's brothers, including his eldest brother.[4] He was that devoted to the family. He also taught the technique of teaching, something not everyone knows! It is something apart, a separate skill. Teaching—a different thing altogether. Thirakwa Sahib[5] was a *very* good tabla player, but *in a dramatically lowered voice* does he have any disciple who plays well?

That is why I say, to play well is one thing; to teach someone else to play is something else. You can't just do it. And yes, well—there are numerous sarangi players here—*addressing Regula*: if you had perchance landed with someone else, you would not have progressed this much. No one gives his knowledge easily. First a person has to know how to teach; only then can he teach someone.

So my grandfather gave me a lot of 'help.' True, he beat me, but I benefited from his beating. Because then I kept practicing. In the morning I sat down at 5 A.M., and at 10 he said, go inside and eat something. Whatever 'bread and water' my grandmother had prepared, I ate that. Of course there was no tea at that time, none. In our house, we did not have any tea at all. There was milk, or bread, stew and bread. And then he sat me down again. He let me off for an hour after 10 or 11 o'clock, and then sat me down until 1, when it was time to eat. First he went to say his zohr prayer. When the call to prayer was sounded at about 1 he'd say, "Stop now." Now he went to pray and left me free for two to four hours. I could roam around. After the afternoon prayer (*Asr*) or evening prayer at sunset (*Maghrib*) I again sat down with the sarangi. Then I got off at 10 at night. That's how much he made me work.

After that I went to live with my father, then he made me work hard. I must have been 10 years old. He used to come home once a year in the month of Muharram. You know, we take a break at that time, for 10 to 12 days. Then I sometimes went back with him when he was working in Delhi. So then he was teaching me, as well.

Then, at age 12, I went to give an audition, but I failed it. At 13, I gave another audition, at the old All India Radio building on Alipur Road. That's where I went. I failed that audition as well. Then at age 15 I gave an audition for the Madrasis (the Tamil unit of South Indian music). They passed me right away!

A Passion for Learning More

During this later part of the conversation, Sabri Khan's uncle Ghulam Raza Khan dropped in and took a keen interest in what his nephew was telling the foreign student who spoke and understood their language, adding reinforcement and even prompts to this obviously very familiar account of the family's most outstanding member. Also visiting and waiting quietly was Sabri Khan's most accomplished student, Ghulam Sarvar, who was hoping to borrow a sarangi for his next engagement. Sabri Khan now pitches his conversation to them as well as myself. He is a skillful narrator who often

*initiates his topic with a statement that intrigues the listener and prompts
her to ask for the story behind it.*

Playing from Notation

Sabri Khan: When I first came to the radio (All India Radio), no one
would let me sit near the mike because then my playing would be
audible. I used to play wrong notes. I played in tune—that's why
they gave me the job. But I did not know how to play orchestra (i.e.,
play from notation).[6]

Ghulam Raza: Because of notation!

Sabri Khan: Notation—I did not know it.[7] I had no idea of it. Yet that
is where they put me, in the orchestra (where everyone plays from
notation). That was in the Madrasi Unit, the Tamil Unit. And I did
not understand the Tamil language (or script). They put me there
because "the boy plays beautifully in tune, he will become a good
musician." That's why they employed me at such a young age.

So I went there and learned orchestra notation, (letter
notation) in Urdu, Hindi, English, and Tamil. I can read the Tamil
script as well. You won't find anyone who knows all this in India,
Pakistan, or Saudi Arabia. Hindi, Urdu, English, and Madrasi.
Others don't know Tamil writing, but I learned the Tamil script; I
can write and read it. Then I started to play and became an expert
in it. And when someone came from outside, they would put a page
of music before me, an entirely new page, and I was able to sight-
read and play it.

But at that time no singer asked for me as an accompanist.
I was just 16 years old. I had come to the radio at 15, when I did
not even have a mustache or beard. My job was in the Tamil Unit,
working with Madrasi musicians. So naturally, no singer from our
side (North India) would ask for me. They didn't even like me. I
couldn't play 'light' music, nor did I know how to play classical in
the orchestra. And practice with the tabla? Well, I had very little
of that at home. Of course there were tabla players on staff at the
radio, a few of them boys like me. So we're sitting there and I say,
"Come on, let's practice," so we both sit down in the booth and
practice. It helped me, and him too; he got the idea of accompanying, and I got rhythm out of it.

So I learned everything in the radio, most everything.
How much did I know at 15? I was far from fully trained. What
I didn't get at home, I learned it all during my stay in the radio. I

learned notation; I learned playing in the orchestra; I learned to 'copy' others, to accompany. I learned how to play solo in the radio, how to play from my own mind.

But in the end it depends on God's kindness whether you make progress. We were 20 employees. They are still where they were when they started their service. When everyone went to drink tea, I would practice. At lunchtime, when the orchestra had its break: "Are you coming for tea?" "No, I want to practice." I didn't go. My interest was the sarangi. Everyone would say, "Okay, you've practiced enough, it's been several hours." I used to sit down like this on the bare floor. Even if I was wearing nice clothes, I didn't mind. The booth did not have space to spread out a sheet for sitting, like the studios. It was the small recording booth of Studio 4. So I'd quietly close the door, no sound went out, and I am practicing, alone. Now if a friend or someone else junior wanted to join me with the tabla, I'd say, "Come on in," and we are practicing together.

I had a passion for it. At first I was badly humiliated when I had to play with singers, because I could not manage to accompany at all. So I felt 'insulted' when I could not reproduce the singer's *tan* (fast passages). I felt bad. I'd go to the booth and cry, and ask the Lord: "I feel very humiliated. I don't want to be like this; make me into something good. I want to make a name for myself in India. This is no use; any singer comes and makes me humiliated. My playing is not right; he does not like the way I play; he doesn't like me."

Other people, it did not bother them. But I wanted that the singers should like me so much that they'd ask for me. Instead of refusing me, they should demand to have me accompany: no, I want *Sabri Khan*. Well, thanks to God, the time did come when the singers asked for me: "Give me either Sabri senior or Sabri junior."

Learning from Other Masters

Sabri Khan: Listen Regula! if you want to learn from someone, serve him; it's the only way. We study with our ustad. Later, we also learn from other musicians. But how? Here is someone who has an excellent piece of musical knowledge, but he can't just give it to me. Who would give away his knowledge to just anyone, and why would he give it?

Here is what I did, and it took about two years. There was a poor old sarangi player who knew many unique old compositions, Ali Gulab. First thing in the morning I would go to Gulab and offer my very respectful greeting: "*Adab Arz*" (I present my submission to you).

"Come in, son; come in, brother. Master musician's son, what brought you here at this time?" "I have come to visit you, master musician (*Khan Sahib*). Let's go and have some tea." Well, there was the Hakim Hotel in the Chawli area, between here and the old reservoir (Qazi Hauz).

So I took him to the Hakim Hotel, and "Brother, bring one lamb chop, bring two eggs, bring them half fried, bring one butter, and bring toast!" I treated him to a sumptuous meal (*khub unko khila dia*). He ate and felt very good. "Will you have something more, Khan Sahib?" "No, no, son, that's enough, son; you've done enough."

Alright, then I took him to the nearby meadows. In those days the surrounding area was wilderness, all these shops were not built yet. The entire Minto Road[8] area was a meadow. That's where I took him and asked him to sit down. "Let me massage your legs." That's what I did, like this *makes a massaging gesture*. Then Gulab Bhai (Brother Gulab) said, "Play something, son." "Sir, how can I, a mere junior? Why would you want to hear me?"

"No, son, do play." Well, so I played some, and he played some, and then I said *Sabri Khan's voice is suddenly low and entreating*, "Sir, that composition (asthayi) in raga kedara, which you ..." "Yes, son, what about it?" "Master musician (Khan Sahib), that asthayi ... please give it to me."

Ghulam Raza: And he did give it to you!

Sabri Khan: So these were my actions! But not just on one day—again and again, whenever I met Gulab Bhai. When he had a program on the radio, he came to the house and he stayed here. Then I'd take him to a restaurant. You can't make your request right away: like today I buy him tea, and the same day I ask him for the composition. No! Definitely not! It's only after he kept coming quite a few times; only then, I said, "Khan Sahib, that asthayi in *chandni-kedar* that you sang ... you sang it so very well; please give me that."

"Alright, alright, son. It's a most excellent composition *chiz*."

And so the compositions I obtained are now 'registered' as mine.[9] Nowhere else did I find them. That's a fact!

Raga kedar compositions: raga *shudh kedar, jalbhar kedar, maloha kedar, chandni kedar*. I have all of them in my repertoire, by the grace of God. I have compositions in the different types of kedara, the types of *bahar* and the types of *malhar*. But how do you gather all this knowledge? Your ustad does not have all of it. He simply cannot remember all the knowledge of the world. If he knows something unique, then someone else knows something new too. Now if you want that, how will that person give it to you? He will give it if you serve him. Without that, why would he give it?

Ghulam Raza: Meaning, you make him happy, this is how he will give …

Sabri Khan: There are many ways of serving, not just one. I have spent a lot of money on this! So, in raga *gaur malhar*, for instance, there are very many special compositions. In your shagirdi I played several such special compositions for you in raga gaur malhar, several asthayis, and a tarana. Everyone won't just give them away. Brother, I have gathered a lot of compositions in my 42 years since I came to Delhi to join the radio.

I Have 50 Styles

Sabri Khan: The best minds are those who hear a thing once, and—bingo—now it's as if their father had owned it. I had that kind of mind. I just listened. The moment I heard any passage, I copied it right then.

 On first hearing I would pick up even an intricate melodic passage, and reproduce it exactly. Right? This becomes a habit from childhood, so that the brain 'catches' it instantly; whatever comes out of the singer's mouth is sounded on the sarangi right away.

Regula: Then did you memorize it all?

Sabri Khan: *Who* remembers? Who *retains* anything? We copy you at that instant. At once, the sarangi player takes a picture, at *once*. You are the negative, we are the picture; so we make the photo right away. As soon as you show the negative, we make the print.

 A camera, the sarangi player is a camera! But only the one who can really *play*, whose mind is present (*dimagh hazir ho*), who understands everything. Otherwise there are lots of players who get confused, who play something different from the singer. You say one thing with your voice, I play something else. Can that be a good accompanist? Okay, he plays the sarangi, that's all. To accompany is a difficult job. It's the most difficult of all.

 And then I don't know which raga the singer has prepared. You have practiced a raga for ten years and you want Sabri

Khan to accompany you at your concert, without any rehearsal. I can't rehearse your 'style', the style of your fast passages (*tan*) and your general vocal style (*gayaki*), whether it's Kirana style, Gwalior style, Marathi style, Jaipuri—or Rajasthani—style.[10] I don't have any idea of that! At the time of the performance I sit down and play exactly the way you sing. That's being a good accompanist. And if I don't play the way you sing, then I am not an accompanist.

So this is very difficult for the accompanist to achieve. Then there are genre styles. It's not good enough just to play *khayal*. Of course I have practiced a lot in khayal, but all is not khayal. No! There is also *dhrupad*, of course. Then there is *tarana*; there is *tirwat*; then there is *thumri* and *ghazal*; there is *dadra*, *kajri*, *chaiti*, and *bhajan*.[11] And there is *tappa*, and *mand*, and Bengali song, Gujarati song, *Maharathi bhavgit*, stage song—each is distinct from the other. How do I know which one you are about to sing? Then and there I must recognize the genre and execute it correctly. If I can't play all the genres, I can't be a good accompanist. That's what makes a sarangi player: he should know *50* things, 50 styles, and what can be done in them. Then he will be praised as an excellent accompanist: "Very good, bravo!"

Listen to the point I am making: whatever style the singer uses, I have knowledge of all those styles (*sab hamare pas hai*). How is that possible? Because I remember them. Because I have done a lot of playing. That's how I have an idea of everyone's style. I know Ghulam Ali Khan's style well, also Amir Khan's. I have played a lot with Amir Khan Sahib. But Amir Khan was very choosy about sarangi players at the radio. In those days I was young, so they called me Sabir Junior, as distinct from Ghulam Sabir Khan Sahib of Ambala, who was called Sabir Senior. Amir Khan would say, "Give me Sabir Senior or Sabir Junior, no one else."

Your Ustad Has Not Been Idle: A Splendid Career

This conversation took place eight years later, in 1992, when Saleem and I first visited Ustad Sabri Khan's large modern house in Asiad Village, New Delhi. Here he lived among diverse artists who were chosen for this recognition by the government. Now retired from the radio, Sabri Khan was now at an advanced stage of his career and was clearly ready to stand back and assess his achievements. His two younger sons had become young professionals, starting their careers on sarangi and tabla, while his daughters were all married, one of them to his nephew Nasir Khan, who in 1984 had come to live with the family as his student. Mrs. Sabri Khan, and to an extent Ustad

Sabri Khan too, was missing the familiar world of Old Delhi with bradri relatives all around.

This time our visit was joint and personal, a time to reminisce and look at Sabri Khan's splendid photo album as a guide to the highlights of his long career. The visit culminated in an excellent lunch, served no longer on the sheet-covered floor of a gender-separated music room, but at the family dining table, where we all sat together, eating in modern middle-class style, something that Sabri Khan and his children clearly relished.[12]

About All India Radio

Sabri Khan: Ghulam Sabir is my name from childhood, my real name. When I came to the radio in 1942, that's when they gave me the name Sabri Khan. The radio people did this, because Ghulam Sabir, Sabri Senior, was already there. It's so long ago. At that time they called him Sabri Senior and me Sabri Junior (Bade Sabri and Chote Sabri)—two Sabri!

In my audition for the radio I played raga *bageshri*. "Very good, boy," said the British director general, and "This one is very artistic; he will make a good name for himself, what melodious playing." And the head of the Madrasi unit and S. Krishan Sani, a senior violinist there said, "Yes, this boy plays very well in tune; he will go far, so employ him." And I was in excellent practice. Yes, I was in *top shape*, really in *top shape* (*tayyar*).

Regula: Now you have become an elder among artists.

Sabri Khan: Oh, I am nothing at all! I retired from the radio in '89. I worked in this job for 46 years, by the grace of God. I started at 50 rupees and I received 10 rupees for every 'timed program.' That makes 10 rupees for 12 programs plus 50 rupees per month. At that time one rupee bought 28 or 30 pounds of flour. And 2 pounds of clarified butter (*desi ghi*) cost 4 rupees. You had to taste it to see if it was pure. My grandfather used to take me along when he went tasting.

Regula: Amazing. So 50 rupees was not bad.

Sabri Khan: Now look at this photograph of the orchestra! From that time, they had put me in the midst of everyone. I played orchestra *very* well. I wanted to show you these pictures; they are proof that I was there at age 16 or 17. In those days they did not consider age, just how good you were.

After that, I started composing. I became a very good composer, of light genres like ghazal, *git*, and bhajan. I composed sitting at the piano.[13] And a lot of women who sing light music became my students. Then I went to Mr. Athavale, who was program assistant. I said to him, "Friend, please put me on the staff list as composer; I have decided to be a composer." What he said to me was: "Brother, who knows a composer? He is known just within the four walls of the radio. You are going to be a very good artist. Become an artist, and all the world will know you." Even the director general nobody knows. Who knows the director general? Only those who go to his office, no one else. But the world knows an artist. So I gave up the idea. He gave me very good advice. I value him very much for this. If he hadn't given me this advice, I would have gotten stuck with composing, and who would know me then?

After that, I began to play light music very well. I played 'light' for ten years and orchestra for ten years. I also played in Ravi Shankar's orchestra in 1968.

Travel Abroad

Sabri Khan: Since 1985, thanks to your prayers, I have been going to France every year. They invite me for a solo program. They give me 10,000 francs, at 8 rupees to a franc. They also give me the fare. *To Gulfam, his youngest son, who has appeared:* "Bring a 7-Up; that's very clean."

Here *showing photograph*, this is a very famous cellist in France. He organized a duet performance with me. People told him, "He is a famous musician from India, and you are famous too, so you should play a duet."

Saleem: Cello and sarangi, that's very good.

Sabri Khan: I will show you the write-up that was printed. He came to my house for a rehearsal with his cello. Harvey Parnai. He sat with me for half an hour. But, he said, "In such a short time, I can't play. Next time maybe. At this point it's difficult."

Regula: On the cello it is particularly difficult, with the long distance for the fingers to traverse.

Sabri Khan: No, no, I was not playing extended patterns by any means. Only a composition, in raga *kafi*. I mean *he sings a well-known song*, to play such a composition is not particularly difficult. But, he became nervous. And once he became nervous, the playing didn't work. We could not do the duet together. He said, "I'll try it with you next time." He is famous, therefore he is always busy. But after that, he began to treat me so respectfully, the way you respect a teacher. So now he books me every year, whenever there is a conference (music festival) somewhere, any program that is several days long. And because of these engagements I now have programs booked in Germany too.

Do eat something after all!

Regula: You please eat. If you don't eat, how can I?

Sabri Khan: Yes, all right. I will eat.

Regula: The ustad's permission should be taken even for eating *laughs.*

Sabri Khan: This is entirely your house. Do you have to ask for anything here? You can just take it and eat.

Regula: Okay, I am eating toast and omelette.

Sabri Khan: Just recently, someone else came from France. I am not talking to get praise, just telling you what is real and true. I had gone there in '91. There were performances in Paris. *He again calls out to his sons to get 7-Up for Saleem, asking them to take money and a glass.* So in one program, he organized an entire performance for me; his name is Frank Bernède. Just see how the French people advertise *showing program.* That is something.

Regula: Beautiful. It says "Yehudi Menuhin of the East." Very good.

Sabri Khan: And one more thing, Saleem Sahib. About programs I did outside of India. You see here there was Shivkumar Sharma and so many others. The program went for 24 hours nonstop ... in Paris. It was a full house, and the tickets cost 250 francs. It started early morning and went through the night, 'whole night, whole day.' I had a solo performance. Afaq Husain[14] played tabla with me. Everyone played two items each—Chaurasia, Shivkumar,[15] and all the others—one in the morning and one at night. But I played *three!*

Why did this happen? Because after my second item, the public gave me a standing ovation. That is, they stood up: now we don't want any other item, we want *this*, just sarangi. Malina Salini was the organizer. I had come off the stage, but the public would not accept it; they kept clapping: we want nothing but the sarangi.

They had not ever heard this kind of sarangi playing. Because, *softly* thanks to your prayers, *normal voice* I have many styles of playing.

There are those who are not hereditary musicians; their father wasn't one, nor was their grandfather. They learn from somebody, then they start performing. Yes, they play in tune. But they lack the knowledge of ragas; their raga is not pure! That is why Bhraspati[16] said, "I acknowledge you; your raga is always pure." He used to call me "uncle" (chacha, "father's brother"), even though he was much older than I.

Saleem: I see.

Sabri Khan: "Come here, uncle!" Well, he gave me a lot of respect. What did I want to tell? Yes, so I said to Bhraspati, "How do I know what you think of me?" He replied, "Should I give it to you in writing?" I answered, "Please do!" Then he wrote a *very* good letter. Here is his writing *Ustad Sabri Khan shows Regula the letter, officially signed by Acharya Brhaspati.*

Regula: This is very 'special.' He would not praise anyone just like that. Do you still do accompaniment now?

Sabri Khan: Outside of India I play only solo and never take any engagements to accompany. But here I have done so for really great artists.

And let me tell you about playing a duet with Yehudi Menuhin. Look, here is the photo; Yehudi Menuhin is sitting, and so am I. Yehudi Menuhin had challenged Ashok Sen, the Director General (of All India Radio): "If you have anyone in the radio who plays the sarangi well, then he should play with me." The DG said, "We are having a meeting tomorrow; we will tell you the day after tomorrow." He held the meeting the next day, calling together the DGs, subdirectors, and others. It was decided that only Sabri Khan can play this 'duet,' no one else.

There are people who get nervous in front of a great artist: "Oh, he is so famous, a very great foreign violinist!" They won't be able to play. I already had the experience of playing a 'duet' with the great Indian sarangi player Shakur Khan, face to face with a single mike in the middle. People had started this practice of duets in the radio.

The recording of this duet with Menuhin was broadcast as "India's famous sarangi player with Yehudi Menuhin." Now listen! The newspaper people criticized the DG: "You gave Yehudi

Menuhin the Nehru Award, and the artist who played a duet with him, you gave him nothing?" You see, this came out in the magazine *Mother India* and in the *Hindustan Times*.

Regula: Oh yes, see the heading: "The Ustad's Ustad." How did they know it was you?

Sabri Khan: They came to me, saying "We heard that you played with Yehudi Menuhin." I said, "Yes, I did." They said, "But your name isn't even there." Well, whatever it is, this is what I say: "They (the radio people) certainly don't want their artists to gain recognition." But very fine people gave me compliments.

I played many duets with Yehudi Menuhin, and he was so pleased with me. When he was given a check—and it was quite a bit of money—Yehudi Menuhin said, "Oh, he has played so very well with me, and without rehearsal! He did not even do a rehearsal and played with me just like that. I want my check to go to him." They did not even give me that check.

Regula: Really!

Sabri Khan: 'By God!' That's one thing. Second, I got a lot of praise. The director general's wife came outside afterwards and said, "Khan Sahib, you have really done us proud. Everything he played you instantly played it after him." Whatever he played—'gay music, sad music,' whatever you play—I will play in the same style. But he was not able to play our music. While he played, he kept looking at the written music in front of him. But he only played what was written in front of him, keeping his eyes on it all the time. For us, in Indian music, there is no question of looking at anything. So everyone was very pleased, saying "You played it all without looking at anything." But still, they did not give me that check. They praised me to my face, but did not put it in the newspaper.

And then I had this CD made. Let me tell you the story of this very great man. I mean the man who owns the company Audiorec. It's in London. I did not know him, but I, Kamal, and Ghulam Sarvar were playing, the three of us. It was a solo concert in London, and 'by chance' someone had invited him to listen. The house was full, no room to sit; he did not even get space to sit. It was a very big program. After the program ended, he said, "'By God,' Khan Sahib, where else can I get such a family tree program? Record it just like this. We will give you as much money as you tell us." I said, "Alright, I will give you a date from Birmingham." It takes two hours to get from London to Birmingham by car. So we arrived in Birmingham, at the house of my son—a very comfortable place with two bedrooms, kitchen and bathroom, and a very big hall downstairs—well, we rested for a couple of days, and then worked some more on our program. Now every day he phoned, "When are you giving a recording date?" "I'll tell you tomorrow." I stalled, so that he should get even more eager (*laughs*).

Regula: *Laughs.* These are the methods.

Saleem: *Reciting a verse:* "Oh how you enhanced their pleasure...."

Sabri Khan: It's just a small matter. Well, we did make the record. I said, "Let's give him a date." And the CD which I have just shown you, the owner of Audiorec, Mahesh Patel, he was very happy with the recording. He called in a photographer at 10 at night who took two hours to take 'pictures' and filled three rolls of film! Mahesh Patel gave me the three 'pictures' you see here. From all those pictures, they chose one to make the CD.

I want you to have at least some 'information'; that's why I am taking your time and putting my own time in too. So that at least you should know that your ustad is not sitting idle; he is achieving something.

Regula: About that I never have any doubt *laughs*. How wonderful.

CHAPTER 2

Sabri Khan

The Master and His Disciples

Introduction

This chapter presents Sabri Khan in action as the master of many disciples as I was privileged to experience and record it. It starts with the ritual of sha-girdi *(discipleship) when Sabri Khan made me his disciple and thus inducted me into his circle of disciples both inside and outside his family. The formal ritual is followed by encounters with other disciples and joint practice sessions, all of them taking place under the ustad's (master teacher) wide-ranging guidance in overlapping combinations with different emphases: from conversations with his oldest and his youngest disciple to common practicing and, in the next chapter, a set of teaching sessions focused on my learning efforts. All of this takes place in the changing scene of the music room.*

This takes us back in time to the beginning of my study with Sabri Khan in June 1984. The crucial day when he accepted me as his shagird *(disciple) also marked my entry into the oral world of his extended, yet intimate, musical family of "brother disciples" and their master. Its center of action was Sabri Khan's music room, an informal combination of* darbar *(holding court, literally "royal court") and workshop, where we were welcome to join in a learning situation that was open-ended yet always rigorous and demanding. The ustad's care for individual students extended from music to life itself, from imparting the particulars of the classical heritage to fostering their successful performance careers. But sharing his precious oral knowledge was measured in accordance with the capacity and merit of the student.*

*In 1984 the circle of disciples ranged from the successful middle-aged All India Radio staff artist Shabbir Husain, now deceased, to the ustad's eight-year-old son Kamal Sabri, who is today a well-known young artist. Three other sons enriched the musical home life under their father's tutelage, all three being tabla players: teenagers Ghulam Sarvar, now settled and well known in England, Jamal Sarvar, now an accountant, and six-year-old Gulfam, now a performer and teacher of tabla, voice, and san-*tur *(hammered dulaimer). Also living with Sabri Khan was his nephew Nasir, whose tabla-playing father had brought him to be trained as a sarangi player (now a professional and married to Sabri Khan's daughter). The Ustad's most accomplished student then was Ghulam Sabir, a highly compentent young professional and a prominent visitor to the music room, especially during the initiation ritual. Another faithful disciple was Nathu Ram, who provided expert restoration and repair service. Even international students maintain the bond, as is most eminently exemplified by my* shagird bhai *(brother disciple) Daniel Neuman, through whom I first connected with our ustad.*

Once he had accepted me as a shagird, Sabri Khan ensured that I became part of the entire circle. He also welcomed senior relatives and community members who came to socialize, to assess, and to contribute to the disciples' progress. The rich gift of his ustadi *(teachership) is simply invaluable in the true sense of the word. It is a gift to be shared with the world, and also to be rewarded by it.*

The Ritual of Shagirdi—A Tie That Binds[1]

Accepting Regula as a Disciple

Ustad Sabri Khan has agreed to accept me as a disciple! It is June 1984 and I have a summer of intense music study before me, under the guidance of this renowned master of the sarangi and master teacher of many successful disciples, including several foreigners. Together with my husband, Saleem, we land at the Ajmeri Gate, enter the old city on a bicycle rickshaw, and make our way to Ustad Sabri Khan's house, past the water pump, tea stall, goats and chickens. Then we climb the dark staircase, and suddenly, a different world opens up, when Ustad Sabri Khan welcomes us into the music room. Already present are his sons and disciples, as well as several senior members of the community who have come to witness the shagirdi.

The formal proceedings of the shagirdi are embedded in informal musical conversation, both social and technical. An important part is for the master to have his students perform something to show their and the teacher's

Figure 4 Sabri Khan guiding Kamal on sarangi and Gulfam on harmonium during shagirdi ritual, his music room, Old Delhi, 1984.

competence. But the central ritual is the ceremony of tying the thread (ganda bandhan), *a symbol of the student's permanent tie to the teacher. The teacher ties the thread and feeds a sweet to the new student, iconic of the nurturing paternal role he is assuming. He recites a special prayer requesting God's blessing for this lifelong relationship.*

Sabri Khan is the attentive host and pivot of the informal, sometimes multifocal event. He keeps a watchful eye on all the goings on in the music room, not only as the impresario and main actor, but also as the facilitator and nurturer, ensuring that everyone present is comfortably engaged according to what suits them, while also playing their part in the main agenda, which he is in charge of. Today, this means to initiate teaching the new student and to create conditions for learning, including setting the student up with a good instrument. This is happening at the shagirdi, where two instruments are being tested. It also means to establish connections with the new student and her husband by finding common conversational ground.

The ustad welcomes us to the shagirdi ceremony and introduces his sons Ghulam Sarvar, an accomplished young tabla player, and nine-year-old Kamal Sarvar, a beginner on the sarangi and the ustad's youngest disciple. He also presents Ghulam Sabir, his most accomplished student, who is a very fine professional sarangi player and also sings very well. Ghulam Sabir's nephew Nasir Khan is introduced, as well as a teenager who has come to

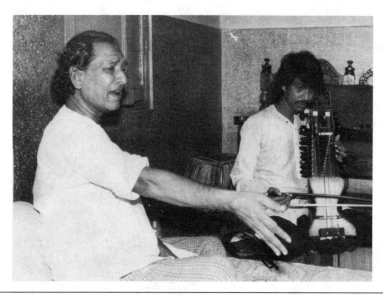

Figure 5 Sabri Khan demonstrating an old composition, accompanied by Ghulam Sabir, his music room, Old Delhi, 1984.

Delhi to live with Sabri Khan and become his disciple. Both are also related to Sabri Khan.

Hosting an Informal Gathering

Ghulam Sabir is plucking and tuning the 37 sympathetic wire strings of a newly repaired sarangi.

Sabri Khan: *Converses with Saleem, introducing a community member who is visiting from Lucknow, the city of Saleem's family.* His father was a very good sarangi player. He was also a sarangi player, but he left it—stopped playing about 20 years ago.

Visitor: I changed my 'line' (of work), went into the film 'line.'

Sabri Khan: *Takes the tuned sarangi and shows it to Saleem, since Regula will need to get her own instrument.* This is a new instrument, sir. Actually it is old, it only has a new 'polish.' It was cracked. Now see it. I don't like a new instrument; I like an old one. Now see, it was cracked at the bottom, so I put a brass plate on it; now it can't come apart. I had a special 'polish' put on; my student Nathu Ram does this. He learns *dilruba*[2] from me. I have a dilruba here. I got him an audition in the radio (All India Radio), and he passed it with a B grade. Now with a B grade he has begun to get programs. Well, he does very good repair work on everyone's instruments:

harmonium, sitar, *sarod*, etc. He's the one who fixed this sarangi. *To the visitor:* have a glass of water; it's cold.

Testing Instruments: The Star Student Performs

Ghulam Sabir is ready to play, and as is proper, he asks permission from his ustad, Sabri Khan, and from the visiting musician. Then he starts playing a brief alap (introduction) in raga gaur sarang. *Now he picks up the second sarangi and tries it out by playing what he calls a 'light tune' in raga* pilu.

Visitor: The instrument hasn't become quite 'set' yet. After two to three months of playing it will sound fine.

Sabri Khan: I haven't yet made a hole in the skin (that covers the belly; this is easily done with a burning cigarette).

Saleem: This one has a bigger tone than the other one.

Sabri Khan: *Testing Ghulam Sabir:* Why is that? Can you tell why it sounds like that? Let me tell you. Can you see a difference between the two playing strings on the two instruments? That one is thin, this one thick.

Ghulam Sabir: Yes, that can be. Actually, putting a block under one foot of the bridge will make the sound bigger!

Sabri Khan: Yes, this will raise the playing strings. It will sound better if you tighten the strings some more, raise the pitch.

Ghulam Sabir: *Raises the main string and briefly intones a light and highly ornamented tune.*

Saleem: Play again, so that I can take a picture.

Ghualm Sabir: Should I sit the way I do now (*legs crossed in front*)?

Saleem: Sit the way it's done for playing.

Ghulam Sabir: Actually, the proper way to sit with the sarangi is kneeling, with legs to one side. *To Regula:* Have you been told that before? *He assumes the kneeling position for the picture and now begins to play* mian malhar *on the better-sounding sarangi, outlining the features of the raga.* This a very big raga. I owe all this learning to Ustad Sabri Khan's prayers (*du'a*) and to his teaching … everything he has done for me.

Sabri Khan: After two or three months this instrument will sound well.

Ghulam Sabir: Yes, you have to keep playing it and tuning it. Do you want to play it? I'll tune it first. I have an even bigger instrument at home. *He does more tuning.*

Regula: Is this a double-brained instrument *domaghza*, and what's the difference?

Ghulam Sabir: This is a domaghza. In the *yakmaghza* (single brained) there are no pegs above the face.

Sabri Khan: *Testing Regula's knowledge:* Do you know the names of all the parts of a sarangi? They all have names.

Regula: Please tell me. I have heard them from others, but you will tell me correctly.

Ghulam Sabir: Well, she speaks very good Urdu.

Sabri Khan: Yes, her Urdu is very good.

Saleem: Oh yes; with me, how could she get away with wrong Urdu?

Sabri Khan: Mmmh *laughs*, that's Doctor Sahib speaking!

Regula: Yes, you can see. (*Eagerly:*) So please tell me the sarangi parts.

Sabri Khan: I'll tell you some time; it's not needed right now. Did you understand what one-brained means? This top part is the brain, and if you take that away, it's a single-brained instrument. But all that is really the face (*chehra*). Below it is its chest (*sina*), and below that, the belly (*pet*).

Saleem: And the legs?

Sabri Khan: *Laughs and points to the base.* These are its tiny legs (*pair*). *All laugh.* And this is the string holder (*tar gahan*). This one (above the fingerboard) is also a string holder; it holds up the three playing strings. This lower part, they actually call it *kothi* (villa, house).

Ghulam Sabir: *Resumes his performance of raga* mian malhar *while referring to the raga's season.* This raga will really sound well in the rainy season; you will really like it then.[3] *Now he takes the other sarangi again and plays a thumri, an expressive light classical song.*

Saleem: Bravo!

Sabri Khan: *Addressing Saleem:* Ghulam Sabir plays excellent sarangi, but he is also a singer; he sings *ghazals* (art songs based on ragas and romantic poetry) very well. (*To Ghulam Sabir:*) Why don't you take the harmonium and sing?

Ghulam Sabir exchanges the sarangi for the harmonium and begins to sing and play the same thumri he has just performed on the sarangi. On Sabri Khan's urging he changes to a ghazal, noting that Saleem savors ghazal poetry. Sabri Khan's eldest son, Ghulam Sarvar, brings his tabla and starts tuning it to match Ghulam Sabir's chosen tonic. Their performance is punctuated by lively verbal applause for the song and for Ghulam Sarvar's brilliant tabla interludes. Sabri Khan applauds, highlighting special phrases or accomplishments to the other listeners. Then he welcomes a new visitor. The song ends, followed by warm applause. Ghulam Sabir starts a second ghazal, now singing especially to Saleem who applauds vividly, repeating verse lines sung. Others applaud as well, and the singer as well as the drummer gain enthusiasm.

Shagirdi Ceremony

Now one of the boys brings in two trays, one filled with rock sugar, the other with laddu, *a ball-shaped sweet, and places them on the floor in front of the ustad. These are the designated sweets for the shagirdi.*[4]

Sabri Khan: *Explains the special significance of the sweets.* This is what they call *shakar dori* (literally "sugar and thread"). Ustads who do a shagirdi ceremony often don't remember the special invocation called shakar dori. Ask them the question: "As you are making someone your disciple, do you recite a shakar dori?" Our elders have a *bandish* (composed text) for everything, so there must also be something for this undertaking, something that makes the occasion auspicious, like saying *Bismillah* ("I begin in the name of God," the opening phrase of the Qur'an) when you begin anything. There is a "Bismillah" for everything. For learning the English language the "Bismillah" is ABCD, just as for Urdu it is Alif Be Te.[5] But for shagirdi there is something like that, an "opening" that gets recited in a special way.

Saleem: I see. Who will recite it?

Sabri Khan: Everyone does not remember it right, sir. *Turning to the first visitor, from Lucknow:* Many people do not recall it, isn't that so, sir?

Visitor: That's true.

Sabri Khan: It is done by special request.

Saleem: I was worried that you might ask *me* to recite *laughs*.

Sabri Khan: No, no! But if you get a chance to see a shagirdi-ustadi (literally "master-disciple ceremony") somewhere, do ask them: now that you are doing a shagirdi, please also recite the shakar dori.

Now the sweets are being served and commented on.

Saleem: These sugar pieces are like rocks.

Sabri Khan: *Laughs and responds to several guests who discuss the size of the rocks and whether the pieces should be cut.* The rock sugar is fine as it is for the ceremony; afterwards take it into the other room and break it in smaller pieces.

More guests have come. Eating arrangements are being made for them, and plates are passed to everyone.

Sabri Khan: *Turns to Regula:* Let me tell you something new. We have a special shagirdi, for the sarangi. Singers have a different one. Tabla players have one that is yet different. This you won't even hear about from others, you understand?

Now you'll see what a fine composition (bandish) I will recite for you. *To his senior student, Ghulam Sarvar, softly:* You have already heard it in your own shagirdi, of course.[6] (*To all:*) As I said, every undertaking has its Bismillah, and if God wishes, the outcome will be blessed (*barkat*). A little teaching will produce a big result (*thora sa sikhaya-zyada ban gaya*). So it becomes 'God's gift.' *To Regula:* This recitation is to invoke 'God's gift.' I will of course teach you. But it is up to God to make it effective. To gain for you praise from others—"bravo, ahahahh, very good, very good"—this comes from Him; we humans cannot make it happen.

Saleem: You just say so, and I'll applaud *laughter*.

Sabri Khan: Yes, well … but she is a 'musician' and will mostly be among musicians, so she will sometimes see a shagirdi. Then you ask some of those big ustads who sit there! They carry out a shagirdi but do not know how. *Shakardori: shakar* means "sweet," and *dori* means "this string." And this string, once properly tied, is such a strong bond (*bandhan*) that it lasts your whole life. It is the same relationship as our *piri-muridi*, the Sufi bond between spiritual guide (*pir*) and his spiritual disciple (*murid*). Only here the bond is between a master and a disciple of music (ustad and shagird).

*In the background, the call to early afternoon prayer (*zohr*) is sounded.*

Saleem: That kind of tie we had with marriage.

Sabri Khan: And it is also similar *laughs*. I guess the custom is not observed that much now to putting a comb in the bride's hair. Though in India we still observe it some. But in a 'love marriage' there is no need for it; you just go to the court and get married.

Saleem: What's different about a 'love marriage'? We had three marriages: in the court, the mosque, and the church. *While this conversation continues, a senior visitor comments on young Nasir's impending shagirdi with Sabri Khan.*

Sabri Khan: *Addressing the visitor:* Once Nasir's father reaches Delhi, we will go through the same customary ritual (*dastur*) with him. He will absolutely have to have the ceremony; it is a very necessary thing.

Saleem: If you had told me earlier, I would have invited Regula's father too. *Everyone laughs.* You know, her father has visited Delhi before. *The laughter gives way to surprise.*

Sabri Khan: I see! *He pauses and now turns to the ceremony.*

Tying the Thread

*Sabri Khan has prepared the special raw cotton thread (*ganda*), dyed alternately red and yellow.[7] He now ties it around my right wrist and recites the shakar dori in a low voice (but this text is not to be recorded). He ends with a humble request to the Prophet for help in asking God to bestow his gift of blessings and that He may give the student success in the endeavor which has brought her here.*

Sabri Khan: So this is a tradition (*parampara*) that comes down to us from our ancestors (*buzurg*). *Now he feeds Regula a piece of sweet laddu, but rather than putting it in her mouth, as is the norm with male students, he offers it to her in his hand, for her to pick up herself and eat.* This is another custom (*dastur*), to feed all the other students who are present as well. I did not invite too many, because some live too far away, or they are busy on a Sunday morning. I also did not consider it necessary. But the students who live close by are here. *To Saleem, who has been taking photos:* Please take one more picture.

Saleem: Yes, certainly.

Sabri Khan: This practice (*rasm*) comes to us from our forefather. Now, from this day on, she now stands in the same relationship to me as my child (*aulad*). It is the duty of the master to teach the disciple the way one teaches one's child. And likewise, it is the duty of the disciple to learn.

        Now he puts several laddu in a paper bag, which has been brought in at his request, and says to Regula: These are for you to distribute as a blessing. *Then he invites Saleem and all those present to take some sweets and partake of the blessing.*

Senior Visitor: *Offers a laddu to Nasir, who hesitates but is urged to take it.* You also play something, so that everyone can hear.

Sabri Khan: Yes. But don't tape him, not yet.

Regula: No? Alright. *Regula shuts off the tape recorder while Nasir takes the tuned sarangi and plays a brief piece in raga* marva.

Sabri Khan: I remember a very special shagirdi held many years ago in Muradabad (his home town). Laddan Khan of Rampur was present, an incomparable sarangi player who was also my uncle. They all played on that occasion, so he performed too. Laddan Khan's own ustad, Chutke Khan, was also there. Chutke Khan was a very good sarangi player from Kanpur (city near Lucknow). That region has produced excellent musicians, a lot of them!

To conclude the event, Sabri Khan, the ustad and musician of highest standing, emulates the shagirdi of his elders by presenting a performance himself, using one of the sarangis that is already tuned (his own instrument remains at the radio station). He decides to show us raga malhar, *which his student Ghulam Sabir has intoned earlier. His eldest son Ghulam Sarvar accompanies him on the tabla. At my request, he allows me to record his playing for my own study.*

Sabri Khan: These are old compositions that few people remember today; I do remember them. I have played them in New York, and a tape of the performance was sent to me. I remember all the old songs, of *dhrupad* and even *dhamar* (both venerable archaic genres). I did not just make them up myself!

He continues playing alap, then starts the vilambit *(slow) composition, accompanied by Ghulam Sarvar in slow* ektal *(cycle of 12 beats). After about seven minutes, he switches to the faster-paced* drut *composition in* tintal *(cycle of 16 beats), and almost immediately starts playing a variety of tans, including virtuosic rhythmic patterns full of syncopations, a range of bowing techniques, and a variety of melodic shapes from bold upward leaps to circling around one or two single pitches. This too is concluded within five minutes. Enthusiastic applause follows, with clapping and then exclamations of* Subhan Allah *(God be praised),* shabash *(bravo), and others.*

Ghulam Sarvar: You had mentioned that old composition in malhar?

Sabri Khan: Yes. *To Regula:* I'll sing it for you; it is a very special composition. *Turning to the junior family members present:* And, *bhayya* (brother), get the food ready; it's high time and everyone is hungry. *They leave the room.*

This is a dhamar. He sings while clapping the outline of the 12-beat cycle (ektal). First the asthayi, then antara (first and second section of a composition),[8] and then the return to the mukhra (principal phrase), concluding on the sam, the downbeat of the cycle. It is a serious, formal composition, executed with flair and competence.

Visitors: *Approvingly:* Yes! Wonderful indeed!

Sabri Khan: This is a very fine composition (*bandish*) *he repeats, emphasizing the importance of such musical knowledge. Then he calls across the terrace:* Bhayya, bring the lunch quickly!

A sumptuous lunch, prepared by the women of the family, is served to celebrate and conclude the shagirdi-ustadi event.

SHABBIR HUSAIN, OLDEST DISCIPLE: DEVOTION TO THE USTAD

Introducing Shabbir Husain

An important lesson I learned during my study with Sabri Khan is his lifelong support of all his students, and their lifelong devotion to him. Sabri Khan's oldest student, Shabbir Husain, shared with me his own enactment of this lesson during an unforgettable conversation between master and disciple. His visit culminated in a touching song of praise for his ustad.

Shabbir Husain traveled to Delhi from his village in the nearby province of Haryana. His family belongs to a local community of hereditary musi-

cians who remember that their ancestors were once Hindus from the Jat community. At the age of nine he became a disciple of Sabri Khan, living in his care. Thanks to Sabri Khan's teaching and guidance, Shabbir Husain successfully auditioned for a position at All India Radio and became a staff artist in the "Rural Programme." His repertoire combines the folk songs of his region with the classical ragas he learned from our ustad.

With his family in the village, Shabbir Husain commuted to Delhi and always kept in touch with his ustad, also inviting him to perform in the countryside. Barely literate, he turned to Sabri Khan to get schooling for his child beyond the limited opportunities in the village. Shabbir Husain was a thoroughly humble musician full of eternal gratitude for what his teacher had done for him; he personified genuine devotion.

The Musical Family in Action[9]

I arrive at Sabri Khan's music room as usual, but Sabri Khan is not there. Nasir, his nephew and new student, is practicing, so I join him and we both do scales together. Now the ustad comes in, having changed into a sarong to be comfortable in the heat. While he checks over my scales, his young son Kamal joins in the playing, and now all three of us play together to our teacher's instruction.

In the middle of our practice session, Shabbir Husain comes in and sits down, waiting for his ustad to attend to him. He needs help in getting a child admitted to school, starting with the admission form; he cannot read the Devanagari script of Hindi (only Urdu, which is written in Perso-Arabic script).

Later Ghulam Sabir, Sabri Khan's senior nephew and most advanced student, also comes to the music room, and the practice session turns into a conversation, with informal performances by both senior students. For all three of us junior students, listening to our advanced brothers play for our teacher was a musical family treat and an inspiration.

The session starts with Sabri Khan teaching scales. Nasir, Kamal, and Regula all play to his instructions. Now Kamal valiantly plays the sequence sa re ga, re ga ma (123, 234), struggling with intonation; in the background, Nasir does the same thing faster. At the same time, Sabri Khan proudly jokes about Kamal's efforts and also corrects him in between. Then he turns to me:

Sabri Khan: Out-of-tune playing must be corrected, otherwise bad intonation (*besurapan*) becomes embedded in your hand and fingers. *Now all three are playing a scale slowly. Sabri Khan pays close attention to Kamal's fingering.* Pancham (5)! Do it again in tune! Now go further up the scale to re ga (2 3). *They play it.* Now to ma *pa (4 5). It sounds less in tune.* Back to re ga (2 3). *Now it sounds quite in tune, and they keep playing it. Nasir and Regula speed up, and he has us go all the way up the third octave (it sounds messy) and eventually down to the lower octave and back. To Regula:* Lighten your bow so that it does not scratch so much in the lower octave.

Now the ustad introduces Shabbir Husain who, upon being greeted, says:

Shabbir: God's blessing (*Allah ki mehrbani*)!

Sabri Khan: He has my prayers with him. With the help of my prayers, God had him receive land worth 20,000 to 30,000 rupees.

Regula: Oh really!

Sabri Khan: He is very devoted and serves me a lot. A lot! Learning is one aspect of being a student; 'music' is there, of course. But making the teacher happy also gets the student his blessings.

Shabbir: Yesterday Munir Khan (a senior sarangi player) told me that the fragrance of your ustad's sarangi is present in your playing, not in that of his other students. I played raga *gaur sarang* and *shriraga* (raga *shri*), and thanks to Khan Sahib's prayers ...

Sabri Khan: Shriraga is a very difficult raga. And *marwa* is difficult. He played marwa "straight" (unaccompanied) at the Harbhallabh Music Conference (*Harbhallabh Sangit Sammelan*) in Jalandhar[10] before an audience of thousands. And he got clapping applause (*aur claps lia*).

Regula: Excellent, bravo!

Sabri Khan: He played for one and a half hours!

Shabbir: Master musician, Khan Sahib, I wanted just to relay what Munir Khan said.

Sabri Khan: Yes, Munir Khan too is a pedigreed (*gharanedar*) person (also a member of a recognized musical lineage). Yes, I consider this real praise.

Regula: So you started as a boy?

Shabbir: I have been in the service of Khan Sahib since I was nine years old. Now my age is about 42 or 43.

Sabri Khan: His father was a sarangi player, so he wanted his son to play sarangi too. He came from a village, Goana. So he got his son started. He had heard many, many great sarangi players, excellent ones. But he did not become the student of any of them. He came to me. And it is his father who brought him to me. His father said, "Khan Sahib, please ..."

Shabbir: My father wanted that Khan Sahib should teach me; he had heard him and thought most highly of him.

Sabri Khan: Shabbir was very young. But his father said, "I want to place this boy in your service."

Shabbir: And he invited Sabri Khan to a restaurant ('hotel').

Sabri Khan: Listen, many people wanted Shabbir Husain to come to them for training. Those people were quite annoyed. But Shabbir's father, Dhulia Khan Sahib, was himself a sarangi expert (*nawaz*). He knew the world; he knew who had what to offer.

Shabbir: *To Regula:* Our Khan Sahib (Sabri Khan) has all 'styles' at his command. Khan Sahib plays the four kinds of sarangi music. I haven't the time because of children and family obligations; otherwise I could have reached much further with Khan Sahib's training.

Sabri Khan: I have many 'types' of music. One type of sarangi music I have been thinking of playing in the morning is raga *lalit*. In this music you cannot play with technical brilliance ... raga *lalit*.

Shabbir: Alright, Khan Sahib, I am in great difficulty right now. Now I ...

Sabri Khan: *With reference to Regula:* First do something for her; she is making a tape recording, so tell her something about sarangi players, about your father, and important sarangi players in your family; tell her some of the names.

Shabbir: Hmm ... but I have brought along the form for that child's school admission. I just want your advice.

Sabri Khan: Alright, tell me. But first drink tea.

Shabbir: Oh, just give me water.

Sabri Khan: Here is water, have it. *He reads the form.*

Shabbir: I left Khan Sahib's service for this child (*kai dafa neora, bachche*).

Sabri Khan: Now he wants to take the boy away from Gwana, his village, and leave him here with me, to learn the sarangi. His children are there, his house. There is a bus route from here; it takes about an hour.

Regula: So you travel to Delhi every day.

Shabbir: Yes, since I am employed at the radio. Thanks to Khan Sahib.

Sabri Khan: His level is B high grade. None of my students has achieved anything less than B high grade, thanks to God. Whomever I prepared for an audition got B high grade. It is a very good grade.

This is a most excellent shagird of mine. When he received his first pay, he placed all of it before me. "This, Khan Sahib, is all yours." I just picked up 100 rupees, but he insisted "No, no, I won't take it." And now he has given 5000 rupees for the wedding (of Farzana, the eldest daughter of Sabri Khan).

Shabbir Husain's Radio Audition

Sabri Khan: And hear this, a very big story. At his audition, Shabbir Husain played exactly like at that music conference, and people said, "It was actually Sabri Khan who was playing; it sounded just like him." When he had his audition here is a story about faith, having faith in someone. When he had his audition, I did not attend it.

Shabbir: He thought, "Well, how will this fellow be able to play? He is useless."

Sabri Khan: What do you think! Oh come on! He said *assuming a pleading tone*, "Khan Sahib, please you come along to my audition."

Regula: So why did you not go?

Shabbir: If I did not play well, or play something that did not make sense to him, then he would … He did not have confidence in me.

Regula: Oh?

Sabri Khan: That's right; I was not sure. So Shabbir said, "Please, give me your cap." So he put on my cap and went. The cap that I put on in winter, when it is cold, he took it and put it on his head. And he said to me, "Now I 'feel' as if you are standing in front of me."

Shabbir: This token was on my head, but I felt dejected: Khan Sahib did not treat me well by not coming along. My stars are not good. There was a choice of two ragas, *marwa* or *sham kalyan*. So I played marwa. Inder Lal was standing there, and Mushtaq Husain (a sarangi player and a famous singer, both staff artists).

Sabri Khan: Marwa is a 'difficult' raga!

Shabbir: So I played. It was a half-hour tape. That tape was examined by the director and passed, and they said, "We can't recognize Shabbir Husain! Yesterday Khan Sahib (Sabri Khan) was quite doubtful about him."

Sabri Khan: They gave him a grade of B high. Another point: Shabbir Husain is a 'specialist' of 'Haryana music', that is, of 'folk music'. He does 'rura'l—the "rural program." His 'father' was also a 'specialist' in folk music. And in the entire radio, in all of India, there is no one else who knows this; the only person who does is Shabbir Husain. His 'basic' competence is rural. His classical competence—that he has learned from me.

Regula: He is at the radio, that is in addition to Inder Lal?

Now Nasir and Kamal are starting to play scales again, one fast, the other slowly.

Sabri Khan: True, Inder Lal is also there, but there is greater demand for Shabbir Husain.

Now the conversation turns to the prospect of Shabbir Husain's child living in Delhi with Sabri Khan, including the issue of school expenses.

Sabri Khan: *Enumerates:* His 'dress', 'uniform,' his 'pocket money', and his 'fees.' *Then he fills out the application form.* And the principal's name? Write "Shri. K.C. Mehra."

Having received his ustad's help, Shabbir Husain now starts tuning his sarangi.

Sabri Khan: Will you have some more tea? No? *Turning to Regula:* I never tell any of my students what they should do, what they should give. Never; I don't make any demand.

Performing for Regula

Shabbir finishes tuning and starts playing long notes; then he intones raga madhuvanti *(a lighter raga). Meanwhile, Sabri Khan fills me in with information about Shabbir Husain.*

Sabri Khan: His village, Goana, is on the side of Panipat. His community is the Jatowale; there have been some excellent sarangi players among them. The forebears of these people were Hindu; they were Jat. Jat, you find them in the police service. Then these people became Muslim. This happened hundreds of years ago, 500 years. So they are called Jatowale. The ones who practiced a lot became good players.

Shabbir: *Now introduces a light piece in a similar scale and starts singing a Haryana song, accompanying himself with ornamented interludes on the sarangi.*

Sabri Khan: *To Regula:* Yes, now this is what he will perform, a song from Haryana. *Turning to Shabbir:* Present a bit of it; don't make it too long. And then sing something more lively.

Shabbir: *Complies, ending with a song about Lord Rama.* To play and sing at the same time is difficult.

Sabri Khan: Oh yes, it is, to play with your hand and sing with your mouth. There is one song that Shabbir Husain has composed for his guru.

Long Live My Ustad

Shabbir: Yes, I have written one devotional song (*bhajan*) about my guruji. A bhajan about Khan Sahib. Khan Sahib had gone to America. I remembered him a lot when he was away so long.

Sabri Khan: He sang it a lot, for everyone, and also sent it to me in writing. It's a matter of faith. He saw me in his dream.

Shabbir: I have written it myself, and every word is worth listening to. *Accompanying himself on the sarangi, he sings in a* bhairav-*like, but more chromatic scale:*

1. Ustad Sabri Khan abad raho!
   Tane jag mein rosan nam kiya.
   Aisi sarangi baji teri taine
   Pura apna kam kiya

1. Ustad Sabri Khan, may you live long!
   You have made a name for yourself in this world.
   You have raised the sarangi so high
   That your life's achievement is complete.

2. Koi gavayya aya bharat mein,
   Tei kisi se nahin ghabraya.
   Agle ne ek kahi tanen char kahi,
   Tu hazir jawab khara paya.

2. You played with singers from all over India,
   But none of them could phase you.
   You matched their passages fourfold,
   Proving yourself a master of improvisation.

   Tum Khuda Rasul ko manne wale,
   Karam Ilahi tere sir par chhaya.
   Nike chaliye jhuk ke miliye,
   Khuda Rasul ne farmaya.

   You believe in God and the Prophet,
   The blessing of God is upon you.
   Go straight and be humble toward others,
   That is the divine command.

   Ho re rat dina taine mehnat kari,
   Aram subhe nahin shaam kiya.
   Aisi sarangi baji teri taine
   Pura apna kam kiya.

   You have worked hard day and night,
   And now you are reaping your reward.
   You have raised the sarangi so high
   That your life's achievement is complete.

3. Amrika England Germany:
   Bides ki kari ghumai.
   Tum ne kam kiya Khuda ne nam diya
   Aur achchhi kari kamai.

3. America, England, Germany:
   You have traveled across foreign lands.
   You did the work, God gave you fame
   And made you prosperous.

   O re thare bina, Dilli ka radio
   Suna jo deve dikhai.
   O kitne chele kare taine
   Sabki kari bhalai.

   Without you, the Delhi Radio Station
   Seems a lonely place.
   You took on so many disciples
   And did much good to all of them.

   Khuda se dua kari aur madad kari, Yeh
   hukam sahi Islam kiya.
   Aisi sarangi baji teri taine
   Pura apna kam kiya.

   You prayed for them and gave them help,
   Thus you followed the tenets of Islam.
   You have raised the sarangi so high
   That your life's achievement is complete.

4. San ikyasi men professor bane.
   Tane kala ki dhum machai.
   Ho angrejan ne tere pani puje,
   Aur hogai sufal kamai.

4. In 1981 you became a professor.
   You made the arts thrive and flourish.
   Even the foreigners worshipped you,
   And you were crowned with success.

   Tere jaat paat ka bhed nahin.
   Hindu, Muslim ho Sikh, Isai,
   Jo fariyadi darbar pahonch gaya,
   Tei dil se jaan larai.

   Caste or creed did not matter to you.
   Hindus, Muslims, Sikhs or Christians,
   Whoever came to you with a need,
   You put your heart into helping them.

   Hind men kise sarangiye se
   Vakt mila tene sabse alag mukam
   kiya. Aisi sarangi baji teri taine
   Pura apna kam kiya.

   You have gained a special place apart
   From all the sarangi players in India.
   You have raised the sarangi so high
   That your life's achievement is complete.

5. Jitne chele thare the
   Sab guru charan ke das hue.
   Guru ne jhanda gad diya bharat mein
   Anand barah mas hue.

5. All the disciples you have had
   Have learnt at the Guru's feet.
   They raised their Guru's banner across India
   And enjoyed happiness all year long.

Bhagwan ne daya kari,
Guruji ki mehar phiri,
Ham sare chhokran pas hue.
Shahinshah kab darsan doge Bharat men?
Hamen us din ki kare as hue.

God bestowed his blessings,
The Guru provided his support,
And all of us students passed our audition.
Oh Emperor when will you show us your face in India?
We are all hoping for that day.

Shabbir Husain huane ke na guru ko
Bar bar parnam kiya.
Aisi sarangi baji teri taine
Pura apna kam kiya.

Shabbir Husain says that he touches
The feet of the guru again and again.
You have raised the sarangi so high
That your life's achievement is complete.

KAMAL SABRI: BEGINNER TO RISING PROFESSIONAL

Introducing Kamal

It was late in his teaching life that Sabri Khan decided to teach his own instrument to one of his children. Hailing from a family of singers and sarangi and tabla players, he chose the tabla for both his two older sons. At the age of 19, Ghulam Sarvar was headed for a professional career, whereas Jamal Sarvar, at 15, was studying commerce, playing tabla only as an amateur. At the age of 9 years, Kamal had already been learning the sarangi for over two years, but he became a diligent student only recently, when his older cousin Nasir arrived in Delhi and became a second sarangi disciple in the family home. Gulfam, the youngest brother, got an early start on the tabla, but he had a clear talent for singing and harmonium playing. The two boys learned the same fundamentals and sometimes practiced together; sometimes Gulfam was also asked to play tabla, but he as yet did not have to follow the stringent regime of practicing. Eventually he was to become a tabla player as well as a singer.

Kamal was a steady presence in the music room, diligently practicing his exercises: a scale up and down, sequential patterns up and down, and at his father's request, he and his younger brother Gulfam would play a special teaching composition or sargam *in raga* yaman kalyan, *which has been passed down from the family's ancestral master, Bahadur Husain Khan. In the presence of his father and other elders, Kamal did not say much; he listened and did what he was told. But away from the sarangi he could have fun with his younger brother Gulfam, on the large terrace separating the music room and the family portion of the house, where they could slip away until they were called back to practice or to bring water to a visitor.*

Figure 6 Kamal Sabri on the terrace at home, Old Delhi, 1984.

Playing for visitors on request was also a normal part of life for both brothers, and obligatory at special events like a shagirdi, when a brief performance from each student present was expected, in ascending order of accomplishment. This practice shows the strength of the master's circle while exposing the students to performance, their own and that of their musical brothers. Of course Kamal and Gulfam always went first, being the youngest. For Kamal, playing his difficult instrument was a challenge. While his younger brother was able to sing and play tunes on the harmonium with some ease, Kamal struggled to control a scratchy bow, to stop the thick gut string with his small fingernail, to find the exact spot on the string for each note to sound in tune, and to maintain the correct sitting position that would always put his leg to sleep. He and I, together with Nasir, often practiced together, sometimes with their much older brother Ghulam Sarvar, who enlivened our simple exercises with his impressive virtuosity on the tabla.

Today, 20 years later, Kamal Sabri is leading a new generation of young emerging sarangi players. He has already made a name for himself as an accomplished sarangi player who sounds much like his father, yet has a bold personality of his own. He plays in India and abroad, including appearances with his father and, most recently, in a three-generational ensemble that includes Sabri Khan's daughter's young son Suhail. The ustad is once again imparting his sarangi training to the youngest of the family; the master's lineage continues!

Kamal and His Brother on the Terrace (1984)

This conversation with my youngest musical brothers came about following the teaching session on July 30, 1984 when Mrs. Sabri Khan and her daughter joined me in the music room for a rare family chat (see the dialog for session 2, in Chapter 3). The ustad had gone to the mosque for afternoon prayer; so we sat on the terrace to talk and take pictures, away from the music room where Kamal and Gulfam rarely spoke. Both continued to maintain a respectful distance toward me as their senior, even if a fellow beginner, compelling me to take more of a lead in the conversation than I would have wanted.

Regula: How long have you been learning music?

Kamal: I began learning the sarangi two and a half or three years ago. But then I stopped and only started when he (Nasir) came here.

Regula: So you started from the beginning again? What was the first thing your papa taught you?

Kamal: He taught me everything, starting with the first notes: sa re ga ma (1 2 3 4).[12] My Papa first of all placed my fingers and told me the notes, and how to hold the bow. First I learned to draw the bow, without fingering (open string): sa sa sa sa (1 1 1 1), then re re re re (2 2 2 2). Then came playing sa re ga ma (1 2 3 4). I learned to put the fingers on the string one by one: re re re re (2 2 2 2) with the first finger, ga ga ga ga (3 3 3 3) with the second, that way, going up the entire scale.

Regula: What notes or raga did you learn first?

Kamal: There is the day *sargam* (notes, scale) and the sargam for the night (or evening). My teaching started with *bhairon (raga bhairav).*[13] Papa put marks with a pen for each note on the sarangi, so I could see where to put my fingers.

Regula: How did he have you play—separate bows?

Kamal: Yes. (*He plays the bhairav scale very well, one bow stroke per note, but adds two notes on the same bow stroke a few times.*)

Regula: Bravo! You also played some tied notes; that is more difficult. When did you learn the evening notes?

Kamal: After six or seven days I learned the evening scale (raga *yaman*).[14] And then, after some days, came the *paltas* (sequences): sa re ga (1 2 3), re ga ma (2 3 4), in both the day and the night scale.

Regula: Do you play the night scale only when you sit to play at night, or do you play it any time?

Kamal: No. At night you play the night scale, in the day the day scale.

Regula: But when you go to school and there is no time to play in the morning, then can you play the morning notes at night?

Kamal: No, only in the morning—so we can play bhairav on holidays.

Regula: Your sarangi is smaller than a full-sized instrument, but not as small as some I have seen. Did you have a smaller one when you first started playing?

Kamal: My maternal grandfather (*nana*)[15] brought this very sarangi and gave it to me. He has also created a new instrument, *sabroz sabrang* (all colors for every day); it is like a guitar but played with a bow. He made it along with making the sarangi for me.[16] My grandfather first taught me how to hold the bow.

Regula: So your grandfather is the one who gave you your first start.

Kamal: Yes, he did.

Regula: When your papa started teaching you, did he sing or play on the sarangi what he wanted you to learn?

Kamal: He does both, and I have to imitate what he shows me. *He plays an ascending and descending scale of raga yaman (with a raised fourth), using separate bow strokes.*

Regula: When he started teaching you this scale and the sequence patterns sa re ga, re ga ma, ga ma pa (123, 234, 345), did he tell you which finger to use on each note, or did he let you use any finger?

Kamal: No, the fingers are fixed. He shows me by playing the first sequence up and down the octave.

Regula: That's very good. Did he have to correct you a lot?

Kamal: *Demonstrates out-of-tune notes.* He would correct out-of-tune notes right away. If anything is wrong, he corrects it—any note. Sometimes dha (6), sometimes pa (5). Also, sometimes the bow scratches or moves up the string; then he has me lower it. He'll say "down, down." And at first I used to miss the rhythm. Now he has taught me, by clapping the beat. That's how I learned to keep it in mind. One, two, three, four *he demonstrates, clapping while counting.* He clapped and counted out the beat with everything.

Regula: Did he ever tell you to play two notes in one bow, instead of playing each with a separate bow stroke?

Kamal: No. *But he attempts to play the scale and sequences by connecting two notes on one bow here and there between the separate bow strokes*

Regula: So this connecting, you did it on your own! *He nods.* Bravo! Now tell, when you started learning, when would your father teach you every day?

Kamal: Any time at all, whenever he had time. And if he did not have time … not every day.

Regula: And did he tell you to practice for a particular length of time, or any time?

Kamal: Do it any time, but it should be two to three hours.

Regula: Oho! So how long did you do it when you started?

Kamal: At first, one to two hours. Then I was playing sa sa sa sa, re re re re, etc., practicing bow strokes and fingering.

Regula: Did you ever practice too little and get scolded?

Kamal: Oh yes.

Regula: Did he beat you too?

Kamal: Yes, when he got angry.

Regula: Well, teachers do beat. It creates fear. Does that make you play or practice more then?

Kamal: Yes, it was during those days when I stopped playing. Then I started again when he (his cousin Nasir) came, in Ramzan (Ramadan, the Muslim fasting month)—he arrived on the third fasting day.

Regula: So why had you stopped playing? Did you get fed up?

Kamal: No, I just did not feel like it when I was playing all alone. Even Gulfam hadn't started playing the harmonium.

Regula: What method of sitting did he teach you?

Kamal: This one. *He demonstrates a position with both legs folded (like kneeling) on the right side, holding the instrument.*

Regula: Does it not hurt after a while of sitting like this?

Kamal: No, but my leg goes numb. Then I can't walk for a while.

Regula: Our sarangi is placed on one side, resting on your knee, right—not in the middle. Has your father said anything about that? Or some people hold it with a tilt or turn.

Kamal: He said to hold it straight, not to tilt or turn it.

Regula: What other special things about the sarangi did your father teach you?

Kamal: Putting rosin on the bow, but tuning the strings will come later.

Regula: Did he teach you any composition yet (bandish)? Like that song in raga bhairavi, or that sargam teaching tune that you and Gulfam played together earlier?

Kamal: Oh, you mean ni dha pa ma, ga re ga ma (7654, 3234, 764, 5- - - a famous sargam or teaching tune in raga yaman kalyan).

Regula: Yes, that one, when did he teach it to you?

Gulfam: *Interjects:* That came before.

Kamal: Papa had taught it to Gulfam on the harmonium.

Regula: I see; so you both picked it up. It's much more difficult on the sarangi, though.

Choosing an Instrument for Both Sons

Regula: Was it your wish to learn the sarangi, or did your papa tell you to?

Kamal: No, I wanted to play it. Papa said, "I'll teach you sarod," but I did not want it.

Regula: And you, Gulfam? Did you want to learn the harmonium? Didn't you also learn tabla?

Gulfam: Yes.

Regula: And did you also first have to sing the notes, or did you play them right away?

Gulfam: First I was taught by singing, and only then by playing. It's to remember; if you forget, then you can say it (the names of the notes). First I was taught tabla, when I was little.

Regula: And now you aren't little any more? I see. How long ago was that? You tell me, Kamal. When you started the sarangi, is that when Gulfam started tabla?

Kamal: Yes, for a while.

Regula: What did he teach you first?

Gulfam: On tabla, dha dha ti te, dha dha tu na (basic drum stroke syllables). On the harmonium, sa re ga ma (1 2 3 4).

Regula: On a big tabla? Is there no small tabla?

Gulfam: No, I started out on a big one. But sometimes my two hands were not together; they moved separately.

Regula: So did you get scolded, or beaten?

Gulfam: Yes, both.

Regula: Then you stopped the tabla? Why?

Gulfam: Yes. I didn't like it. My hands would not move together. Then I started playing the harmonium.

Regula: So what did your papa teach you on the harmonium?

Gulfam responds by first playing the evening scale of raga yaman, *slowly and correctly: srgmpdns (12345678, with a raised fourth degree), followed by the same sequence of 123, 234, 345 that Kamal had played earlier, also with a fixed fingering. Then, at my request, he searchingly plays the morning scale of raga* bhairav, *correcting himself when his finger played a wrong note. The second time the scale is flawless as well as the sequence 123, 234, 345. He also plays the second sequence, which is a string of four notes, srgm rgmp gmpd (1234, 2345, 3456). Next he sings and also plays a unique Muslim devotional hymn in the same raga and in a rhythmic cycle of ten beats, the first raga composition both boys were taught.*

> *Asthayi:*
>   Kar le tu ab yad (6- 5-6 45 3-4)
>   Bande Allah ke (22 345 34 2-1)
>   Jo kuchh bhi bhala hove tera (12 3-4 56 782 78 65)
>   Tu ab yad kar le (6 45 3-4 6-5-)

> *Antara:*
>   La ilaha Il Allah (34 6-6 77 8-)
>   Muhammad ul Rasul Allah (8 77 8-1 78 6-5 …)
>   Nabi ji ka kalma subha pahr (45 434 56 782 78 65)
>   Tu ab yad kar le (7 65 3-4 6-5-)

> *Asthayi:*
>   Now do remember (God),
>   You creature of God,
>   Whatever misfortune may befall you.
>   Remember God now.

> *Antara:*
>   There is no god but God
>   Muhammad is His Prophet
>   Recite the creed of the Prophet in the morning
>   Remember it now!

Regula: That is a beautiful morning song. Were you taught to both sing and play the song at the same time?

Gulfam: Yes, Papa always did it that way.

Regula: *To Kamal:* But this is not done with the sarangi, or is it?

Kamal: No, there you just play.

Regula: So, do you two practice together?

Both: Once in a while.

Regula: So, anything else I should know that you learned from your Papa? No? Alright, thank you very much. Now let's go and practice!

I take photos of Kamal and Gulfam, as well as their cousin and brother disciple Nasir, who joins us on the terrace. And I consider myself fortunate for the gift of this musical as well as verbal conversation and its precious insights into these two remarkably focused young musicians and their perspective on what learning music in Sabri Khan's family is all about. Since the ustad is still absent, I offer a good reward for both Kamal and Gulfam to Mrs. Sabri Khan, wishing to observe elder etiquette.

Forging the Profession Today (2005)[17]

An entirely new Kamal, self-possessed and eloquent, now speaks of his mission and career in articulate English on his roving cell phone. Our conversation reveals a remarkable transformation from struggling beginner to a "complete musician" for the world of the 21st century.

Regula: You remember that little interview that I did with you way back? When you now look at yourself, as a musician, did you follow the footsteps of your father?

Kamal: When you're a kid and a student of a teacher who is a milestone of musical greatness and can properly teach you music on the sarangi, then you follow him. I was very fortunate to have him there in my family. After that, after you've learned, you've crossed to that stage where you need to look for work by yourself.

Regula: How does that happen?

Kamal: My father is the kind of musician that would never phone someone to get his students or son work. He was confident enough in his teachings, and the blessings of Allah. And some things, your teacher doesn't teach you, and you learn by your own mistakes and by your own experiences—there are so many things. You cannot simply say that this is enough for you to become a great musician; this is what you should do. It's not that simple. There are so many things which are counted in becoming a great musician.
The first thing is that you have to have a good teacher. You have to have belief in God. You have to have appreciation from people. As long as you are a student, you should always respect what your teacher has said to you. And then as soon as you become a musi-

cian, you look to other musicians as well and you try to follow their qualities as well. And you have to enrich yourself with a vast knowledge of music, otherwise you can never be a good accompanist. To be an accompanist you have to be humble, you have to be nice. Your attitude towards your role as an accompanist has to be complementary to the vocalist, not disturbing him. You have to add fragrance to the flower, because you are a team and you are working together with the vocalist.

Regula: You're so right. Tell me, didn't you just have a tour of Rajasthan? Are there new things that you are doing?

Figure 7 Kamal Sabri, on tour, Italy, 2005.

Kamal: I have composed sarangi music, all-together instrumental, for four to five sarangis together layered on different channels, on different tracks. This music is called "Dance from the Desert," and that CD is going to be released by *Music Today* in July. It's something experimental, the first time ever in the history of sarangi playing.

Regula: So these are different sarangis? Like, Rajasthani sarangis?

Kamal: No, these are classical concert sarangis, but they are played in a very folk way, a Rajasthani folk way of playing sarangi. A sarangi player has to be versatile to be outstanding. He cannot just play *lehra* (metric tunes for tabla or dance), or just play solo, or just play accompanying the vocalist. I call myself a versatile sarangi player because that's what my father is and what he taught me, to be able to adjust yourself, even with other music. I have played with Egyptian musicians, with English musicians, with musicians from Finland and from India. Nowadays, other areas are open to sarangi players, to experiment with different types of music.

Regula: That is something new.

Kamal: My father used to say, "The teacher must be competent, the student must listen, and God's help must be with you" (*Ustad ho kamil, shagird ho amil, Khuda ho shamil*). And he used to say "Become the type of fragrance that the air will take around the world."

Regula: Looking back, when you were playing and talking to me 20 years ago …

Kamal: That time was such that sarangi players were having difficulty. Because, Ustad Sabri Khan, then Ram Narayanji, then there was the time of Sultan Khan, and then there is a big gap. Then suddenly Kamal Sabri appears. Sarangi players were having problems. My father used to tell me that you should not be a sarangi player; you should be a vocalist, do something else. But I used to think that the time will come for me. I can't just give it up like this.

Regula: So did you like the sarangi? Did you come to like it? It must have been very difficult.

Kamal: I started living for it. I started to think that maybe I will lift this light up, because this has been the dream of my life. And there are so many musicians that had been an inspiration for me to be challenging. Like Zakir Bhai, Pandit Ravi Shankarji, they did so much for their instruments, so the sitar became synonymous with Pandit Ravi Shankarji. Tabla became synonymous with Ustad Zakir Husain. I used to think that there should be a time for the sarangi as well. What I was liking in other sarangi players, I started working on that. Becoming articulate, working hard to speak good English, working hard to become a world-class musician, listening to other music, and speaking to other musicians. Traveling around. I'm playing other music. I used to think I had to do something exceptional for the sarangi.

I traveled to Bihar, where I went to small schools to play. And yes, of course, I traveled around to India where I played for small villages. People come to know about my instrument; they enjoy it. If you don't travel to these places, and if someone asks you to play a Bihar folksong, you cannot play because the vibrations are not there; you never traveled to that place. How would you play? So this is what made me travel to those little villages in Rajasthan where I went. I heard the music and felt it, the soil, felt the people, vibrations. Then I went to UP to understand what is *kajri*, how you should play it. Why is only when Bismillah Khan plays it, it's like he has brought Benares in front of him.

Regula: When did you start traveling and who organized these things?

Kamal: I started traveling when I was 13, because my father had a tour in England, and that tour was appreciated very well. I hadn't traveled in India much, but I used to travel with him to the *Harbhallabh Sangit Sammelan* (Harbhallabh Music Conference), where I performed when I was 11, and that was a turning point of my life. That's when people first started talking about my future as a musician and of how well I played. It encouraged me towards sarangi, not to give it up but to keep playing. Later I had the opportunity to work with Jan Garbarek in Norway. I was the only Indian who was playing. From Pakistan it was Fateh Ali Khan Sahib and from Norway it was Jan Garbarek. When I was playing with him I was so young, and he was a great maestro, but he said no, no, I shouldn't feel like that. I should play what I know. And I learned so much by the presence of that great musician.

Among singers, Girja Devi was the first one that heard me and she wanted me to play for her. And then I tell you an incident where I was playing with Shrimati Gangubai Hangal. In that performance I didn't tell her that I am the son of Ustad Sabri Khan. I just went; I said that I have been invited to play sarangi for you.

And then she said, okay, okay, come on. And then I was playing, and after the concert she immediately asked me, "Are you the son of Sabri Khan, or are you his student?" I was shocked that she could tell by my playing that I should be either his student or his son. It was a great, great award for me. I am not saying I am like him, but that a small glimpse of my father could come into my hand. It was something like a great blessing for me from my forefathers.

Being part of a seven-generation musician family, you always pray to God, because it's a big responsibility for a musician like me. So becoming a reasonable, or somewhat mediocre sarangi player is not enough. I have to be exceptional; I have to be outstanding. So I used to practice all night and pray that God may put power (*shakti*) into my notes, and make my music effective (*tasir*), so that people may like my work. What you achieve by practice is command over your instrument. But to make such an impact on the audience, leaving them what is called spellbound, this can only be achieved by prayer and by playing for the Almighty. He can give you that. And by the blessings of forefathers, and of elder musicians. You serve them, receive their prayers, and make people happy with your presence. I used to see the great example of this that Zakir Bhayi gave—so down to earth; he always asked for blessings from people.

Regula: He is very humble.

Kamal: Yeah, this is what made him great.

Regula: You are really the kind of sarangi player that your father has always talked about—the sarangi can do anything and turn in many different directions. What would you say is your special thing?

Kamal: Often, when you become a sarangi player, you don't get a position in classical music. You start looking for other avenues; you start going into fusion. But you shouldn't do it. You need first of all to make your classical background strong, and then once you've come to a level that people are able to appreciate, then you start listening and looking for other music. I would call myself a world-class sarangi player, because I am not just sticking to Indian classical music, but also experimenting with other music. I could be different from sarangi players, because the way I can play, the way I can imagine a phrase of sarangi is more versatile than other sarangi players.

Regula: In those days, 20 years ago, you and your brother Gulfam were practicing together. Do you play with him now? Do you have any kind of family duo? He plays tabla.

Kamal: Well, he switched over from one instrument to another. He couldn't focus on one instrument. In the beginning he started singing, then he switched over to tabla, then he switched over to santur, then he started singing again. Now he's concentrating on singing; he has a band as well, in which he sings.

In the beginning, we used to practice together. He used to play with me. And you know, we learned many things. We are more like friends rather than brothers. We went to school together; we used to have fun together; we used to play in bands together, in school and in college. We were the cultural secretaries in our college. We were the best-known guys in our college. So we used to practice; when he was playing tabla he used to practice with me. Then we went for tour in Finland. When we came back, he decided to learn santur. He switched over to santur; now he switched over to vocal. We did one concert of santur and sarangi *jugalbandhi* in England, which went really well. And after that, he decided to be a vocalist. I haven't performed any concert with him, accompanying him as a vocalist, but I might do it in the future.

Regula: That's very interesting. So you took quite different paths. That's really great. And what about Ghulam Sarvar in England, have you played with him?

Kamal: I do quite often. I just finished a CD with him with Virgin Records. It's called "Swar Alankar," in which I've played a rag called *saugand*. And I played three different compositions. One in *tilwara tal*, one in *teental*, and *ek tal*. The best thing about this recording is that I have played a *tappa* (a highly ornamented light classical genre), which is rare to hear in any sarangi recording. So that's been quite a big hit in the market in the classical world.

Regula: I have to look for that; I love tappa, it's a very special thing. And you also have a nephew, Suhail?

Kamal: He is my eldest sister Farzana's son, a very good and a very promising sarangi player, the eighth generation of the family. And he's very bright; he was a child prodigy. He started learning sarangi when he was only two. He's doing very well, and he has performed with us in many cities. He toured with us in England

and Norway. He was ten when he went for tour with us, in a three-generation concert.

Regula: He is the promise. He is where you ...

Kamal: When we come together on the stage, people look forward to it, what kind of music they are going to hear. There's a very

Figure 8 Three generations: Ustad Sabri Khan with his son Kamal and grandson Suhail, Delhi, 2001.

big music magazine and there was a big article on us. The first family of sarangi players, in which three generations are working in their own fields. We push each other. Like my father never pushed myself, but I can never push Suhail.

Regula: That's fantastic. Listen, I want to thank you very much. It was great to hear, for you to give me this update. It's wonderful.

Kamal: No problem *laughter*.

Regula: So now, you're going to Paris?

Kamal: Yeah, I'm going on the 19th for a tour in Europe. I'm going to France, Italy, and England. I did music for an Italian film as well. Google search, and put my name "Kamal Sabri," you'll get all of the information.

Regula: Very good. I'm impressed with the way you present yourself. You have a really clear picture of where you are going, and that's very impressive.

Kamal: I think that's God's blessings and my father's blessings.

Regula: And I wish you everything good on your tour. We'll talk again.

Kamal: *Inshallah* (God willing).

We say goodbyes, and I then call Ustad Sabri Khan in Delhi to congratulate him on his son's achievements and on receiving the Padma Bhushan Award from the President of India on Republic Day, March 23, 2006. He is very proud of both!

CHAPTER **3**

Teaching Regula
I Will Make You into a Sarangi Player

Introduction

In 1984 Ustad Sabri Khan taught me all summer, creating for me an intense and comprehensive learning process. Starting from the competence I had from my earlier study of the sarangi, he began by teaching me a raga (maru-bihag) and at the same time integrated into this teaching the very basic practice routine that his junior students shared, attending to flaws in my bowing and intonation. At first, Sabri Khan was cautiously assessing my commitment and ability. The teaching sessions that follow are the beginning of his commitment and show in a most remarkable way the holistic concept of his teaching that encompasses the whole range of concerns for a sarangi player, from playing the notes in tune to shaping a performance. A most crucial dimension is composition or how to create the structure of a raga improvisation into the form of a classical genre. Finally, Sabri Khan seriously addressed my future as a sarangi player in North America.

Foreign students were not new to Sabri Khan; he had experience teaching several Westerners, most prominently his long-time disciple Daniel Neuman, my friend and colleague. What made his sessions so precious was being able to join in the unmediated flow of interaction in Urdu that Sabri Khan used in a pithily idiomatic and richly referenced way to get his teaching points across. Sharing the language also activated a bond of shared meanings that quickly dispelled the inherent awkwardness of a foreign woman planting herself in the all-male music room where women were simply not part of the company.

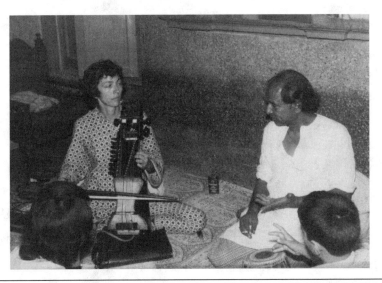

Figure 9 Sabri Khan's approving gesture of Regula's marubihag phrase, with visiting Polish student on tabla, music room, Old Delhi, 1984.

The three sessions that follow are interconnected by the common reference point of a short performance I was to do on national TV—a test for the new student. All three took place within a span of a few days; each offers a slice of life of the music room, and within it a slice of my learning curve under my ustad's comprehensive guidance.

Session 1: Preparing for a Performance[1]

Present are one or two visitors from the bradri, *perhaps to listen in on the new student's progress. Both Sabri Khan's nephew Nasir, and then his young son Kamal Sarvar join me for practicing. This session is really a preparation for the brief performance and interview that I have been invited to do on national TV a few days later. At first unsure of my competence, Sabri Khan now fully supports my appearance, once he has heard the result of my intense practice.*

Music in Sabri Khan's home is framed spatially by the walls of the music room. It is also framed temporally by the call to prayer, which can be clearly heard from the nearby mosque five times a day: at pre-dawn (fajr), after 1 p.m. (zohr), in the afternoon after 4 p.m. (asr), at sunset (maghrib), and at night, after 8:30 p.m. (isha). The call reminds Sabri Khan to walk over and perform his prayer; he returns within half an hour except when he meets neighbors and relatives living nearby, or attends to errands. Unless told otherwise, I stay and practice until the ustad returns.

Figure 10 Sabri Khan welcomes Regula in his New Delhi home after eight years, 1992.

This is a uniquely short, but focused, teaching session, fitted in before the afternoon prayer (asr). With full-time duty at the radio (All India Radio), followed by a late lunch, Sabri Khan often takes a brief rest before embarking on the many activities that fill the later part of his day. Accommodating a temporary student's need for intense teaching can be a problematic interference with ongoing commitments that count more toward providing long-range sustenance than even a well-paying stint teaching a foreigner. In this brief span of time, Sabri Khan covers the studying work that needs to be done and what it takes to pull together a performance. The session is focused on strategies for practicing. It is also an opportunity to try out the strategies together with my fellow students and feed on the cumulative enthusiasm of three eager beginners.

Sabri Khan: *Intones the composition and passages* (tan) *in marubihag, the raga that I will be performing on TV.* Some people say if the instrument is good, the playing is good. But it is not the instrument; it is the hand that plays.

Regula: *Begins to play marubihag passages, but the intonation is a bit shaky.*

Sabri Khan: It sometimes happens in tans, the way you are "feeling" right now; different notes are not quite in tune. You have to make a real effort to correct the intonation. Put your mind to it.

Technique and Fingering

Regula: I sometimes get confused regarding fingering, which finger patterns to use in different tans? For instance, should I use my first or second finger on *madhyam* (ma, the fourth degree of the scale)? That's the only point.

Sabri Khan: Use the first finger. That's not a small point; it is a very big point. It won't solve itself. If you use a wrong fingering, then your tan will not come together. But if the pattern changes this way, then use the second finger.

Nasir comes into the room to join Regula with his sarangi.

Sabri Khan: *Introducing Nasir:* This is my brother's son. He is getting my teaching free. He is my disciple, but before that he is my paternal cousin's son. If you have to spend money to get something, then you appreciate its value. What you get free, you don't understand its value. Whatever it is that you are getting for free, a sarangi or a tabla, you won't value it; alright, you just leave it lying around here or there. But if you know that you've spent so much money on it, then you will know its worth. Then you'll practice the life out of it and value it. You get me; you understand Urdu very well!

Yes, so you just keep playing this pattern. Don't leave it until it is completely in tune. That's it! I will fine-tune your sympathetic strings; that will help the intonation. A scale pattern: don't ever start it downward; that's wrong, always upward first and then down. Whatever you do, it should be correct.

Sabri Khan demonstrates practicing a scalar pattern in raga marubihag, first up to one octave, then to two, then gradually extending the scale further to the third scale degree, then the fifth and the uppermost tonic, playing many notes.

Sabri Khan: My 'idea' of practicing is only this. I don't do anything else. It's my special thing. I do it for half an hour and that takes care of my practice (*riyaz*).

Regula and Nasir continue to practice sequential tans up and down.

The Way to Practice

Sabri Khan: You should play each tan 100 or 200 times, at the very least. Then what will happen? It will turn into *gold*! This is the way to practice, according to Mamman Khan Sahib and other great masters of the past.

Regula: That's what they said?

Sabri Khan: Not what they said, what they *did*. And I have seen their offspring; they too are dead now. I saw his son, Mammu Khan Sahib, he just kept working away … Okay, you've spent an hour practicing the same tan over and over, for at least one hour. No other tan! Once you have practiced the same tan in this way for a whole week, what's the result? The tan will flow like *water*; it will become liquid. You will be able to toss it in at any point in your performance, and play it as brilliantly as can be.

That's the method. But the task is difficult. Why? Because you feel restless for a "change," any change! To kill your desire is very difficult.

Now just repeat your tan. *That's* the way!

Regula plays the tan over and over, now joined by both fellow students in the house, Sabri Khan's nephew Nasir Khan, and his young son Kamal Sarvar. The music room resonates with the bright sound of three sarangis, when a guest arrives.

Sabri Khan: Come in, come in, Salam Alaikum. *Addresses Regula:* This Khan Sahib (respected musician) is a very knowledgeable person.

Regula: *Resumes the tan repetitions, worried about the impending performance.* There is also the matter of *alap* (melodic improvisation introducing the raga). May I play it, and you please stop me wherever something is not right.

Sabri Khan: Yes, absolutely. That's fine.

Regula: *Begins to play; it sounds out of tune.*

Sabri Khan: Your sarangi is not tuned. It doesn't matter, just leave it alone; don't let it bother you. Occasionally there is no time to tune; then just put a cloth over the resonating wire strings so that there is no false resonance.

Regula: *Keeps playing while Sabri Khan and his visitor discuss something.*

Sabri Khan: *Turning suddenly to Regula:* Listen, did you memorize this from the tape of my performance that I gave you?

Regula: I did.

Sabri Khan: Very good. Your playing is absolutely right.

Regula: I listened and listened, and then I wrote it down, I mean, as much as I could. Now I am playing it.

Sabri Khan: What a good mind! *To the visitor:* She did this just from listening to a tape. Listen Regula, if you do intense practice for four months—do it until you leave and continue practicing back in Canada—then after four to six months give a concert. But for at least two months you need to have a tabla play with you. Don't worry about the cost! Why? What will come out of it? It will bring you reputation and 'respect.' I mean, in the area of performance. Theory is something different; this is practice! And when you give a concert, you will get paid for it! The entire money you spent will come back to you. Don't be worried about the expense, but make sure you engage a tabla player.

Returning to the upcoming performance: Now I will put it in a sequence: first you play alap the way you just started now. *Yes!* Play it *just* this way! It will sound far and wide as if Sabri Khan is playing. Absolutely!

Regula: I have copied you. As the Sufis say: imitation leads to the real thing (*naql se asl paida hota hai*).

Sabri Khan: That is absolutely correct. I mean, just seeing a Sufi always reciting "Allah, Allah, Allah" will turn a person into a Sufi himself. Imitation leads to the real thing; that's a correct saying. Just play the way you were playing. I liked it. That's why I said it. So just give this 'idea' of the raga, and then start the song. And do play *jor* (pulsed improvisation) too; after all, you have three minutes.

Regula: Jor is easier for me to learn, but I can't do it today; it will be ready by tomorrow.

Sabri Khan: Alright. And you need to do some 'timing.' They gave you three minutes? Even if you play for four, it will be fine. And ask them how long the interview is to be. If it is a 15-minute program, 10 minutes will go for the interview, and you get 5 minutes for the sarangi "item." *He lowers his voice.* And do tape the whole program, do it yourself. Just put your recorder to one side. Then we will listen to it, and when you return to Canada, play it for people there. And then, do some more practice on it, just polish and polish it, and practice hard. After that, ask one of your societies or organizations to sponsor your concert.

Turning to his visitors, who showed surprise at how Regula has progressed so fast: Her in-laws' home is in Lucknow. Actually, she plays the cello. But the real thing is that she has music in her head, that's how.

(*Back to Regula:*) Right now, practice whatever "material" you have, I mean written from the tape, practice all of it very well, for at least two days. And on the third day play it for me. Whatever you have done from the start: alap, jor, put all that "material" together into what you are going to play and time it. I will listen to it with my watch. But you must practice it all thoroughly, including the tans. Those five to seven tan passages, they come at the end. First play each tan once; each tan will conclude on the *sam*. Second, what will you do? Join two tan passages together, that makes one separate tan out of the two. For example, if you have eight tans, you play each of them, that makes eight; then you combine two each, that makes four more, a total of twelve.

Regula: I see. How about the straight up-and-down tan?

Sabri Khan: Absolutely! Toss your hand up the scale (*upar maro hath, bilkul*). It will require some practice, however.

Regula: Oh yes, I have to improve that. Otherwise I'd have to do it slowly, but that wouldn't sound good.

Sabri Khan: Why play it slowly? It won't sound good in performance. Rather don't play it at all. Keep it as practice for now. Once you can play it fast, then add it to your performance. Okay? This entire little collection of material, practice it, polish it up completely for two days, and make it completely smooth. Then it will become very good. And then play it for me.

As we talk, the call for the afternoon prayer resounds from the nearby mosque.

Visitor: The call for prayer has sounded!

Sabri Khan and the visitors get up and go to the nearby mosque to pray. Meanwhile, Mrs. Sabri Khan and her daughter Babli come to the music room to talk about my "rehearsal" with Jamal Sarvar, Babli's younger brother, who is to accompany my TV performance on the tabla. Then their mother tells a story about Gulfam, the youngest boy, and a white monkey in a tree outside her mother's home, in the nearby city of Merut. With the senior men's departure, the music room has become a different place, dominated by conversation about nonmusical matters, though Babli shows great interest in learning Western staff notation because it is often used by studio composers in India. Her husband, too, is a musician who plays the sitar for All India Radio, and her father-in-law, Ali Raza Khan, is a well-known sarangi and vichitra veena player.

Session 2: Generating Ideas—An Ocean in a Cup[2]

It is late afternoon two days later. Sabri Khan has returned from his work at the radio station and now resumes teaching me a second session today, the day before the TV recording. Also present is Raza Husain and the respected older musician from the previous lesson. Today, Sabri Khan's wife is in the room to listen and to meet me. Jamal Sarvar, the ustad's second son, is present too because he has been designated to play tabla with me on the TV program. His tabla training is basic; he studies full time in a business college. Today he plays tabla with me, and also with his father.

This session shows how Sabri Khan teaches technique in conjunction with composition. He also demonstrates here how much beyond traditional sarangi playing his study and competence has taken him.

The ustad is trying out the sarangi he has procured for my use this summer. He uses the occasion to demonstrate what he calls, for my benefit, 'types' or genres of sarangi playing: a thumri, *then a* khayal *in raga madhuvanti.*

Sabri Khan: Nice sarangi! *He now intones alap of marubihag, the raga that Regula has been learning.*

Regula: Very nice, very nice. It has a very good sound.

Sabri Khan: *Mashallah* (By the grace of God)! ... Say "Mashallah"!

Regula: Mashallah! … oh yes, you mean so that no evil eye may strike a good thing?

Sabri Khan: Yes indeed. *Both smile. He continues playing, moving from pulseless alap into pulsed jor improvisation by using separate bow strokes to mark the rhythm. He also includes playing a rapid tremolo, short bow strokes repeated on a single pitch, and shows Regula how to do it with a light grip on the bow.*

New Techniques

Sabri Khan: Now see, for this I support the bow lightly, with only two fingers, taking the rest of the hand off the bow stick. If I hold the bow with my entire hand, then that makes the hand "tight." This is what they call "technique." Once, at the radio, I was scheduled to play a duet with a violin player. So I started doing this technique. People are jealous, you know: "Why does 'Sir' (the director) ask for him?" Other sarangi players ask, "Why is he in demand? We too can play!" He selected me to play a duet with a violinist from Madras, Sadiyo Pavari. He plays very fast. I said, alright, I'll play. Which raga? So-and-so raga. Okay, go ahead. For zzzzzzzzzzzf, he tossed out a fast tremolo (*lai phenk di*), so I tossed out a tremolo too. *He demonstrates a tremolo.* This bow is a bit heavy, a light bow will move faster. You can also use tremolo to do a triple cadence (*tiya*), starting from the sam (first beat and arrival point of the cycle).

By the way, tonight on the radio you can hear a program I played together with Rajan Sajan Mishra, the famous vocal duo, sons of Benares sarangi player Hanuman Mishra (see Chapter 10). I have played a solo piece in it. *To Jamal:* You dub it for her.

Now he intones a straight tan [scale passage] starting on the lowest string, with changing variations. You should play this as well, from time to time, moving around the two lower strings. It's a new idea. Other players don't do it. It will take practice, but anyone can do it, if he works on it. *He gradually expands the scale upward, to three octaves, always shifting accents.* This is an idea too. Do you understand it? *More accents.* This is difficult, to play cross rhythms within the cycle (*lay banana*). The strong bow strokes and accents require strength. *Now he shows Regula how to bring the scale to a sudden end with a cutoff* (sur chhorna*). Finally he takes the scale all the way up to four octaves.* To go this high, the string length should be changed, making it longer to create more space for finger placement in the fourth octave.

Regula: What is the advantage of playing up there? The sound is very high and does not resonate.

Sabri Khan: Nothing, really, just to show that we can play four octaves!

From a Single Idea Come 50 More

Now the ustad comes to special turns of phrase for raga marubihag, especially a lovely descending series of sinuous mordents from the raised fourth scale degree down to the tonic: ma ma ga ga re re sa (4433221).

Regula: I'll certainly play this one in between, it is so attractive!

Sabri Khan: *Continues teaching the pattern.* It is amazing how a person can shape one thing in so many different ways, not just one. *He demonstrates ma ga re sa (4321) in many ways: ma sa ma ga re sa (414321), sa ga ga ma ga re sa (1334321), sa sa ga ga ma ga ga ma ga re (1133433432), and more.*
     Suddenly, he says softly, with significance: You stay here for six months, only six months and you'll become a sarangia (sarangi player).

Regula: I do want to come.

Sabri Khan: But you have no time! And why am I saying this? Your 'mind' is capable of it; it's very good. It 'catches' things. *And*, I can teach you. I *want* to teach someone who has talent. But to teach someone who is dense, I find bothersome.
     The teaching process continues: You should get 50 ideas from this, at least; that will be worth something! But you know, this is very difficult work. I have done research; I have immersed myself, immersed, meaning that I lost myself in it: What more is there in the music? What more can be drawn from it? I have practiced a great deal. Eventually I became so 'expert' that I could handle everything.
     Now listen to one "idea," out of it come 50 more ideas. *He shows Regula how to create numerous transformations of a typical marubihag phrase: ni sa dha—ma pa sa (786, 458), singing the syllables to make the notes clear to me.*

So I have decided in my mind how many ideas to present.

Regula: But you have already mastered all this!

Sabri Khan: You will master it too. I am demonstrating it for you. First of all, you have to create the "idea" of a whole performance in your mind. You are too involved in alap (introducing the raga); there have to be tans (passage work) too.

With significance: This is not a one-day task. And you can't master everything at once. I have given you the "idea" for one note; there are only seven notes in all to expand on (*barhat*)—or only five, if you take out ga and ni, (as in raga *bhopali*). Out of this one idea you generate five, six, or eight more ideas. Eight ideas come out of one note, then eight more out of the next note, and so on. Imagine how long your vilambit (slow section) can go on; you can play it for one and a half hours!

Now, proceed the same way as you did that first variant phrase. *He demonstrates pa ni re sa (5728).*

Regula: If I am to try this, it will be completely plain. *Plays: ma pa ni pa sa (45758).* It doesn't sound good.

Sabri Khan: It doesn't sound good because you did not play in tune.

Regula: *Tries to play ma pa ni pa sa (45758) again, this time in tune.* But it is plain, isn't it, without grace notes (*murki*) or ornamentation, because I don't know how to place them.

Sabri Khan: You want ornamentation too? Look, first you produce it plain; only then can you produce ornamentation. To produce murki (grace notes) right away? You want to become a Sabri Khan right away?

Regula: *Laughs.*

Sabri Khan: *Laughs too.* Here I have spent over forty years in radio and I've done seven more years of playing before that, starting from age seven. And you want to master everything in four days? Now let me tell you: leave your job for some time, that is, if you want to become good. My advice is: take one year. Do you want to become a good sarangi player? Then you just have to leave your job for a year, that is clear. Tell them, "Listen, give me a year off. I don't want money, but keep my job for me."

  You stay here for one year. Then tell me, what is it that your hand won't be able to produce *kya nahin nikal rahi hai mere hath se*! It's only one year for you. For someone else it is ten years. For you it's only one year because your mind is good, you catch on. At the most by the third telling. Also because you will work hard, and you have nothing else to do, only to practice all the time, and you have no interest in reading novels or watching movies, or in sleeping a lot, or roaming about. You'll just practice. And if you practice and learn, and gain understanding *samajh logi*, then in one year you can become very good! So that is your problem; you can't leave your job.

Regula: Then there is my husband!

Sabri Khan: Yes, that is a problem. But your husband ... the point is, even in Canada, and in America, there isn't anyone who can play sarangi that well.

Regula: My fingers can do it, I know that.

Sabri Khan: But you have to tell your husband: I want to become a good sarangi player. I mean, not in theory, but in practice. To become good in practice, I will have to stay in India.

Regula: That's true, I accept that. But you see, the alap you just showed me, by singing the notes, can you play it on the instrument, so I can see what the difference is. The same thing, expanding on the sa, just two or three ways. I mean, could you translate from the voice to the instrument?

Sabri Khan: Pay attention to what I am saying. First you must ask me, "What do you do to develop variations on phrases?" Do you know what this process is? It has its own name. I will tell you.

Regula: Do you mean what you just showed me. Is it called *bahlave* (expansions)?

Sabri Khan: I want you to *ask* me this question: What is this process of developing the notes? The job I am doing, to present *one* thing as ten different "ideas." I am showing it in ten different ways. What is that called? I want you to ask me!

Regula: Alright, please tell me. What *is* its name?

Sabri Khan: That's the way! You will not get this knowledge elsewhere; others will not tell you. That's right, *he* won't. But I tell you that *I* do it.

Regula: And the answer to the question?

Sabri Khan: The answer is: this is called *mir khand*. Do understand. That is, out of one note ... exactly what I had told you one day about one and two notes. Take sa re; are these two notes, or ten? Between two notes, how many combination ideas can you produce sa re, and re-sa, that's all, correct?

Regula: Yes, right.

Sabri Khan: But I can produce ten notes. So, what is this called?

Regula: Mir khand.

Sabri Khan: It is called mir khand. Only someone who has received proper instruction and has studied mir khand can produce it; otherwise, he can't.

Regula: I have had a singer teach me a raga, but he can't tell me how to produce it nicely on the sarangi. That's why ...

Sabri Khan: I have given you an "idea" of fingering. Then what are you afraid of when you play?

Regula: I am afraid because I don't know the proper ways of doing it.

Sabri Khan: You just move your fingers the way I gave you ideas. Like ni sa dha, ma pa sa (786, 458). Can't you just play this?

Regula: *Plays, trying ways of approaching the two notes.*

Sabri Khan: Mir khand is not taught (among sarangi players), but I have training (*talim*) in jor. I have properly studied alap, jor, *jhala* (free, pulsed, and rapid ostinato-based improvisation). If you come for three hours, I will perform one raga for you for three hours! I will create its combinations out of my mind and play them for three hours; you will not get bored (*boriat nahin hogi*)! Within the same raga I will play some compositions, in different rhythmic cycles: *ektal* (12 beats), *jhaptal* (7 beats), *tintal* (16 beats), *rupak* (7 beats). And of course alap (unmetered improvisation) ... Once at All India Radio I was to perform raga *desi* and the tabla player was missing. Two minutes before the program, Gopal Das arrives and says, "Khan Sahib, I am a little late." My program starts at 8:10, and he shows up at 8:08! I said, "Now I don't want a tabla player." In two minutes, how can you go and fetch the tabla and also tune it? I took my sarangi and played solo alap, jor, and jhala. I didn't need a tabla player at all.

With the tabla I play khayal. I have also played with a *pakhavaj* player, in Los Angeles. I played jor and *dhrupad* in (raga) *bilaskhani*.

Uncle: Bilaskhani todi is difficult.

Sabri Khan: I played only alap and jor. Jhala I started a bit but stopped it, because while it sounds good on the violin, on the sarangi the fast scraping sound on the string—"ghis ghis ghis ghis"—doesn't sound good, because it has gut strings. If it had wire strings, it would sound good. This is why I have rarely played jhala.

So there in Los Angeles, Taranath played pakhavaj with me. I played *dhamar*, for two hours. For one and a half hours I played alap in bilaskhani. I have the tape, and although people made requests in Chicago and New York, I only played khayal. So what I want to convey to you is that music is an ocean. An ocean. When you are in the middle of it, then you realize that this really is a very huge thing. But this huge ocean can fit into a drinking cup; it can fit into this glass!

Uncle: It fits into a cup.

Sabri Khan: It can fit into this glass! The entire ocean will fit into this cup of yours here. I mean the little cup that is in your brain. No need to put it in writing. It can all fit in here, in the mind. Our music is not "written" at all. I have stored it all right here in my brain, and that's where it comes from when we play. You ask me to perform and I'll play for three hours, or ten hours, or the whole night. Sometimes even that kind of concert has happened where only the sarangi is featured all night.

In Kashmir there lives a music connoisseur, Ved Lal Dhar, who plays the sarangi; I once stayed at his house in Kashmir for a performance he had arranged especially for the sarangi. "Sarangi Khan Sahib has come, so he should play solo," he said. It started at night and ended at five in the morning. At about midnight or 1 o'clock I started playing raga *darbari*. Well, this is a rag that lasts for two and a half or three hours. While I was playing darbari, I saw that the girls who were sitting in front were crying. I asked Rageshri, "Why were you crying?" Their names are Rageshri and Jaijaivanti. Ved Sahib had named his daughters after ragas: Jaijaivanti, Rageshri, Bageshri, Sarswati. "So, child, why were you crying?" She said, "I don't know. As the sounds came to me, tears fell from my eyes."

Uncle: The notes should be just right, then they will have their effect.

Regula: *Keeps playing slow marubihag.*

Sabri Khan: Okay, listen. *Softly:* This is an uncle of mine, on my father's side. I had been thinking to introduce him, but it slipped my mind a bit.

I realize that an offering to this senior relative of my ustad would be an appropriate gesture. I stand up to present an appropriate monetary offering to him. Then I practice the fast passages (tan) of raga marubihag.

Sabri Khan: *Upon hearing Regula:* Now look at the way I play this tan. (*He plays, forcefully articulating the phrases with the bow.*) Your playing is 'soft.' *He continues playing, slowly and deliberately intoning the tans that Regula has prepared in raga marubihag, including the difficult ga ga re sa, ni ni dha pa (3321 7765).*

Regula: Where should the pressure come from in the left hand?

Sabri Khan: Don't give too much pressure; don't let your hand become a block of wood.

Regula:	*Laughs.*
Sabri Khan:	Oh yes *laughs too.* Your fingers should remain 'soft.'
Regula:	I see, because you yourself have a very soft hand.
Sabri Khan:	So it should be. Just squeeze my hand and see, it is "like a woman's hand." It has been made that way.
Regula:	Your uncle, my Ustad Hamid Husain Khan's hand (see Chapter 11) was like that too. How is that done?
Sabri Khan:	I have *made* it soft.
Regula:	But *how*?
Sabri Khan:	Well, now you tell me how!
Uncle:	It's done by kneading bread dough.
Sabri Khan:	Anyone whose hand is hard, tell them: use the dough for making chapati bread. Yes?
Regula:	Oh yes, I make chapati bread myself.
Sabri Khan:	You knead the dough with the back of your curled hands, the way our women do it at home.
Uncle:	Do more kneading with your left hand.
Sabri Khan:	Because this is the hand that needs to be softened. Keep adding a bit of water and knead, then add a little more water and knead, and do it again, for 15 minutes.
Uncle:	Then your hand will become soft (*mulayim*). You do it at least for 40 days.
Sabri Khan:	Then your hand becomes like this. My father had me do it. In my childhood, when my hand was hard. I was playing sa re ga ma, and my hand was not soft. Also, with a hard hand you cannot advance in technique. A soft hand is more agile.

Okay, for the tabla you need a hard hand, but for the sarangi your hand needs to be soft. When I shake someone's hand, the person often says, "What a soft hand you have." But how can anyone know why? I did it myself.

Uncle: Now we told you the method to do it!

Regula: My husband will like it, because that way he will get chapati to eat. *Starts packing up her instrument.*

Sabri Khan: Do you have to go somewhere?

Regula: Oh, it's time for me to go to Nizamuddin Shrine. Will you ride along to go to the radio?

Sabri Khan: Alright, let's pay our respects at the shrine (*haziri dena*) and then each go our own way. A last piece of advice: Practice tans, and do it slowly. If you do it fast, it won't be in tune.

We leave and hail a motorcycle rickshaw that takes us to the Nizamuddin Auliya shrine, my long-time musical and spiritual home in Delhi.

Session 3: A Holistic Approach to Musical Competence[3]

Sabri Khan is, as always, sitting against the wall in the center of the music room. At the far end of the room, his son Ghulam Sarvar is practicing tabla and Nasir accompanies him with a lehra *(cyclical tune) on his sarangi. I sit down facing the ustad and start playing alap, the slow introductory improvisational phrases that introduce the raga. Today, he is pleased with me, with the way my performance went on national TV, and with the interview, which gave me the chance to acclaim him as my ustad. He offers me tea, betel leaf, and even lunch.*

But today the music room is also a sarangi workshop. An old instrument is being re-covered with a new goat skin, a major undertaking that requires softening the skin in water, then stretching it tightly across the hollow belly of the sarangi, and finally trimming and gluing it along the edges with a mixture made of flour and water. Nails are used to hold the skin in place as well as the leather strap that is then stretched across the belly to make a strong base for the bridge that will have to hold up the instrument's 40 strings. Sabri Khan has been teaching Nasir how to do this work and lends a guiding hand where needed. Instruments are part of the music and are personal.

Sarangi players set up and repair their own instruments, and this skill is also passed on within the family.

Now Nasir stops playing and gets back to fixing the sarangi. Ghulam Sarvar continues practicing tabla. At the same time, Sabri Khan is teaching me. Music is ongoing in Sabri Khan's house. The two instruments, sarangi and tabla, can always be practiced simultaneously, as is the case today. Boundaries between practicing and teaching and performing are permeable, one easily moving into the other. Equally easily, one is stopped to make room for the other, as happens today, when Nasir stops playing his lehra (cyclical composition to accompany tabla playing) when I start playing for Sabri Khan.

This session encapsulates Sabri Khan's remarkably comprehensive teaching: he addresses instrumental technique, musical knowledge, professional strategy, and above all conveys musicians' wisdom. His method of teaching is multivalent and intertextual: he moves between verbal and musical interaction; between playing, singing, and skill demonstrations; between situational responses and strategic messages.

Sabri Khan: This sounds good; it is not wrong. Just keep playing. When something is wrong, *then* I will say something.

Regula: *Plays alap in raga marubihag.*

Sabri Khan: *Today offers Regula tea, and takes a betel leaf. In between teaching Regula, he tells Nasir how to work on the sarangi, showing him how to cut the edges of the goat skin that has been stretched over the belly of the instrument and glued down along the wooden sides, and then pounding nails into the glued sections to reinforce them.*

Regula: *Begins jor, the pulsed improvisation.*

Sabri Khan: *Tutors Regula by singing the correct notes by name [sargam]. Then urges Regula to drink her tea while reflecting on how her study should progress.*

Now that I have acquitted myself as his proper shagird *on national TV, Sabri Khan is treating me with increasing generosity, like a real member of his musical family. It is now that I experience the full range of his concern for my progress, here, and after my return to Canada.*

Sabri Khan: For the morning time, you should also prepare a morning raga with lowered *rikhab* (second scale degree). Would you play *yaman* (an evening raga) in the morning? *With warmth:* I have told you something important (*main ne tum se ek bat kahi hai*). It will take me five years to teach someone else, but with you it will take only one year. You have a brain, and you can play. Don't worry too much about this and that, recording and making videos, checking your bow, your hand, your fingers, your alap, your jor. All this has kept your mind preoccupied.

Regula: That's how I learned this much.

Sabri Khan: No, no, no. That's not the way. You just have to understand the raga in order to play. That's all. If you worry about everything you'll be all over the place. We have a proverb that says it all: "Mastering one raga, means mastering them all." Mastering four ragas means mastering enough for your whole life. In fact, even one raga will do it. Now ask me, why! *Softly:* The tans are the same, alap and jor will be the same. Only the raga brings changes.

The ustad demonstrates this by playing a different raga, malkauns. Starting with slow improvisation (alap), he builds the raga step by step, then expands into faster passage work (tan). Then he stops and points to my bow.

Bowing Technique

Sabri Khan: The way you bow gives jolts or jerks. I can't ever play like that. This is not the way the sarangi is played, it never will be; it's completely wrong. *He demonstrates, using the same raga malkauns.* Here is sarangi bowing: smooth, continuous bowing, without any jolt or unevenness. Even in separate bow strokes there is no jolt, just even strokes.

Regula: We cellists especially work on changing the direction of the bow smoothly, without stopping in between.

Sabri Khan: That's no problem; you just have to control the bow (*gaz ka sadhna*), nothing else! Just practice running the bow all the way and back, on an open string, keeping the hand and wrist steady, running the bow in one place. Just practice this bowing for ten minutes. Many musicians used to say: "He still hasn't learned how to hold the bow (*gaz pakarna*), and he doesn't know how to *draw* (*chalana*) the bow either!" They say this when someone isn't competent. And they won't correct him, either.

Stories are part of Sabri Khan's teaching. They become parables to convey a message; here it is the value of having the right relationship with your teacher. From correcting my bowing at my request, he highlights his own proper action with two dialectical opposites, both of them unfortunate: a player who does not receive correction from his own ustad, and one who tries to obtain another ustad's advice without first becoming his shagird.

Sabri Khan:　　One young boy had his hand set wrongly, like this. Someone else was teaching him. He asked *me* for help, that fellow. He often comes to my program at the radio and watches me and listens. So he said: my finger gets stuck here, it won't go up to the upper tonic, it gets stuck there (*tip par atakti hai*). Please tell me how to do it. I said, "You, sir, are *his* disciple, so go and ask him. How can I teach you? I can't. And why should I correct your 'defect'? Is this a proper hand position?" The teacher isn't checking what the student is doing with his hand! He can't progress; there is no way he'll become proficient, when his hand is crooked from the start. He had come here to audition for the radio.

Regula:　　He didn't succeed?

Sabri Khan:　　These things are a difficult challenge: how to hold the bow and how to place the hand. That's the first thing to learn. If the hand is right, then your playing will come out right too.

Regula:　　What about my hand?

Sabri Khan:　　Your hand is fine, it's doing fine, and you also keep checking; you understand everything. Just keep practicing your bowing. *He turns to check on Nasir's work with the instrument repair, and looks at his own instrument, commenting in a sad tone:* This sarangi of mine, I have lost my affection for it, because it got a crack.

Posture and Presentation

Regula:　　*Returning to her own concern:* How should one sit for playing? I sat with my legs back and to the right, as I see others, but it hurts my back.

Sabri Khan:　　*Calmingly:* Just sit the way you can sit comfortably.

Regula: How does one hold the sarangi? The way you hold it with your feet?

Sabri Khan: You won't be able to hold it that way; it will be difficult for you.

Regula: And the way I hold it now, my sarangi sits too much to the center.

Sabri Khan: Not at all, it's just right.

Regula: You too place it in the middle; I never noticed (*ghaur*).

Sabri Khan: *Sarcastically:* You don't notice anything? Do take notice! These are little things: how to hold the sarangi, how to sit. First learn how to play! You can always change the way you sit! Don't worry about sitting posture. Learn how to *play* the sarangi. You won't be able to sit the way I do. But it doesn't matter; I also sit the way you do sometimes. Only the sarangi can't be stabilized very well. *He sits cross-legged.* This is the real way to sit with the sarangi. The kneeling style is only to make it "beautiful," to present a picture of yourself that looks good. But sitting cross-legged, holding the instrument with both your feet, that is the real sitting style for a strong player, a man or a woman. Then the chest presses against the sarangi, and that's how tans come out well. Without that pressure, tans come only from the fingers and have no force.

Now let me tell you what you should practice: for at least ten minutes practice bowing. That jerky bow is no good; get rid of that habit. Play long bows, and practice it so that your bow will run well. Second, for fingering: do alap and jor; that's all. And if you want, spend 15 minutes playing khayal in marubihag, including passage work. But mostly practice alap and jor; that's what you will need more for performances, especially when you don't have a tabla player. But then always keep a *tanpura* player with you on stage, it provides 'help' with intonation, and it looks good to have two, rather than only one, person with you on the stage. If not two, then at least one tanpura. This also makes you more powerful; one lone sarangi player means nothing, but if a tanpura player sits behind you, and one or two listeners with you on the stage, then do you know the impact it makes on the stage? Have you seen Ravi Shankar? He puts five to ten people on the stage, just to see, and the public watches, is impressed. It's his 'policy,' that's all.

What a 'policy' that is! These are all 'techniques' for playing and making one's style strong. When you seat ten people on the stage, what will they do? They won't sit still. They'll certainly move their necks in approbation. Now the audience sees them and thinks: 'Very good.' Even what a listener can't understand, he applauds with exclamations because he sees those ten people on the stage applaud.

Creating a successful performance is part of making a musician professional. Sabri Khan's own experience concertizing in North America sensitized him to managing a performance in an environment that often lacks tabla players.

Sabri Khan: *Offering final advice:* What you hear yourself play, tape it and then listen to it again. Now if it sounds good to your ears, it will sound good to everyone. And what you don't like yourself, others won't like either.

Someone brings nicely wrapped betel leaves, and Sabri Khan invites me to have one. I take it, we talk a bit more, and the session is over, signalled by this final gesture of hospitality. This is also the beginning of a cordial and affectionate relationship that has lasted over the years. Whether I practice or not, Ustad Sabri Khan's house has become my second home in India.

Bombay: Freelance Center

CHAPTER 4

Ram Narayan
The Concert Sarangi

Introducing Pandit Ram Narayan

Ram Narayan, born in 1927, is famous as a pioneer of the modern solo sarangi in India and across the world. A hereditary musician of an unconventional background, he entered the world of the classical sarangi mainly through teachers outside his community (Bhai Lal, Madhav Prasad, and the legendary Abdul Wahid Khan), and he eventually developed a distinctive solo style of his own. Like other excellent sarangi players, he obtained a position at All India Radio, first in Lahore and, following the partition of India, in Delhi. But in 1950, after only eight years at AIR, he moved to Bombay to freelance in the film and recording industry while tenaciously pursuing his goal of building a career as a sarangi soloist. It took until 1956 for the Indian concert stage to accept his solo performance; by the 1960s there were solo recordings, and foreign tours followed, the first one to Europe and America in 1964. For the past three decades, Pandit Ram Narayan has continued to concertize and record in India and all over the world.

Pandit Ram Narayan is also known for his teaching at modern public institutions like the National Centre for Performing Arts in Bombay and the American Society for Eastern Arts. In addition to his Western students, he has turned his attention to passing on his knowledge in India. Above all, he has trained his daughter Aruna, making her the first female Indian sarangi player, though ironically she has been living in Canada for years now.

*Most importantly, Pandit Ram Narayan has been an overarching influence
on the contemporary concert sarangi. Unique for the sarangi, his early and
numerous recordings have helped enable younger players to adopt aspects of
his style, particularly his tone production and improvisational style.*

Pandit Ram Narayan and Regula

*When I first wrote a letter to Pandit Ram Narayan in 1968, requesting him
to teach me during my first visit to Bombay, I was already initiated as a
shagird of Hamid Husain (see Chapter 11) and had previously learned some
basics of music and instrumental technique with Mirza Maqsud Ali in Lucknow (see Chapter 7). After encountering their traditional hereditary milieu,
my surprise was to find in Ram Narayan a sarangi player who lived in a
contemporary urban setting, with a teenage daughter who spoke English
and a journalist from the* Times of India *visiting my lesson and writing an
account of Panditji's new teaching project with me.[1] And then he invited us
to a high-profile inauguration of a film on Urdu's greatest poet, Ghalib, for
which Ram Narayan had composed and performed the music. Clearly, this
musician and his sarangi were part of a modern cultural milieu of Bombay
and its vibrant musical scene.*

*But in our lessons, tradition reigned and oral knowledge was carefully
measured out, with the admonition to guard it carefully. This was a master
who had developed a personal style of playing characterized by an intensely
beautiful tone and impeccable intonation, even in the most rapid passages.
He tested my intonation by teaching me raga todi, a thoroughly nondiatonic
modal combination lacking the fifth scale degree, and then had me play it for
the* Times of India *journalist. I passed the intonation, but where I stumbled
was in keeping track of the rhythmic cycle! Leaving Bombay was a wrench,
but we would meet again, in Canada and elsewhere on Panditji's international tours.*

*My next intensive visit with Panditji was in 1988, nearly two decades
later, now as part of my search for knowledge about the sarangi in the hands
of this remarkable pioneer, and from a broadened horizon that included
a panoply of players, strategies, and musical results. I was a teacher at the
National Center for Performing Arts and a professional researcher, though
still learning and playing the sarangi. And Panditji had been an honored
guest at our house in Canada. All this added a new kind of collegiality to
discipular respect and prestations to which Panditji responded graciously
and personably.*

*Language is a powerful means for activating connections in the multicul-
tural and multireligious social universe of Hindustani music. While Pandit
Ram Narayan's mother tongue is the dialect of Rajasthani, his main language
is Hindi, with its Sanskrit-derived vocabulary and references to Hindu reli-*

Figure 11 Ram Narayan, portrait, 1960.

gious experience. But he is also enculturated in the Urdu-speaking milieu of hereditary Muslim musicians and quite easily adapts his speech to my Urdu, choosing Persian-derived vocabulary along with typical Hindi terminology. For instance, he used the Urdu terms ustad *and* shagird *instead of the Hindi* guru *and* shishya. *This adaptation was present both in 1969 and 1988, but 1988 brought, in addition, a great deal more English into the conversation, reflecting Ram Narayan's considerably increased fluency, his desire to use it, and also an increasing reliance on English terminology in his Hindi conversation. All this reflects Westernized Indian usage in major cities, reinforced by Panditji's frequent concertizing and teaching outside of India.*

Like Coming Home[2]

After nearly two decades, I easily find the house where I had my first lessons from Pandit Ram Narayan. He welcomes me into his apartment and we sit down in his music room on the farsh, *a soft, sheet-covered floor space with bolsters for making music and socializing. His daughter is now in Canada, but his son Brij, a well-known sarod player, lives downstairs with his wife and children. Now Panditji's daughter-in-law brings tea and snacks and stays on, mostly as a listener to our conversation.*

We catch up on each other's news since his recent visit to our Edmonton home, and we talk about my present teaching stint at the National Centre for Performing Arts, where he himself held master classes years ago, a first for the sarangi. Pandit Ram Narayan begins to tell me about a new interest arising in the sarangi, and I ask for his permission to record our talk on this important topic.

Regula: *Having set up the tape recorder:* Please, just talk.

Ram Narayan: Alright, I ask you, what should I say?

Regula: *Taken aback at the question:* But you were already telling me about …

Ram Narayan: *Laughs heartily at his playfully formal response to Regula's cue for turning the conversation into a recorded interview.*

Regula: *Joins in laughter:* Please pick up from where you had left off.

A New Life for the Sarangi

Regula: You said that there are a lot of people who want to study the sarangi?

Ram Narayan: It makes me very sad that the sarangi is in such bad shape (*durdesha*), and it also makes me angry. That is why, wherever I get a chance, I do *anything* for this instrument: teach, give a lecture or a concert. And now there is quite a bit of interest, quite a few people want to learn.

Regula: Earlier, no one was learning it. What has happened now?

Figure 12 Ram Narayan on the Indian concert stage.

Ram Narayan: Now? They must have started enjoying sarangi music! *He laughs, an obvious reference to the impact of his own concertizing and recordings.*

I am teaching a number of youngsters and putting my heart into it. Some are children of the old-style sarangi players who did not get much from them, or they have no elders left to teach them. Now they are saying, "We will start learning sarangi again."

But these students cannot come to me, especially to a place like Bombay, where living is so difficult and expensive on top of it. So that is why I give them some lessons when I go to the places they live in, and they keep practicing. Just last month, I had a concert in Delhi, and quite a few sarangi players came to attend—old ones, and new ones too, they all came. In fact, there were more "musicians" than listeners in the audience. There is a sarangi player from Benares, the father of Rajan and Sajan Mishra (Hanuman Prasad Mishra, see Chapter 10), he had come. And Ahmad Banne, whose son is my disciple, he also came. He was a staff artist at the radio (All India Radio) and has just retired. He had a very beautiful hand; at one time he played very well.

Regula: He is not teaching his son himself?

Ram Narayan: No. What has happened, Regula, is that the work that should have been done on this instrument, has not been done. For 400 years there just hasn't been any work done on it. No one has had time for it—these poor traditional players have been too busy with making ends meet. So they just play whatever they are told; if a singer tells them to play only a little, they play only a little. On the other hand, those players with a great deal of talent gave up the sarangi and took up singing, like Bade Ghulam Ali Khan Sahib, Abdul Karim Khan Sahib, Amir Khan Sahib. *He attaches sahib (Sir) to the names, the polite form of addressing a senior musician.*

So how to turn this around? I have played the sarangi a lot; I have played this instrument in every lane and every voice *har gali aur gale men. Regula joins him in laughing at the pun combining gali = 'lane' and gale (gala) = literally throat.* By now people have begun to realize that the sarangi is very good and it should stay around. And if you look at it seriously, this is the "perfect Indian instrument."

Regula: That is true. And you have helped perfect it by correcting its weaknesses.

Ram Narayan: Absolutely. Because in order to play "solo," I had to do a lot of work to expand the musical range that is required for playing solo. So that even at a performance of four to five hours, the music should not be limited.

The Temptation to Become a Singer

Ram Narayan: You know, once I myself had an opportunity to leave the sarangi and become a singer. Here is how that happened. We used to have a festival in Jalandhar for the last 100 years. Now it has now been closed down because of the troubles in Panjab. (Note: Ram Narayan uses a Sanskritized version of Harbhallabh.) The Mela of Harvallabh, that's what they called it. The festival had music day and all night. Even in winter, people brought blankets from their houses and they kept sitting there. It went all day and all night, with only a small "gap" when people would eat a meal and wander about. So this happened when I played a concert there in 1974 or '75. A *lot* of people came to listen to me. I mean, I had a lot of fans there: 10,000 to 15,000 people were in the audience. It was afternoon, and I was playing raga *gaur sarang*.

I have mentioned this raga particularly because to play or sing *pure* gaur sarang is very difficult, even though its notes are very simple. I was developing the raga (what is called *barhat*), and people were listening with great enjoyment. You see, once in a while it happens that each and everything is just right: the tanpuras are well tuned, my instrument is sounding in tune, the tabla, too, is comfortable, everyone is sounding good. So with all this going so well, I thought, "Well, I should also explain to these people what is going on *inside* me."

Now what I was playing was the *asthayi* (first part and refrain of the song), and it was very beautiful. I was saying the words of the song inside and developing the words on the sarangi, presenting each text phrase (*bol*) in five or six different ways. Hmm. Well, I was getting pleasure out of this, and so I thought why shouldn't the people who are listening get that pleasure too? They should know what the words of the song are. So I sang the words. A hush came over the audience and they listened very attentively. After the asthayi, I sang the *antara* (second part of the song) as well.

After that I presented the improvisational passages (*tan*). Now to understand the notes (*sargam*) that make up these fast passages is very necessary, because they are a rapid interplay between bow and left hand fingering. But on the sarangi I obviously can't verbalize the notes. *He sings a passage naming each note:* ma ma ma ga ga ga ga re sa ni, re re re re sa ni dha pa—I can say the words only if I sing them, but on the sarangi, how is that possible? People are gracious enough to listen to my playing and even like what they hear. But if it were 'explained' to them, they would like it even better.

Regula: So you did it by singing the same passage.

Ram Narayan: Yes, I did it by singing, and then I topped it up with some more improvised passages. All this singing took about seven, eight, nine minutes altogether. And then, when I picked up my bow and started playing again, people began to say, "Please just keep singing." *Starts laughing.* Then I said: I have already played sarangi for 1 1/2 hours; let me play for another 15-20 minutes and I'll do a vocal program another time. After this experience, I found out that this is a dangerous matter. If I did the same thing a few more times, I would become established as a professional singer (*gawayya*).

Regula: Why, you did not want that?

Ram Narayan: Well, I do sing, I still sing today for teaching, and I have the competence to teach singers. Among today's singers there are quite a few whom I can teach something—I mean, even practically. Like how the voice should be used, where tan patterns should be placed, how to sing on the vowel a—, all this I know. But then I thought that this would be the same thing over again that Ghulam Ali Khan Sahib, Amir Khan Sahib, and Abdul Karim Khan Sahib had done. So I did not sing publicly again, ever.

Regula: You remained faithful!

Ram Narayan: *Absolutely*! That's what I told myself, afterwards. Even though, if I had taken up singing, I would have profited very greatly. But I have never been greedy for profit. Nor have I pursued my music for that, ever.

Regula: You certainly have dedicated your life to it.

Ram Narayan: And I enjoy it. With no obligation on anyone, that is good enough for me.

Being an Accompanist

Regula: I know that you only play solo, but earlier you accompanied many great singers.

Ram Narayan: There are two kinds of accompaniment. One is to give very nice support to what the singer is singing. Then when he reaches pa (5), play sa (1) softly. The sonority will please him. Another kind of accompaniment is to disturb him, even to hide the sa (tonic) while he stops singing to take a breath.

Regula: Oh yes, I have heard about this, but would you have done it?

Ram Narayan: You know Sharafat Husain of Agra, he sang very well. Once I was accompanying him. *He stops to think how to explain this to Regula.* Take sa, the tonic and ground note of the central octave; then take pa, a fifth above it. If you use the same notes in your scale but establish pa as the ground note or tonic, it will result in a different raga, won't it! When I got that little bit of a "gap" for playing (in between the singer's phrases), I established the octave between lower and upper pa (5), and that way pa (5) became sa (1). And really, Sharafat Husain became confused: "Oh, something has changed here."

Regula: You mean for instance in (raga) todi, if you turn dhevat (dha), the 6th degree of the scale into sa (1), it will become (raga) *bhopali.*

Ram Narayan: Exactly, exactly! In the same way pa to pa (5 to 5) becomes something different. There you have to consider which raga will fit with those notes. Say you go from ga to ga (3 to 3), what combination do you get?

Regula: I see. *Both chuckle.* So this is a special art of sarangi players!

Ram Narayan: Yes, only those who are very expert in it can carry it off. This is not a job for everyone. You can't change the notes of the raga; that would be totally unacceptable. But here you keep all the right notes; you just have to shift the ground note, that's all!

A Musical Contest

Regula: I have heard a lot about contests (*muqabila*) between different musicians, especially between sarangi and singer.

Ram Narayan: Regula, there have been very, very few people among sarangi players who were well enough prepared for a contest. I am one of those few. The other was Gopal Mishra, of Benares. And the third was Ghulam Sabir, Senior, of Ambala.

Regula: So you actually did a contest.

Ram Narayan: A contest was like this: I myself took part in a most remarkable contest. It was in 1948, and Amir Khan Sahib had come to sing at Delhi Radio for the first time after Partition. There are still a few people around today who were present at that performance. It was a morning broadcast, and I was on duty to play sarangi with him. This was a half-hour item, and he sang only a fast piece (*drut*) that lasted for half an hour. The raga was todi; there is a *tarana* in *ektal* (a fast 12-beat cycle), that's what he sang, and so he stayed in a fast rhythmic cycle for the entire half hour. So because he started in a fast tempo from the beginning, there were a great many fast passages (*tans*). Amir Khan could sing five to seven elaborate passages (kaj tan) in one sweep. When he arrived at the *sam* (end/beginning point of cycle), only then did I pick up my bow to play. And I reproduced the whole thing, articulating the phrases with my bow exactly as he had sung them.

That is a contest, isn't it? Now to do this also requires a perfectly sharp memory: of what the first tan was, and where he started it from. Then what he did in the middle. And then, how he brought it to an end. You must have that much power of comprehension to keep the whole design in your mind. And then, you must have control over your hands, so that you can execute what you memorized. It must always sound in tune. And it must stay within the rhythmic cycle so that it hits the sam in the same way (as the singer did).

So that is what I did, and this back-and-forth between us continued for half an hour. All the listeners were musicians, the staff artists on the radio, and also the 15 to 20 members of Vadya Vrinda, the newly established National Orchestra. These were fabulous musicians, from South as well as North India. They were all present because everyone had heard the name of the Amir Khan Sahib, and of course everyone liked his singing. So I said to myself: this is his first performance here, so it should be a special pleasure. Particularly because Amir Khan Sahib's singing had a number of the sarangi's special idioms in it.

Regula: Well, he himself … his father was a sarangi player.

Ram Narayan: Yes, exactly. That is what I enjoyed; this was a chance for me to make a statement with my playing. So this chain of interaction between us *silsila* went on for half an hour. Later he gave a three-hour-long performance. There, too, the same thing went on. And in that performance people gave me as much applause as they gave him.

Regula: Oh, and he didn't mind?

Ram Narayan: No, he *did* mind. And from that day on, Khan Sahib stopped using sarangi accompaniment altogether. You see, the point is that once the applause becomes divided between two people, the soloist gets upset—which is a very wrong thing. It shouldn't be like that. In South India, this doesn't happen.

Regula: Oh yes, the violin and *mridangam* players get a chance to play solo.

Ram Narayan: Yes, those singers give them an amazing amount of (solo) opportunity, and they get so much respect, just like the soloist. And why not! Well, I became fed up (*tang a ke*) with the whole situation of being an accompanist, and said to myself: "Friend, this is not right. If this is life: just to get a piece of bread and be happy, then that is no life at all." It's over this that I left my 'service' at the radio.

Creating Recordings and Film Music

Ram Narayan: In 1949 I came here, to Bombay, to the HMV Company, and with those people I was very happy, up to a certain point. There was Pandit Krishna Rao Shankar of Gwalior. Have you heard his singing?

Regula: No, I haven't. I don't have his record.

Ram Narayan: Alright, if you get a chance at NCPA (National Center for Performing Arts), they have one recording of his in which I have played. Though even at that time he was already quite aged. One thing, however, you will certainly notice: to accompany him was very difficult. That singing is so difficult for the sarangi player that it can't be measured (*us ka hisab nahin*). Not every player is up to putting his hand to the job.

    The very first solo recordings I made on the sarangi were done in the 1950s. And I made these recordings under the most difficult conditions, because the "recordist" was a most rude and crude Englishman here in HMV. He was extremely ill-tempered, and at that time I did not understand any English. *He illustrates by intoning loud, imperious, British-sounding commands:* "Come here!" "You have to do!" "Near to the mike!" "Play!" He acted as if he was obliging me. Both I and a tabla player were already worried when we arrived at the studio. The British sahib's rude way of talking upset us even more (*aur dukhi hogaye*), so I said "Friend, let's get through this and leave."

    G.N. Joshi Sahib was producer at HMV at the time. I spotted him somewhere and said, "Please save me from this man! I don't understand what he says, and his behavior is so haughty. Joshi Sahib, you please sit in front of me when I play." He answered, "Yes, sure, I will sit there; let's go in." Regula, this was the best recording. I mean as regards time, it was 3 minutes and 15 seconds long. Among Indian musicians, that was the best adjustment (to the 3-minute norm) ever. Only Bade Ghulam Ali Sahib and I achieved this. *And* I played each side only once! After each piece, that Englishman just shouted *in a clipped voice* "Okay!" As for doing a second take, he shouted "Nothing! Nothing doing!"

    First I recorded ragas *lalit* and *marva*, and then *gujri todi* and *pilu*. I made these two records in *one* hour. And they are as appropriate, timewise, I mean: how long the first and second parts of the composition/asthayi should be, the antara, how much alap there should be, how many tans there should be, and how it should end.

Regula: Most remarkable!

Ram Narayan: It is fantastic.

When I Worked in Film

Ram Narayan: It was in 1950, '51 when I became more involved in film. In addition to playing, composition was part of the work in film music, and it was easy for me. The other people who did this work, they often asked me to compose their songs, saying, "I just can't get this song done, could you?" (*yeh gana, yar, yeh kaise hoga*). So I made up quite a lot of songs, because it's not very difficult to do. For us (classical musicians), how can it be difficult, when we compose every time we play a concert? *Laughs.*

Regula: Obviously, you *are* a composer! So *you* would provide the composition? Although they did not give your name; because they don't do that?

Ram Narayan: Yes, yes. But in this way, indirectly, I did a lot of compositions that are really good. I did songs in seven films; let me remember some: "Do hanson ka jora" ("Two swans together" in the film *Ganga Jamna*), "Yun hasraton ke dagh" ("Wounds of suffering" in the film *Adalat*), "Has jia roe" ("My heart is Weeping" in the film *Milan*), and four classical songs in the film *Hamdard*.

Regula: These are wonderful songs, especially the "piece" (interlude) between verses.

Ram Narayan: I started that, you see. Film music at that time was good. One music director was my very good friend, and he was also very knowledgeable (*jankar*). So for him I put my mind to work. But as soon as I got the opportunity to leave film, I was gone.

Regula: *Laughs.*

Ram Narayan: *Laughs too.* You see, I played there, but my heart wasn't in it (*halanke main ne dil laga ke nahin bajaya*). I had to earn a living, since I had stopped accompanying singers.

Sarangi, Voice of Separation?

Regula: The way I think, in films the sarangi expresses a certain kind of feeling like the pain of separation, like someone gets married and loves someone else. You know, when the heart breaks, the sarangi plays.

Ram Narayan: That is okay, Regula, but it depends on what the situation is, for any instrument. If the player knows how to play it, he can give it any shape.

Regula: So you mean, the sarangi can do other things also; not only this.

Ram Narayan: *Absolutely,* absolutely!

Regula: But isn't it true that films have had this effect that sarangi is always giving that feeling?

Ram Narayan: You see, there is this illiteracy; people have no idea about any music in our country. I also said this recently in an interview I had on Delhi Television. I mean, whenever some great person has died, continuous sarangi music is playing on the radio, on television. Now the performers, they really don't know how to do this, so when they play the feeling of "sad," it sometimes sounds like "funny." *Laughs.* But those people have this very thing in their head, namely: sarangi means sad.

Regula: Like upon the death of Indira Gandhi.

Ram Narayan: Alright, consider Indira Gandhi's death. If someone should tell me to play the sarangi in a way to make people dance, I can of course do that by playing some light tune or something (*dhun waghaira*). However, if Indira Gandhi's death gives me and everyone great pain, and they ask *me* to play, then I would definitely make them weep.

But the radio people think, "What do we need Ram Narayan for? We can take someone from our staff," and when *that* person plays, you see, then it sounds a bit like a joke, because the player is not concerned about it, he was just put on duty and told: "Come on, just continue playing, as long as the music is without tabla." *Chuckles.* It is wrong just to insist on this use of the sarangi without any understanding. Upon Indira Gandhi's death, the sitar could have been played sadly too. Conversely, I can make the sarangi sound cheerful.

Teaching: Learn Properly, Don't Just Imitate

Regula: Your example is also being followed by some young sarangi players who are working to be soloists.

Ram Narayan: Yes, there are some that follow my records; they follow my style. But there are certain things, Regula, that cannot be mastered unless you sit down with a teacher and learn them properly. Without that, some things just develop wrong.

How to place the fingers, how to draw the bow, what phrase to play, what bow stroke to begin with—this is not a joking matter. If you want to handle anything in a hurry, it means that there is something wrong somewhere. What you develop systematically, that will always remain with you, and for a long time to come. To follow a bit, listen a bit, and play is just for the moment; there is no depth in it. The same way a person spends money more wisely when he has earned it himself. If before you leave you just give me some dollars *laughs*, I will spend them very carelessly *laughs heartily*!

Regula: When did you decide to pass on your art to your daughter? I remember her as a schoolgirl listening to the lessons you gave me in 1969, but then she was not learning sarangi.

Ram Narayan: First I found her a sarangi. It was in Tapovan, where Lord Rama lived with Sita.

Regula: A holy place!

Ram Narayan: Yes, with many temples. There I saw a sarangi player begging for alms; he was singing devotional hymns and accompanying himself. His instrument sounded very nice, so I asked whether he would sell it. He said: "It will cost you!" I paid him the 150 rupees he asked for and also made sure he had another instrument to use. Then I gave him the telephone number of a friend in nearby Nasik so that he could get help if he needed it.

Regula: This was an auspicious beginning. When did she begin her study?

Ram Narayan: I started teaching her only after she finished her BCom (Bachelor of Commerce degree). I spent two years teaching her everything. Above all, I taught her the way to learn, so that she progressed quickly.

Regula: That is remarkable. She has certainly made a name in Canada.

Final Advice

Regula: Alright, would you look at my sarangi?

Ram Narayan: Yes, certainly.

Regula: *Starts by playing a thumri composition in raga bhairavi from 1969 lesson notes.* I don't know whether it is correct or not, but this is what I had notated.

Ram Narayan: No, it's alright.

Regula: And you had told me some sequences (*palte)* plays *ga re sa re—sa, ma ga re ga—re* up and down.

Ram Narayan: Alright. Now play simple sargam.

Regula: *Plays a slow scale.*

Ram Narayan: Good. Now tell me, do you do any practice, any performances, or not?

Regula: Sometimes there are occasions when someone asks me to play. Then I practice. But in between, practicing is left behind. You please tell me, when I have so much work to do in between, teaching and research, I am writing, doing other things, so …

Ram Narayan: But the best work of all is playing.

Regula: That's true. You get the most happiness from it. But how do I do it, what do I do?

Ram Narayan: Practice!

Regula: Tell me, what should be a daily minimum?

Ram Narayan: One hour in the morning, one hour in the evening.

Regula: It's too much. It's not possible.

Ram Narayan: Alright, then let it be just half an hour. At least set apart half an hour.

Daughter-in-Law: And how about getting up early in the morning to practice?

Ram Narayan: No, they have a lot of work to do over there. Here is what you do: practice half an hour in the morning and half an hour in the evening. And do sargam in all three octaves. Practice slowly rather than fast. Playing slow will make the hand more steady for playing fast. You better take this a bit more seriously; only then will you get somewhere.

Regula: I know, that's what I should do. But you have to practice; otherwise it is not possible to play in tune.

Ram Narayan: Yes! Now if you decide, once some of your jobs are done, or if you think that you want to play, you see, you must get instruction *and* some changes in the instrument also, especially the strings, and the left hand too. If you stay with me for a few days, then only this will work. Also, certain notes you play come about with sound strained. And then there should be some "phrasing," some "discipline" of the bow, you see. Like the tongue of the singer, the tongue of the sarangi is the bow.

Regula: Yes, I remember. You had already told me this very thing *laughing* 20 years ago!

Ram Narayan: *Laughs too.*

Regula: Right, I have heard everything already *laughs*. And "your fingers should have eyes."

Ram Narayan: Absolutely, absolutely! But now this is the thing: take out a bit of time and practice. And ultimately, Regula, this is what will serve you well. No matter how many lectures you give, books you churn out, there will be some or the other mistake in such research.

Regula: *Laughs.* That's true.

Ram Narayan: You see, here we musicians have been committed to music for so many years, and we consider it (scholarly activity) pointless. Take this raga *mian ki todi*, what proof or evidence is there for it, just tell me!

Regula: *Pauses.* "I don't know!" *Laughs.*

Ram Narayan: Indeed! So these are absolutely useless matters (*fuzul ki baten hain*); some people remain stuck in them all their life! But, as the scholar-performer Ratanjankar Sahib once told me, the best thing is to prove by doing (*kar ke batana*).

Words of Wisdom from 1969

Hearing Panditji tell me that "the tongue of the sarangi is the bow" leads me back to the first time I had heard his words of wisdom during our first set of lessons in 1969. It was from January 29 to February 12 of that year that Pandit Ramnarayan was my teacher for ten intensive days in his Bombay apartment. Every day I traveled to Banda by commuter train from Marine Drive; then we sat in his living room, often with his daughter Aruna present as well. One day, a reporter from the Times of India visited and took a picture for a big spread about the first foreign woman coming to study the sarangi with Panditji. Aruna had studied English in school and translated for her father where needed, but she was not visibly involved in the music at all.

On our first day, Ram Narayan spoke about the importance of his teaching and the relationship between teacher and disciple:

Ram Narayan: For the shagird, the ustad[3] is everything. For him, there is no god; god has no meaning. There is only the ustad. The shagird has total devotion to the ustad. When I was learning from Abdul Wahid Khan in Lahore, I kept only the little money I needed for my lodging and for eating in a hotel. The rest of my salary from the radio I gave to my ustad. Because my ustad never earned any money.

      When we learn from an ustad, he shows something once; then the shagird is expected to absorb it. If he makes a mistake or if he makes the same mistake that the ustad corrected once, he may get a slap, or the ustad sends him away. But, Regula, that way one really learns.

      American students don't understand this; they are always asking questions. They even question basic facts of the raga, and they ask things again and again, expecting to be told and helped over and over.

The first principles of playing are concrete:

Ram Narayan: Before you play any raga, you have to get your technique perfected. Your fingers must know their places. But don't look at your fingers. As we say: let your fingers grow their own eyes (*unglion ki ankhen banengi*). And your bow is your tongue (*zaban*). It speaks, makes rhythm. Understand and use its characteristics.

Having control of the bow is most important. And then both have to be independent. For instance, you should be able to play a pattern (*palta*) of six notes with your fingers in a rhythmic pattern of seven beats with your bow.

Palta patterns are very important. Out of them comes improvisation in ragas. Work them up to a very fast speed. Then you can make infinite variations rhythmically with all these patterns. The same pattern or scale can be varied rhythmically a thousand times by different bow accents and bow changes. The pleasure you get from rhythmic variations, it is a wondrous thing. (January 29, 1969.)

But ultimately, making music is transcendent; this theme returns throughout the intensive practical course of Ram Narayan's teaching:

Ram Narayan: Most important is to have devotion (*bhakti*, i.e., religious devotion). Those who do not have that devotion in their heart, their playing can't be really good. One who thinks he is great, who thinks he has nothing more to learn, is no good. You have to feel it in your heart (*sur ki as hona chahie*). (January 31, 1969.)

You see, the real essence of music no one can teach or bring to you. You have to experience it yourself; it comes out of your own heart. But that transportation, into another world—"into heaven"—it comes only rarely. In my whole concert tour of six months (abroad), it came only once, in Paris. I started feeling that I am all alone, immersed in music; all the people before me became meaningless, unwanted. I was flying, moving toward heaven. Then I looked back and saw that the people are following me; I am pulling them up with me. I felt one with them; some of them were weeping. (February 4, 1969.)

Nobody can teach you the real thing. It has to come out of you. True, I can lecture you about ragas, and you can write down, but that is far from anything. You can learn by sitting with a teacher, but in the end, it will come automatically, out of your own mind. It takes a lot of intelligence, but without cleverness. And above all, devotion (*bhakti*): remember, there should be devotion in your heart. (February 6, 1969.)

ARUNA NARAYAN KALLE: FIRST WOMAN
SARANGI PLAYER OF INDIA[4]

Introducing Aruna

Aruna Narayan Kalle is the only daughter of the celebrated Pandit Ram Narayan and the first professionally trained woman sarangi player of the 20th century. Shortly after Ram Narayan's first female student arrived from Canada, he also took the gigantic step of passing his personal art to his only daughter on an instrument that had been the exclusive purview of men. Thanks to Bombay's cosmopolitan environment and modern performing arts institutions, Aruna was able to join her father's master classes at the National Center for Performing Arts, a public enhancement of her traditional study at home.

Aruna brings a finely developed musical temperament to her father's legacy of cultivating an idiom of serious raga music for her instrument. Her sarangi playing is marked for its graceful nuances and a sensitivity that is both rare and refreshing. Combined with that is a very strong technical background, grounded in her father's playing technique, that facilitates a free expression of musical ideas well formed and executed.

Although Aruna began her music training at the rather late age of 18, she made fast progress, specializing in solo sarangi playing, and has since demonstrated her artistry in numerous concerts in India, Canada, and in several other countries. In India she performs regularly on All India Radio's classical programs. Living in Toronto with her family since 1984, Aruna is a true artist, totally devoted to her instrument and to upholding the classical raga tradition of Indian music. Her artistic integrity is manifested in her recent video collaboration with Canada's leading Baroque ensemble, Tafelmusik, in Mychael Danna's Four Seasons Mosaic.[5] *She clearly has internalized her father's purism.*

I first met Aruna, during my lessons with her father, as a bright and confident young teenager who dealt with her father's correspondence and translation from and into English as needed. I saw no indication of her future as a musician, but she grew up surrounded by her father's sarangi music and by the musical training of her elder brother Brij Narayan, who became a well-known sarod player.

We got reacquainted at a Toronto conference in 1989, where her performance instantly evoked the unique style of her famous father, for me an inspiring and also moving experience. She had recently moved to Canada and was building a new musical life centered on deepening and expanding her artistic scope through intense practice, while also maintaining her performing con-

Figure 13 Aruna Narayan Kalle, 2002.

nections in India during the concert season there. But it was a decade later, at a concert held in Edmonton, that Aruna astonished both Indian and Western listeners with her evocative and deeply expressive raga improvisations, enhanced by a flawless and always tasteful virtuosity. I had the privilege to explore this superb artist's view of her music on that occasion and in subsequent conversations. What most impressed me is her courage to pursue her art, to follow her own path while continuing her father's musical heritage.

Aruna speaks in English, only switching into Hindi occasionally where it offers her better wording. It is a special pleasure to be connected with her in Canada, a country that has welcomed us both.

Playing with Depth at Home Abroad

Regula: When I came to Bombay in 1969—which is so long ago *laughs*—that's when I first met you.

Aruna: All I remember really is that … I was so amazed that you were speaking in Urdu, you know. When we were children, it was very rare for foreigners to speak in our language; so that really stood out for me.

Regula: And I was impressed with your English and wondering how you were really like a research assistant for your father because you did all the things in English for him, his correspondence, and you were just there for him.

Aruna: Yeah, from a very young age—I mean, I was maybe 12 or so since I started looking after his correspondence because he didn't write English then, and I used to make his phone calls too *laughs*. It is so strange, because you know, later on his agent from Europe, Michael Jean, who was from London, he subsequently got married and Bapu ("father," i.e., Ram Narayan) was there for his wedding and everything. And when they had a daughter, he called me up; he said, "Can I name her Aruna?" *laughs*. So I said, "Oh, I'd feel honored if you did that." And then I met Aruna—she's of course a young lady now—and I asked her: "Do you like your name?" And she said, "I love it." She's never found it necessary to change it or anything.

Regula: That's beautiful.

Aruna: Yeah, so from a very young age I was really, you know, looking after his paperwork *laughs*.

Regula: That is what amazed me when I was in your house. You spoke English very well and, well, you obviously went to a good school. And you must have been just 12, 13 years old.

Aruna: Yes, I was, and of course we went to English schools, you know Catholic schools, really. So we were educated in English.

Regula: That's good.

Aruna: *Laughs. Han* (yes), it was very useful.

An Unusual Training Path

Aruna: I started learning sarangi while going to college and practiced about two hours a day. But from the beginning, my father's systematic method helped me progress. He says he can get a sarangi player trained in three years, and he has done it. I started when I was, I think, 18 or 19. I was still in college; that was in 1973, I think. Yes, I actually started exactly with Joep (Bor), when he came to India from Holland to study with my father.[6]

Regula: That's about four years after I had come to your father.

Aruna: Right, so Joep and I actually started together. I remember because I was just getting my instrument when he came. And so our initial screeching of the beginner's bow on the strings was together. He was a beginner, so we practiced our paltas (sequential patterns) together.

    When I was able to play, Bapu and Thirakua Khan Sahib, the tabla player, and Annapurna ji,[7] they gave three master classes at NCPA (National Center for Performing Arts). Actually that's where I really started learning.

Regula: I didn't know that; that's fantastic.

Aruna: So these three people used to teach twice a week there, and that was really my most formal kind of learning because Bapu and I used to go all the way there from the house, and there were other students who came too. We first practiced an hour of exercises, and then I had my father's teaching. The two straight hours, it was like the most productive kind of training that I got, because there was no escape there, and no distractions, you know, just that room, a fabulous practice room.

    We stayed in there for two hours and occasionally even longer—three hours, as long as there was no other class scheduled. I learnt so much there. And Dr. Narayan Menon, the director, of course wanted me to be known as a student from the NCPA. So he wanted to make sure that I would come there, you know.

    Even later, when I lived in Pune, I used to come to Bombay every week and stay for three days. Every Monday I'd jump in the train and travel straight to the terminal, take a taxi or bus or whatever to NCPA and meet my father there, have the class, then drive back home with him to have lunch. This went on Tuesday as well, and on Wednesday I traveled back to Poona (Pune).

Regula: Impressive!

Aruna: I did that for several years *short laugh*.

Regula: So they had these classes over a long time?

Aruna: Oh, they had them for a long time, and I don't know why, it's so unfortunate that they stopped that; it was one of the best things. There were fewer students, of course, because they wanted professional-level students who can take advantage of the master classes. I wish I knew why they don't do this anymore, because it was so useful for all the students who were from that time. And you know, the commitment from the teachers and from the students was tremendous. Because they were all sort of ... forced to be in this place. It went on for three hours and they couldn't help but, you know, do some real work there. And now there is nothing held in the name of music other than seminars, so I don't know what NCPA is, really. It looks like, more like a theater.

Regula: Well, tell me ... can you remember what years these were? You were already married and were living in Pune.

Aruna: No, I went to those classes for several years before I got married. Then, in 1977, I got married and I continued to go there till I think 1984, at which time I think the classes stopped. I went there till almost the very end of the session. And soon after that I played my first full concert.

Regula: That's so interesting. I mean, no woman was playing sarangi then, at least not in public, though maybe some women played privately.

Aruna: Well, I probably was the first one to play it in concerts. But many years before, a lady had asked my father to teach her sarangi.

A Special Role Model

Aruna: The lady was Leela Mundkur, my husband's aunt, who actually has been mentioned in my father's book. When my father first arrived in Bombay in 1949 or '50, somewhere there, she actually heard him accompanying some vocalist, probably Krishna Rao

Shankar Pandit, in a concert. She approached him and said that she wanted to learn sarangi. So my father said—he had just come and was obviously struggling at that time, and he lived very far away from Bombay, in the suburbs—so he told her that, you know, I live so far away, and of course he couldn't speak any English and then she didn't speak any Hindi. So she said, "I have two apartments in Bombay, very close to Malabar Hills and Kemp's Corner (a very central location), and you can rent one of them."

So he actually lived in that apartment, and then a few years later my mother came and I was born there. So she became very close to our family. She was my father's mother's age, so she was like a mother figure for my parents and for all of us too. I mean she was—Regula, I think, you have some women who really stand out in your life.

Regula: That is beautiful.

Aruna: Yes. She passed away a few years ago, and she was a woman way, way ahead of her time. She was one of the founding members of the Handicraft Board. She used to design temple jewelry. And she sold saris, you know the temple saris. She was immensely talented and… she was also at that time very revolutionary, in the sense that she was a divorcee.

Regula: Oh, that is revolutionary.

Aruna: Yeah, at that time it was. And she could hold up her head high. And you know she had this business going and she traveled everywhere. Her only son still lives in the U.S., but she refused to go to the U.S.; she lived on her own till the very end.

And so she wanted to learn the sarangi, that's how this whole thing started. My father said, "I can't," so she taught him English, actually. He said, "Okay, you teach me English and I'll teach you sarangi" *laughs*.

Regula: That's really amazing. I mean your father was also very modern, very ready to do new things.

Aruna: Oh yes, that's why he did what he did. I mean, within the kind of social environment that he grew up in, there was no way he could do something like this if he was not, you know, adventurous.

Regula: That's right, that's very right. And what is really amazing is that your aunt actually would want to learn sarangi. Even that is most unusual.

Aruna: Even that is fabulous. She practiced and played, but of course it was not like a full-time thing for her. It was just a tremendous interest of hers. She was just so steeped in art and music and everything cultural that this was just one of her passions.

Regula: And you said that she comes from the same family as your husband.

Aruna: My father-in-law and she were first cousins, which is also how my husband and I actually got married, that's how we had met, too, through her. In fact, in her own community she was not very well liked, because she had left her house and separated from her husband. But there were scores of other people who had the highest admiration for her.

Regula: She sounds like a fantastic lady. Someone, maybe you, should write a book, or at least something about her.

Aruna: Yes, yes, absolutely. And you know, if you ever go to Bombay you will see some really nice things in my father's house: antiques, paintings, and even some jewelry. She would buy these to sell, from the South of India, and she would sometimes come straight from the airport and tell my father or my mother, "You must keep this, or you won't get this again." Even my wedding sari came from her, hand-woven in the ancient vudhrak style and over 150 years old, like a museum piece.

So she was this kind of person, a very strong influence in our lives. And really the first woman sarangi player I know of *laughs.*

Regula: I'm amazed. Because this was quite out of the ordinary.

Aruna: Right! Though of course she never really performed. But she at least had the courage to say that "I want to play this."

Regula: Yes, and so it would then be a natural thing that you would also play.

Aruna: Of course. And you know my father, in his book he also says that it was during the time that he knew her that he started actually playing solo. And the first time, of course, that he played solo he was booted out. And he said, "I can't tell you how much I'm grateful to Leela Bai for encouraging me after that." He said that he was so depressed, but she kept telling him that this is something great you're doing, you have to continue. And she started organizing small solo concerts for him, and he said, "I can't tell you how much confidence that gave me." So she was a big part of his career too.

Regula: You know, I'm so happy to hear about Leela Bai.

Aruna: Yes, we miss her just like my mother.

My Father's Teaching

Regula: So when you started playing, did you just start playing at home, with your father? How did you learn? Last time we talked here in my house, you told me that he taught you in a way that you actually progressed very rapidly—it was a sort of condensed teaching.

Aruna: Right, totally. And he is continuing to do that with my brother Brij Narayan's son too. Harsh Narayan is his name. He is about 22 now, and Regula ji, he is phenomenal, a fabulous sarangi player. I mean, he wants big things, and of course he started at the right time, when he was eight or nine years old.

And I think you know that he also learnt in the same way that my father taught me. In fact, now he has sort of perfected the technique of teaching sarangi so everybody starts really playing within about three to four years. Which is fantastic, as opposed to 30 years ago when people were struggling with the instrument forever.

So this is his way of teaching now. But I think I was one of his first students, so I think it was difficult for both him and me, because I started at a later age. But then I've put in a lot of time in the first few years, eight to nine hours a day. And I continued to do that even after I got married. My practicing was just like office timing.

Regula: You mean, he went to the office, and you sat down to play?

Aruna: I sat down to practice, just got up for lunch, then practiced again till evening.

Regula: That's impressive, for any musician.

Aruna: I've put the time in, for sure. But the thing is, the technique of teaching somebody the sarangi, for him, was probably one of the most frustrating things to do. I mean, these masters, what for them is a very easy, small thing, for a student it's huge and very difficult just to produce that.

Regula: For sure, they have to become very patient.

Aruna: Yes, yes. And he was also very fond of me, as his daughter. So he also sort of had to learn patience, and that must've been very difficult for him too.

Regula: Well, I always remember how I needed to write down everything that he taught, but he was extremely patient with me.

Aruna: *Yes*, he still is, I don't know how he does it. In fact, when I called him in India a little while earlier, he was teaching and, you know, there are three or four sarangi students from different places in the background, all playing away, and he just sits there and listens to the whole thing.

Regula: Oh absolutely, he has talked about that a lot.

Aruna: He feels that it is important for him to do it. So he has to listen and he has to teach properly. So he's doing that, which is, I think, a fantastic contribution.

Regula: So are you seeing a change when you go to India and perform?

Aruna: Oh absolutely. I think, you know, the good thing is that a lot of people are actually playing the sarangi. There are a lot of young people from Delhi, children of musicians, who are playing.

Now the only problem—I don't know whether it's a problem, and I hope it won't be—is that apart from Bapu's students, a lot of sarangi players are still sort of stuck in the groove of just accompaniment, and that comes because they do not have the training to play solo. If you are an accompanist, you have to really step out. Your sarangi technique, and the total perspective of playing the instrument solo, that has to be so well-defined that I think there still are very few sarangi players who can really carry one whole concert.

You know, I mean, even if both their fingers and their minds are agile, when they have been stuck in the business of accompaniment, then there is still a bit of a problem that they won't be able to give the sarangi real "stage stature." But I feel that some of Bapu's students are doing well.

Regula: Of course, he pioneered the solo sarangi, really.

Aruna: Yes; so the thing a lot of people don't understand is that playing solo sarangi is a completely different thing as opposed to an accompanist. When we're playing a solo concert, we have no escape. There is no singer to take the edge. So the work that we do has to be continuously and consistently solid in every way: in the musical ideas, the raga, and in building and developing the piece.

Then there is the matter of 'style.' We can't play only in a singing style; after all, we're playing an instrument! We need to combine singing and instrumental, to make that instrument work—that's a big, big challenge.

Regula: Well, you have also spent a lot of time working on this; I mean, your playing shows a lot of very serious thinking and a deep kind of emotional power.

Aruna: That's what I mean; that's what I'm saying. That's the kind of training one needs to know for the sarangi: the capacity to make a presentation on their own.

Regula: I guess part of staying accompanists is just that they have to make a living.

Aruna: Yes, absolutely. That's what I was going to say, that you can't begrudge them that, because of making a living, and also because, for the sake of the sarangi, as long as this instrument is in use, that itself is a big thing.

From India to Canada: Does Being Female Matter?

Regula: Tell me, for you, has it been a factor that you are a woman rather than a man, playing the sarangi? And how has being in Canada affected you as a musician? And where are you going with that now?

Aruna: Well, for me, being a woman and playing the sarangi has never really been a factor at all. The focus has always been to play well. I see everywhere in the world, especially in the West, that women are doing all things that men do. And, you know, you have enough women musicians here (in Canada), violinists and …

Regula: Of course, yes.

Aruna: So, I don't think that has ever been a factor. I think that the sarangi did not have women players because, first of all, it was over the centuries considered really technically difficult to play, even for men. So that was a handicap for both men and women. And on top of that, there was the social connection of the sarangi, you know, with all the *baijis* (courtesans) and so on. It was absolutely a taboo for women to be anywhere near that, which is also one reason why women didn't play that instrument.

    And if you'll notice, in India, with any instrument, you'll have fewer women playing than men. Women are mostly vocalists, singers. Probably the reason may be physical capabilities. Playing takes a lot of energy; if given a choice, audiences will obviously opt for a stronger, faster sitar or sarod player, and that will obviously be a man, as opposed to a woman who's playing the same instrument. So the bias against women instrumentalists has always been there for the sarangi. Added to that is the technical difficulty plus all the social connections. I think it was an area where no woman really went.

Regula: It's true.

Aruna: For me, the sarangi was in my house, it was given to me, you know; it was just part of my growing up that I took up sarangi. For me there was absolutely no distinction between playing sarangi and playing another instrument. But I picked it because I really loved it, and my whole goal has always been to play it well than rather than be a novelty.

Regula: You studied and took those classes with your father till 1984; after that, did you ever start performing or …

Aruna: Oh yes, I did. Actually I started, I think, three years after I started playing. I had my debut concert with NCPA, I think in '76. I think I still have some reviews from there *laughs*.

I did not play too much after that; I continued to study and, you know, I continued to work hard on my practice. It was in '84 when we moved to Delhi when I really started doing concerts, but not the way all the other professional musicians get around. I have never done that because I never believed that I need to sort of be all over the place.

Regula: Yes *laughs*.

Aruna: And, you know, playing a lot of concerts, you sort of develop some things that may not be the right things to develop. Fortunately for me, I've never really had to work as a living; I never had to make this a profession in that sense, to bring in some money—that was never the case. Fortunately, my husband always had a decent job, and I was never that ambitious about making my livelihood. So I really didn't go out and I still don't go out to get many concerts. I'm quite happy with the amount I play.

It is in this sense that from 1984 I started playing more. And then, in '88, we came here to Canada. That was for me a very difficult time. It was very depressing. I mean, it definitely hit me very hard mentally, that whatever I was doing had come to a stop. But of course I was not economically stronger than my husband to say: "No, I can't do this." Of course I had to move.

And we had young children then, so for them, you have to do these things. This is a better place for them for education and in so many other ways.

Regula: So you got totally tied up with that?

Aruna: Right. I mean, I lived here, and although in all these years I've hardly played in many places in Canada, still I was sort of happy because the good thing was that I had all the means to practice here. That's what I've been doing. I have no other activity except, of course, for the house, like everybody does, but apart from that, I've sort of never had a job or anything. So I practice, and I play.

Regula: And you have become an extremely wonderful player. You have a depth in your playing that is just so remarkable.

Aruna: I think that really probably also comes with the isolation. Sometimes when you are alone, and when you're doing your work by yourself, then I think that it really grabs you, the whole of you. You know that you have nothing else, so you put a lot of effort in it.

This is what I do even now, and I mean a lot of people in India might not. My father, he has been teaching a girl; she's playing and actually she's begun performing too.

Regula: Oh really?

Aruna: Yes, yes. So on my last visit she was telling me: "I'm so amazed that you have been away from India for so long, away from Bapu[8] for so long, and that you still continue to work this intensely." And I said to her: "Because I have never known anything else, you know, I've never wanted to do anything else." And apart from my house, there's not much I do. This is all I do. I'm really not sort of ambitious, it's not a rat race for me.

Regula: No, no, I understand you.

Aruna: I really don't care how many people know me, but I feel that for the instrument, it's just something that I can't live without. So I practice every day, and I am with my instrument, so the intensity of the work will never suffer.

But that girl said: "I don't know what I would have done if I didn't have a lesson every day or if I didn't sort of come to see your father every day. I don't know how I could keep this up." Well, you learn. It's a matter of survival.

Regula: That's true. I think you have started exploring some collaborations with Western classical music.

Western Collaborations and Trips to India

Aruna: Right. The reason why I actually even collaborated with Tafelmusik was that I felt that Western classical music is such a strong tradition in itself that the collaboration was not going to compromise either Western music or Indian music. I was bringing something, and I know Mychael Danna[9] very well; I have played for him and some of his students and I know that Mychael is one person who will never interfere with you. He'll say, "Okay, this is the amount of space we have, and I want you to do something that you think will blend with the rest of it."

He has always been like that, and so have I. And you know, I don't play light music, even in classical music, the light part in it, raga pilu, or any light ragas. It's quite a struggle for me to conceptualize light music. So for me, in any collaboration, I'm still thinking in terms of the complete raga and, you know, about the scale and about the actual work. Even in this collaboration with Tafelmusik for Vivaldi's *Four Seasons*, he said: "How about using the *darbari* scale?"

Regula: I see—he knows?

Aruna: Yes, yes, he knows … he's very good; I mean, he's very well acquainted with Indian music, and his wife is Indian too. So he would say, "How about this scale," and so for me the moment he said "darbari," I thought, "Oh, I have to play raga darbari (a famous and challenging raga) *laughs*. Which is what we did, and it worked wonderfully. So basically, to collaborate, I said, it won't do if you're just throwing two or three different kinds of instruments or music together and just waiting for something to happen. But I thought that it was a good example of how sounds can blend, not just because violin and sarangi are different instruments.

Even for the collaboration with Tanya Kalmanovitch,[10] I told her, "You know, we have to do something that makes sense for both of us." It should not be such a huge compromise that she loses what she has (*apna*), and I lose what I have. Doesn't make sense. So that is something interesting for me to do while I'm here, obviously.

Regula: But you also keep going back to India and playing there?

Aruna: Oh yes, of course, every year. Sometimes I go twice a year. And then, in the last few years, there have been a few concerts in Europe when Bapu visits there to play.

Regula: So do you also play concerts with him, or could you even do a performance of three generations with your father and your nephew Harsh?

Aruna: Yes, absolutely. I play with my father and then we can also be together. But Harsh is doing his MBA now, so he's busy with that. And I don't know, becoming a regular professional musician is also fraught with so much.... You can see that professional musicians can't survive unless they do all kinds of nonsense. So for serious musicians like our family, it is a very difficult proposition, not only for me but for these young men also. So this is also a big concern, and that's why he has to have his education.

Regula: You know, you mentioned your father's book.

Aruna: Yes, it has just been released a few months ago; one of Bapu's students has written it in Marathi, and a Hindi translation is just about ready. Someone is also going to translate it into English. I can let you know the publisher.

Regula: That would be lovely. Well, you know, it has been so wonderful talking to you and hearing you talk. I thought that in half an hour we'd be all done, but there are so many rich things that you have told me. Thank you very much.

Aruna: *Laughs.* Not at all.

We say cordial goodbyes, with the firm intention to meet again, either in Toronto, or perhaps even in Bombay, but certainly for her concert in Edmonton soon.

CHAPTER 5

Dhruba Ghosh

The New Generation

Introducing Dhruba Ghosh

Dhruba Ghosh is a different sarangi player. A determined and independent-minded musician of a younger generation (born 1957), he belongs to a family of musicians, but at the same time stands apart from the hereditary lineages of sarangi players. Hailing from Bengal, his uncle was the superb flutist and musical innovator Pannalal Ghosh, who had introduced the flute to classical Hindustani music. His younger brother Nikhil Ghosh, Dhruba's father, was one of the great tabla players of his generation as well as a thoughtful and dedicated scholar of music. In Bombay, Nikhil Ghosh established the renowned music conservatory Sangit Mahabharati (Great Indian Music). Most remarkably, he pioneered an important encyclopedia project for Hindustani music and proposed a notation system for ragas.[1] Dhruba's mother comes from a Maharashtrian (Konkani speaking) family of music lovers and patrons.

Dhruba Ghosh studied music and sarangi under his father's guidance together with his elder brother Nayan, who became a sitar player but also received professional training on the tabla. Remarkably, Nikhil Ghosh imparted essential training to both Dhruba and Nayan. The brothers were part of his vision of a family ensemble of complementary instruments: sarangi, sitar, and tabla. This vision became reality in 1974, when the trio began to tour internationally. On their first visit to Canada and Edmonton, the young Dhruba impressed listeners with the sweet freshness of his sarangi playing. Since then he has systematically explored the technical and expressive range of the instrument to get audiences as interested in a recital

Figure 14 Dhruba Ghosh, 2001.

on the sarangi as on the sitar. He has made a name for himself as a versatile performer whose playing is both innovative and expressive. College educated, Dhruba has also become an eloquent advocate for the sarangi, using English with ease and eloquence; he also writes poetry.

That first encounter with Dhruba Ghosh in Edmonton created an indelible impression of a young beginner's musical promise, and of masterful artistic guidance by his father. I shall never forget the languid simplicity of his playing, reminiscent of the delicate Bengali esraj bowed on thin wire strings. His family's extended visit established a lasting bond of friendship and deep respect for its outstanding leader. In the absence of a traditional student or patron relationship between us, Dhruba and I relate simply as sarangi friends, even though I have learned from him and arranged for him to perform. Our friendship, and my presence, in 1994 at the Sangeet

Research Academy's sarangi conference (Parikh 1994), even enabled me to join the family on his brother's marriage.

It was in 1988 when I was able to visit Dhruba, now an established young professional in Bombay, to learn about his unique approach to sarangi playing. Our meeting at the large teaching academy Sangit Mahabharati was once again a family affair, with his father at the helm of the institution. Dhruba, his brother, and his sister acted as managers and teachers, and their mother had the role of assisting and taking care of daytime meals and tea—a team in action. Dhruba was by then an established young artist, but he had already experienced the handicap of playing an instrument of limited following that was not taught institutionally, even in his family's own music school. Thoroughly modern in outlook, Dhruba was committed to modernize the sarangi even as he lovingly demonstrated its traditional repertoire to his curious Canadian friend. Six years later, at the 1994 sarangi conference, he presented a bold proposal for the sarangi to a special conference on the instrument, the only sarangi player to do so.

Since then, Dhruba has expanded his concertizing in India as well as in Europe and North America. In the years following that first visit in Edmonton, he has returned to Canada several times. He has made a second home teaching in Belgium, but has also joined his brother Nayan in taking charge of Sangit Mahabharati in Bombay, carrying forward their father's teaching legacy. At the same time, the international phase of Dhruba's career continues helping the sarangi take its place among the favorite voices of the 21st century.

The Egg Must Break the Shell[2]

Fourteen years after our first meeting in Canada, I visited Dhruba Ghosh in the impressive Sangeet Mahabharati. In his father's approving presence, I learned about this young musician's chosen path of becoming a sarangi soloist and expanding the instrument's repertoire, all in pursuit of his goal of charting a broader musical course for the instrument. On this visit I also learned of Dhruba's attempt to add a fourth string to the sarangi so as to expand its tonal and figurational range (Figure 15). Remarkably, his father expressed enthusiastic appreciation of Dhruba's experiments to improve the sarangi's playability (Figure 15). The evening ended with a family dinner at a restaurant, to which I was invited.

Our conversation began with reminiscing and catching up with Dhruba's progress and accomplishments, his father enabling him to continue his artistic development while continuing to manage and teach at Sangit Mahabharati. But would a career as a solo performer be possible?

Figure 15 Dhruba Ghosh, demonstrating his four-string sarangi, Cologne, Germany, 2005.

We Must Strike Out on Our Own

Regula: The question was, how can you make a living? Can you manage to do it professionally?

Dhruba: Uh … I think it is possible. If, for example, the artist is mainly a soloist, what happens is that either he has to accompany vocalists, which is again a very unreliable factor, because many vocalists are opting out of the sarangi, they are not taking the sarangi. They'll do the harmonium. On the other hand, there is some scope in the film industry, for background scores, background music. But if an artist really wants to, suppose a sitar player wants to play a concert, a sarangi player today doesn't stand a chance. He doesn't stand a chance.

Regula: That's really terrible!

Dhruba: But there are various reasons also for that, which I, as an old student, have come to feel that the blame is also on the part of the tradition, and also on the part of sarangi players themselves. Let's handle tradition in the beginning. The bias against them is known: the social bias, because of the association with *baijis* (courtesans) and all that. The second thing is followed on by the media. The radio always gives sarangi the background, like even in the national program sessions of one-and-a-half hours, sarangi would never get a full one-hour chunk, except for top-rate artists.

Out of one-and-a-half hours, they would get, I think, about 40 minutes. And so with tabla. Tabla used to get a full one-and-a-half hours by the top-rate artists, until, I think, about 12 years back. But now even tabla players get a half chunk. I don't know what the policy is. The other thing is that the media uses the sarangi for mourning purposes. For example, when a minister dies.

Regula: You know, that's very interesting. I know when Indira Gandhi died, for two days, I think, there was nothing but sarangi on the radio! Why do they do that? And why is that a problem?

Dhruba: Because, I think, the connotation with wailing sound, which I think is a wrong association … because sarangi itself, as it is heard, tends to give a wailing effect, if it is played badly. There are any number of other reasonable factors which have not been explored. So now, I'll come down to the sarangi players now.

Regula: Okay! *Both laugh.*

Dhruba: What has happened is that—this is just my hypothesis—is that the pressure of convention has been too heavy on the sarangi. And the players, because their main subsistence happened to be accompanying vocalists, so nobody really took the risk of doing something … I mean … striking out on his own. They could have if they wanted to. I can't think why they did not. Or maybe they have, and they died.

Regula: Bundu Khan, in a way, did that.

Dhruba: Bundu Khan did a marvelous thing. He was one of the giants. He took a very big leap ahead.

Regula: But see, I think for Bundu Khan, there was a reason. I have studied that quite a bit [as to] why Bundu Khan did that. He had a patron for it (the Maharaja of Gwalior) ... he didn't just do it out of thin air.

Dhruba: That is on one side. Okay, patronage is there. But then why would he evolve his own style? If he had to put the Maharaja to sleep, he could have played in the traditional way.... But he played something very daringly new.

Regula: You are right. You are absolutely right.

Dhruba: He has been one of my main inspirations. In terms of the codes that he left behind. Some of the *tantrakari* (stringed instrument) codes. By codes I mean some of the patterns. When you listen to all his recordings, if you use them, then what happens? With me, I'll tell you, I am calling them a code backwards. Because from each, I could find out many more variations. And that would, if really explored to its full, last quite a while. It will be a full universe base.

Regula: Very interesting. So you have learnt from his recordings?

Dhruba: From his recordings. And also, from one of his disciples: Saghiruddin Khan. He lives in Calcutta, and in 1971, he was visiting Bombay. So luckily, I could get a lesson from him. Just for about an hour or two. That's the only lesson I had from him, unfortunately. I wish I had more sittings, since there is so much to learn.

Regula: But his playing was different; I mean I have heard Saghiruddin Khan.

Dhruba: No, Saghiruddin Khan, in fact, he is so much of a *gayaki* (vocal style) player. Although his sarangi sounds like Bundu Khan Sahib's sarangi. That quaint sound. But the tantrakari part of it, he does not have; I don't know for what reason, really.

Regula: Give me an example.

Dhruba: Yes, I will. *He plays, showing arpeggiation and rhythmic variations.*

So what has happened is that … basically sarangi players have been in a weaker position. If they had to live, they had to live accepting the convention. So if somebody did something, I think the pressure of convention and the peer group was too heavy. What I am surprised by is the number of some geniuses—genii, how do you say it? Bundu Khan belongs to the revolution of which Inayat Khan, Vilayat Khan, Pandit Ravi Shankar ji are a part. Sitar players have been going so many strides ahead. So that has not happened in sarangi. I think one reason is basically that accompanying singers was the thing of the day. And even today, a sarangi player thinks that following vocal is his religion. I mean, his performance religion! What has happened is that when a sarangi recital takes place, what a sarangi player does is reflect the vocal recital.

Regula: So people should be happy, just as they have been very happy at the vocal style that Vilayat Khan introduced on the sitar!

Dhruba: But his style doesn't end at gayaki. He introduced vocal melody on the sitar, but there is the whole region of instrument-specific (tantrakari) patterns on which he has based his vocal style (gayaki). Now that has not happened with sarangi. The sarangi is played purely reflecting vocal melody.

Regula: Do you mean that it has not developed its own instrument-specific style?

Dhruba: That's right! Let's look at it this way: if a vocalist is singing, so why would one want to listen to a sarangi? Because the sarangi does not have words. It's something like a dumb person trying to sing. You can't listen to a dumb person sing, even if he sings a very beautiful melody. And so sarangi is facing something from that major problem. You are still going to miss the words!

But still … In fact, I wrote a very strong letter to the Minister of Broadcasting and to the Director General of All India Radio, saying that their bias against the sarangi, and not giving the full chunk (on the National Programme[3]) is justified to this extent: that traditional sarangi playing cannot hold an audience for more than 30 minutes. I said that I have heard recitals of almost all great masters, past and present, including mine (I have to say that), and I feel I could not stand more than 30 minutes. It is a very candid point—if I was playing the accepted way. For this reason, that it does not have the articulation of words. And although you play the vocalistic style, unless if it is all long notes, it is going to be monotonous, and if it is going to be staccato notes, that is, articulating the words of the song, if you are playing the "tan tan tan," if you are playing that, then it is like a small child learning to talk. It doesn't make sense!

Regula: It is an imitation of ...

Dhruba: It is an imitation. It is a poor imitation, although the tonal quality of the instrument is very rich. So the sarangi does fall behind the rest. Now, this doesn't mean that the sarangi does not have its own dynamics. I mean, performing dynamics? It has to have! If sitar players could get away from the vocal, and play sitar—of course Vilayat Khan came back to a vocal style, that is a different issue. First of all, all instruments, it is generally considered, were used to accompany vocalists. So how is it that sitar players came out (of that)? Is it that there were players who wanted to find out themselves?

Pioneers and the Quest for a New Idiom

Dhruba: Now with the sarangi ... What I feel basically is that if a fusion of gayaki and tantrakari (vocal and instrument-specific) is done, that would really make the sarangi recital valid.

Regula: So, you do that.

Dhruba: I do that.

Regula: Has anyone developed that style? Well, Bundu Khan certainly did.

Dhruba: Bundu Khan, yes, but unfortunately his recordings are very few, and those which are of long length—let's put it this way—I am being very candid. He was a pioneer. But the tonal structure and the musical demands of a modern audience are much more than what Bundu Khan played. The total finesse, the sophistication that the modern sitar would give, or modern sarod would give, for sarangi there has not been a giant player who could give that. In fact, I am really groping in the dark and struggling in order to find an idiom for the instrument. Basically that is it, that is where the struggle is becoming very, very intense. I have been trying, experimenting with using different fingerings and bowings. Bundu Khan Sahib—I don't know if Joep Bor has written that, but there is a technique that I have learnt from his disciple: using all fingers, one on each note of the scale, not to slide one finger from note to note. (*He demonstrates a scale.*)

Regula: Okay, this makes it easier to do fast runs, like on the Western violin, right?

Dhruba: But in the higher parts, *tar sabtak* (the upper octave), it works only if the intervals afford the distance. It will depend on the raga. Otherwise, the distance (between the notes) is too small for placing a finger on each.

Regula: So you really develop your own way of playing.

Dhruba: Really, I am very junior. Trying to break—suddenly for the egg to break the shell.

Regula: The way you played 14 years ago, I remember that innocent beauty of tone every time I hear a beautiful recording of *esraj* (a Bengali bowed string instrument with metal strings and frets), very melodious, not fast.

Nikhil Ghosh: (*Adding his mature perspective to the discussion:*) The base for such playing is vocal training. But from whom will they learn? There is no one left; the masters are all gone!

Dhruba: Yes, there are many sarangi players who have not taken formal training. They have been just accompanists.

Nikhil Ghosh: The point is that, formerly, good sarangi players also studied singing, and they even learned tabla.

Dhruba: Yes, they used to be called "125 percent singer" (*sawai gawayya*, literally "one-and-a-quarter singer"). *Laughter.*

Nikhil Ghosh: *Laughs.* And many musicians, many of the great vocalists, were disciples of sarangi players.

Dhruba: And many great vocalists have been themselves sarangi players. That was a massive revolution in the musical history. So today I think it is ultimately the quest for an idiom that has to take place if this instrument, any instrument, is to survive.

Nikhil Ghosh: That includes *ragdari* (raga competence), knowing the raga, the way it goes. Not just playing the outline of a raga, then take your money and leave!

Dhruba: *Now tunes the resonance strings of his sarangi to demonstrate some of his innovations. While tuning he elaborates further:* The quest for the idiom also has to include the element of excitement. Of gusto. Rhythmic gusto. That, and necessarily the patterns that would evolve from the instrument's special technique, they would create their own rhythmic configurations. There are several such elements that would really go and make an integral idiom. Which would be needed to survive a three-hour concert.

Nikhil Ghosh: *Adding his fervent support to Dhruba's position:* A three-hour concert, yes. May you live long!

Regula: Incredible! If you do all this, then you really have an idiom. Do you find that the attitude to the sarangi in Bombay is different, better than it is in Calcutta, say, where your family comes from? I mean, in the UP (Uttar Pradesh) region, for instance, people are extremely traditional.

Changing People's Attitudes Toward the Sarangi

Dhruba: In fact, in Calcutta, people are more revolutionary in that sense. In fact, whenever I had performances in Calcutta, it created some sort of …

Nikhil Ghosh: Sensation!

Dhruba: And the other thing I noticed was that even with the organizers, they themselves say that they don't use the sarangi because it is a liability. There have been many listeners in my concerts who came and said that till that day they didn't like the sarangi; they hated it, but that day it changed. Recently I was playing at the Maihar festival that is held in the honor of Ustad Allauddin Khan. There, after the recital, a group of journalists came into the green room and said: "We want to interview you. We have not interviewed any artists in this whole place today, for a very specific reason." They said that when the announcement was made that a sarangi recital will be presented now, one section of the audience was going home. They did not want to listen to the sarangi. But by then, they said, your recital had started. And that same section stood there for a full two hours and they listened to all of my recital; only then they left. So the journalists said, "What was that all about?" So they came to interview me.

Nikhil Ghosh: They wanted to know what was the secret!

Regula: How interesting! What *was* the secret? (*All three laugh.*)

Dhruba: This has happened at most of my concerts.

The Physical Instrument—Innovations

Regula: What kind of strings do you use on your instrument?

Dhruba: I use harp strings. This one is a tennis string.

Regula: No, really? *All laugh.* This *is* a new idiom, playing on a tennis string—fantastic! And the bow, it also looks different; what kind is it?

Dhruba: Double bass. To an extent it is okay, but now I am beginning to discourage it. It is light, and doesn't have that energy of the solid arched bow of the sarangi. Still, I won't go back to that very heavy bow but will try the *dilruba* bow.[4]

Regula: But you use very thin strings. Both the tennis string, and this metal string, what is it?

Dhruba: That is a cello string. Because in the thicker gut strings, the chances of having an aberration are greater. *Seeing Regula's incomprehension, he adds:* Because gut squeaks! (*He demonstrates the smooth tone when drawing the bow across the tennis string.*) This has a better effect. So the cello string replaces a thick, lower gut string. *He draws a resonant low tone from the cello string as well.*

Regula: I know all about squeaking strings. Every sarangi player knows that—it's a terrible thing. Now your instrument: did you modify your instrument at all? This looks like a traditional sarangi. Did you make those big holes?

Dhruba: Yeah, I made them for resonance.

Regula: When I first started playing, I got this old sarangi and my teacher took his burning cigarette and burned four holes in the instrument's skin covering. I was shocked! *All laugh.*

Dhruba: It looks like an initiation ceremony! *More laughter.*

Now Nikhilda (Bengali address of respect, with "da" functioning like "ji" for Hindi) introduces his daughter Tulika, a singer, and her cousin from Calcutta, a student of sitar, who have come to join the family at dinner. Then he tunes his tabla to accompany Dhruba, who now presents some of the challenges in different innovations in technique and tone as well as his elaborated outline of a raga performance.

Regula: Dhruba, thank you very much. Really, I am so impressed. I thought you were going to show me just a few fingerings and bowings. But you did this whole panorama of innovative features: cross rhythms and many types of improvisation. And I appreciate your playing raga *shri*, one of my favorite ragas and rarely heard on the sarangi because of the big gaps in the scale. You are obviously learning a lot of difficult things, things that I had not heard of. Thanks a lot. And sorry for keeping you very late.

Nikhil Ghosh: Now let us go for dinner!

The family assembles and he leads us to a fine vegetarian restaurant where good food and good times are had by all.

CHAPTER 6

Sultan Khan

Globalizing Heritage

Introducing Sultan Khan

Sultan Khan is a thoroughly traditional sarangi player who has become an international touring star; the world is his oyster. He is as comfortable in London and Edmonton as he is in Sikhar and Bombay. At the same time, he remains an unabashed hereditary musician from India. An open, pragmatic individual who loves enjoying life in company, Sultan Khan embraces the present but is firmly grounded in his inherited professional musical identity. His career and personality encompass both respect for this inheritance and openness to new ways. As a musician, however, Sultan Khan remains attached to the classical tradition, to which he brings a special musical flavor from his region, the northwestern desert state of Rajasthan. The regional touch is heard most poignantly in the Rajasthani folk songs he likes to add to his classical performances.

Sultan Khan was born in 1940 in the small princely state of Sikhar near the city of Jaipur. He was trained by his father and later learned from the great singer Amir Khan (who had once been a sarangi player). His initial career was as a staff artist at All India Radio in Rajkot (Gujarat); later he moved to Bombay to accompany Lata Mangeshkar and spent some years as a respected studio musician in the Bombay film industry. Since 1991 he has pursued an international solo career in close musical association with Zakir Husain, the world's most famous tabla player, and his illustrious father, tabla legend Allah Rakha. Their close collaboration enables Sultan Khan

Figure 16 Sultan Khan with his father Gulab Khan, Jodhpur, 1981.

to work within the milieu of his own community while internationalizing the horizon of his performances. In contrast to his early recordings—as a usually unacknowledged accompanist—he now has a large number of solo recordings on CD. At the same time, he does not eschew the tradition of accompaniment, as evidenced by his occasional duo recordings with singers and, above all, with Zakir Husain's tabla.

Sultan Khan is my brother; he calls me sister. This makes sense in several ways. We connected for the conversation in this book in 1994 while he was on tour with Zakir Husain, his younger brother Fazal Qureshi, and their father Allah Rakha. All four were staying in the house of another sister, Dr. Srishti Nigam, who has been a close friend of both Zakir Husain and myself. Sultan Khan and I also shared a musical father figure, Alla Rakha: he as the brotherly partner of son Zakir Husain, and I as the disciple of Ustad Hamid Husain (see Chapter 10), Allah Rakha's most beloved friend.

I first encountered Sultan Khan in 1986 in a London flat where he was teaching an English teenager the sarangi. The boy played beautifully, and Sultan Khan dedicated himself fully to this most devoted of students—but to the chagrin of his parents. When we met years later in his Bombay home, Sultan Khan told me sadly that the young man had disappeared and that his sarangi had been found broken in a back lane. In London, Sultan Khan has also taught the best of Western sarangi players, as well as Jaspal Randhava and Saleh Ahmad. In India, his shagirds include staff artist Ikram Khan, of

All India Radio in Ahmedabad, and Subodh Dharyevan, an architect who teaches at an engineering college, as well as his nephew and grandson.

In Bombay, we both participated in the sarangi conference organized in January 1994 by the Sangit Research Academy. I then enjoyed visiting Sultan Khan in his relaxed home atmosphere while he was teaching Subodh Dharyevan, an amateur who loves the sarangi, and during a jovial and intimate farewell gathering on the eve of his forthcoming world tour. Because of his departure, we agreed to have a teaching session during his stop in Edmonton two months later.

To me, Sultan Khan strongly conveys a pragmatic acceptance of both the old and the new, based in self-reliance, a willingness to change, and a genuine love for life and for people. He has taken the sarangi from feudal Rajasthan to the classical and film world of Bombay, and now to the world. In the process, he has returned the instrument to its primal alliance with the tabla, through Zakir Husain, and with the voice. In singing with the sarangi, he dissolves conventional boundaries between specialists and between folk and art music. Whether meeting in a London flat, a Bombay conference, his Bombay home, or my and his second home in Edmonton, Sultan Khan's directness and sense of humor helped loosen the grip of high culture on my interactional style while increasing my respect for this great musician.

Figure 17 Sultan Khan on tour, meeting Ammi and Regula, hotel lobby, Edmonton, 2006.

Respect for the Old and the New[1]

I arrive at my friend Dr. Srishti Nigam's house in Edmonton, where Sultan Khan is staying together with Allah Rakha, Zakir Husain, and his younger brother Fazal Qureshi. Zakir Husain has gone for a media interview before tomorrow's special concert featuring father and son together on the senior master's farewell tour. It is about 1 p.m.; the musicians have just had their midday meal and are enjoying the comfortable informality of this Indian home. Ammi is getting dessert and tea ready while also serving me lunch, while Allah Rakha and I reminisce about our first lunch together, when I dropped in at his Bombay home in 1969 to bring him news from my new ustad, Hamid Husain, his best friend who had migrated to Pakistan 20 years earlier.[2] When Allah Rakha retires for a rest, Sultan Khan and I sit down to talk. Also participating is Srishti Nigam's mother, who has long been the knowledgeable hostess, patron, and caring mother of these and many other musicians. Mrs. Pandit is 80 years old and takes care of all of us; we all call her Ammi (mother). I wanted to follow up on a talk we had in Sultan Khan's Bombay home earlier this year, after an international sarangi conference there (January 1991). He in turn asked me to bring my sarangi, so that we could also have a bit of a teaching session.

Now Fazal Qureshi joins us, and Sultan Khan introduces me as Qureshi Bahin (sister) who plays the sarangi very well. Fazal and I in turn recall our first meeting in Chicago some years back, when we both accompanied the hereditary singer Ghulam Mustafa Khan in concert.

We Are All Descendants of Adam

Regula: *Returns from kitchen.* Alright, so, sir, I have spent a lot of time in UP (Uttar Pradesh) and with musicians from Lucknow, Muradabad, Bundelkhand, but I don't know about Rajasthan.

Sultan Khan: Well, my people come from the princely state of Sikhar, about 80 miles from Jaipur; they were court musicians.

Regula: What kind of music?

Sultan Khan: Look, being a court musician means that whenever His Highness is in a mood—when there is an occasion, a celebration, a religious festival, when it is *Holi, Diwali*, whatever, or *Dassehra*— then there will be a performance (*mahfil*) by every musician who is not engaged otherwise. But the maharaja's "letter" was in force all the time. Their monthly pay was 15 to 20 rupees in those times. And they also got living expenses—grain was provided, other things; they received a ration (allotment) for eating and drinking. It was the same as for other court servants. But we were better off, because by virtue of being musicians, we were able to establish a "direct" connection with the maharaja, while the other servants had only occasional opportunity to offer their salutation to the maharaja, when all the servants would be lined up. Being musicians, our people were in his close proximity; they encountered him 20 times in a year, or personally met him two to four times in a month. That's how it was. Musicians were in a good 'category' in those times as compared to these days, whether they had much money or not. They had respect and honor.

Regula: And their families, their children?

Sultan Khan: People were able to raise all their children without worry. We had our own house; we had land, given by the maharaja, quite a lot of land, nearly 200 *bighas*, and we received a percentage/share (*mauza*) of produce from it. Land, home, we had all of that. That kind of arrangement (*silsila*) was in place since olden times, and it continued as long as there were princely states.[3]

Heredity and Humanity

Sultan Khan: Now, you see, I belong to the eighth "generation" of musicians. That means that this profession has gone on for about 400 to 500 years. And our "family" of musicians in Sikhar was very big. There were at least 300 to 350 households (*ghar*) of khansahibs (musicians). Now, I won't claim that *my* 'father,' my 'grandfather' were some very big standard bearers. They weren't; so what can I tell you? At that time, what world fame could even the greatest artist have? Today, you can say that he went on a "world tour" and so on, but those poor people had not even heard anyone talk about London. But that does not mean that their achievement was any less, or that they were not knowledgeable, or that they were not highly skilled or great artists. I would not say such a thing about them, and it bothers me to hear others say it; it's insulting. Now I have been traveling to the West; this certainly does not mean that my grandfather (*dada*, fathers' father) has become lesser than I because he never came here. Rather, I must be the one to give him the most respect (*ehteram*).

Regula: Are there also rules like marriage that need to be followed? I saw that, among musicians in Delhi and Lucknow, it is said: "Okay, we are all musicians, but we will only marry among these people, not those?"

Sultan Khan: In that there is no high and low. I have told you, we are Sikhar musicians (*Sikharwale*). We will not give our daughter in marriage in Lucknow, nor will we take a daughter of Lucknow musicians in marriage. Why don't we give our daughter, sir? Aren't there any khansahibs in Lucknow? Oh yes, there are khansahibs greater than we are, whose names are more famous than ours. But why go there? We have established that our daughters should not be married just anywhere.

Regula: You mean it feels too strange?

Sultan Khan: Yes, it feels too strange. That does not mean that we don't feel respect for them. But we have a particular region for exchanging daughters (in marriage).[4] There are 10 to 20 villages in the vicinity of Sikhar; those people may be villagers, but they belong to our community. So we give them our daughters and we bring theirs into our families.

Regula: Would you call them members of the *bradri* (*bradriwale*, i.e., people of the brotherhood or patrilineage)?

Sultan Khan: Yes, bradriwale. The point is that the bradri is one thing, and the "community" of all musicians (*gane bajanewale*, literally "people who sing and play") is another. But all this does not mean that we have a bad opinion of other master musicians (ustads), may God forgive me! We have as much love and respect for them, and we consider their sisters and daughters as our own. Because we are, after all, caste brothers and art brothers. I can marry that way too, if I want to. If I can marry a Hindu, if I can marry Uma (*his wife, who had been a singer*), then what objection can I make to marrying the daughter of any Mr. so-and-so Khan?[5] Just to give you an example! It is because most people hesitate to do so, not because of any rules.

Regula: Musicians are called by different terms. What do you call yourself?

Sultan Khan: Please, I'll tell you. Some talk it down; some talk it up. Some use profanity; others use polite speech *Kahin ki gali kahin ki zuban*. Each "branch" of people has its particular "language" and names musicians accordingly. The point is, they remain the same: musicians.

Regula: You mean that in different places they may be considered high or low?

Sultan Khan: Yes, that's what it is. For instance, take me and my people. You can call us *mirasi* (hereditary professional); you can call us Mr. Kalavant (artist) or Mr. Mir (chief). We don't care which one it is. Why? Because we are called this here and that there, but the point is, it all means the same thing.

Regula: This is right. They are all terms to name artists.

Sultan Khan: That's the point: some talk it down some talk it up. It depends on where it is coming from.

Regula: You mean, there are regional differences.

Sultan Khan: That's it, yes. Now in Uttar Pradesh, there are places where people say *dom* (tinker, gypsy, wandering entertainers). How does that make a difference? They are the same thing: musicians. You may call them khansahib, call them phakne khan (master stuffed), top khan (master cannon), lun khan (master salt of the earth), or whatever. What's the difference?

Fazal: *Laughs.*

Sultan Khan: When anyone asks me my opinion on all these distinctions, then my position is this, sister Qureshi: that we are all descendants of Adam, and there should not be any of that. All of those (categories) were made later, but what their reality is I can't discuss, since I have no "knowledge" about it. I just believe as a human being that we are human. Now Muslims came about 1500 years ago;[6] before that, there may have been Christianity, Hindu rule (*Ramrajya* [the rule of Lord Rama]), or whatever else. What will be the difference? Nothing at all.[7]

This morning I was talking about this to Dr. Nigam, that our art has not descended from God. Only the Holy Qur'an has— we cannot say that any human being wrote it from his own mind. Music is different. Our ancestors created music; they created ragas. They made so many that now our generation is passing, and all ragas still haven't been perfected. They also put their religious worship or devotion (*ibadat*) into it. Raga *malkauns*, they have been singing it for I don't know how many hundred years; it has been sung so many times that by now it has been "sifted"; that's how this rag has matured. So when I play it today, people respond to all that. I mean, while a person is singing or playing, a saint (*wali*) is present and blesses him (*dua*). So this "blessing" that he receives, that too is contained within *sangit*, within the music of our elders. To respect our elders is therefore a very big duty for us. *Pensively:* That's what it is.

"My Heart Was Set on This Instrument"

Regula: The sarangi has been in your family. So the decision at the beginning … did you take up the sarangi because your elders told you to play it, or did they see your aptitude or inclination?

Sultan Khan: No, no. My elders told me to become a singer. My father was living mostly in Delhi; there he played with singers. He felt that the sarangi was taking a "down" turn; therefore he wanted me to sing instead. But I had my heart set on the sarangi. Because our entire neighborhood was full of sarangi players. Where we lived in Sikhar, there were at least 300 to 350 houses of musicians; some had one room, some two, some were broken down, some intact. In the month of Muharram, all the musicians, wherever they worked, would come back to Sikhar. And after 13 days of rest (during the days of religious mourning), on the 14th of the month all the sarangis and tablas were opened up and started playing.

Regula: How wonderful!

Sultan Khan: That created a whole special environment in my childhood. And my grandfather played sarangi, my father plays it, so this is what mostly filled my ears. I even received a few beatings over this, because of my father's "opposition." I said, "I like this instrument, and I want to play it." My mother said, "Don't beat him, if he wants that." But my father said, "No, the sarangi has a very bad future. I don't want that this boy should have to see bad days. He has a good voice; if he sings he will be alright."

Regula: He was right about your voice.

Sultan Khan: Yes, what he said was right, but I said, "No matter how you beat me, I won't change." I also got beaten over studying, because I did not like studying at all. By God, I am telling you whatever comes to my mind about my childhood. Today God has enabled me to be as good as I am. You are listening, so I am telling you.

"My Father Taught Me; My Elders Blessed Me"

Regula: So how big were you then, how old?

Sultan Khan: About five to six years old. My father had me start with singing at three years of age.

Regula: But your father, wasn't he away most of the time?

Sultan Khan: No, no. He kept coming home. It was like this: whenever he had earned 100 to 200 rupees, he returned, eight hours by train from Delhi to Sikhar. Then he stayed as long as the 200 rupees lasted. Those 200 took care of us for one to two months, easily. That's the way it was in my childhood. So he looked after his "family life" as well as his "jobs," as they came his way. When I insisted that I would play the sarangi, my father said, "He will have to work very hard. Until he plays very well, he won't be able to earn his living on this instrument." I said, "I will ask God for just one thing: to make me a good player." This was my "confidence."

And today I can say that I am one person who has been playing sarangi and not sold himself. God has bestowed material means and fame on me; he has given me honor (*izzat*), and he has given me love. Today I am contented (*sukhi*) in every way. You have seen yourself, I am comfortable in my home life as well.

Regula: Yes, you are. Your decision was right.

Sultan Khan: Yes, it was right. And then I practiced more and more as time went on, even at the risk of my health, as much as is humanly possible. So I practiced 16 to 17 hours at a stretch. God knows. During those sessions I at most got up to relieve myself, then sat down again. I sat in the sun, because there was not that much space in the house. We all lived in one room and also cooked in it. So I was practicing in the hot sun. But that discipline, it was like *tapasiya* (religious austerity). I also said my prayers five times, at the mosque, and asked God for just *one* thing: Oh God! Make me so that I can take care for all my family.

Well, sir, that prayer was answered. Today I have an extended family (*kunba*) of 100, including my father's elder and younger brothers, their children, and others. Those 100 people think of me as if I were the "commander" of all of them. That's how much they follow my counsel. Even my senior uncles address me respectfully as "elder brother" (*bhayi sahib*). Otherwise, Rajasthan has plenty of sarangi players; you know them all. But God has blessed me. This is His beneficence (*karam*), the blessing of that Supreme Lord (*Maula*). This is why I mostly put my trust in God, sister Qureshi. I don't put my trust in humans, but rather in God.

Regula: Okay. About your early training, I have heard that there was usually an older relative, like a grandfather or uncle, who always stayed at home, while the father worked somewhere else and visited off and on. So when you were small, was there someone who would wake you up early in the morning to practice, perhaps your grandfather?

Sultan Khan: No, no, it was my father. When I turned seven, and he saw that I had really stuck to the sarangi, he decided that now this boy has to be trained and made into something. God knows, he stopped going to Delhi to eat and earn. Now he played with singers within Jodhpur, whoever would engage him for the night, for five rupees, two rupees, four rupees. That's how he took care of our family.

Regula: How far was it to Jodhpur? Could he go there every day from Sikhar?

Sultan Khan: Now, no, not from that old Sikhar place (Sikhar-Mikhar). By then we were living in Jodhpur. In 1947, at the time of the Partition, we ran away from Sikhar and moved to Jodhpur.[8] Our houses are still there, in Sikhar, but then we got a house in Jodhpur as well. So when my father saw that now this boy had to be made into something, then he earned whatever he could earn locally, rather than living away from home for four to six months at a time. And then I asked him to stop playing with singers altogether. Twenty-two years ago, when I got a job in the radio (All India Radio), I said to him, "Now don't play; now I take over whatever responsibilities there are." He did not do that again, not until today.[9]

Regula: During your training (*talim*), did anyone beat you to make you practice? I have heard this from many musicians.

Sultan Khan: No, not that much. My father ... since I made good progress, no one ever beat me over music. And I am lucky that from my childhood people loved me a lot. Very great musicians liked me: "Come on Sultan Khan, you little usurper"—they said it in love. For instance, Rahimuddin Khan Dagarwala, he liked me so much. He had me play with him many times, whenever he saw me. The Dagars certainly did not need the sarangi particularly[10] but, God knows, Rahimuddin Khan Sahib had me play with him and his brother Fahimuddin at least a hundred times throughout his life. You can even see my recordings with them, old ones from the radio.

I am "lucky" in that way, that our elders loved me, and through their prayers and my own practicing, I am earning my bread. I received a lot of love from Amir Khan Sahib, Shamir Khan Sahib, Nasir Ahmad Khan Sahib. And Nisar Husain Khan Sahib, Rahimuddin Khan Sahib, Omkarnathji,[11] Vinayakrao Patwardhanji, Narayanrao Vyasji—God knows, they were very good to me. And Jasraj-ji (the famous singer Pandit Jasraj), when he played the tabla, I used to play sarangi with him. Only the sarangi players were afraid of me—"Whoa! Sultan is playing"—although I was the youngest of all, my beard and moustache hadn't even grown yet. So I have had a lot of blessings from our elders.

Regula: Indeed. This is a great thing.

Sultan Khan: I ask blessings from everyone. I have never had any distress. Whether I played well or not, no one ever turned around and told me off, even though this happens a lot with the sarangi.

Training: My Own Way of Thinking

"Formulas of Our Ancestors"

Regula: Is there any special song used when children are being trained, at the start?

Sultan Khan: *No,* no, no. You see, each lineage has its own, different approach (*andaz*) for giving training (talim) to their children. According to them one thing is right, according to us something else. My paternal grandfather and father were convinced that once the hand is quite set, you teach *tappa*.[12] By teaching tappa, the left hand gains speed and suppleness.

Regula: So you mean the standard tappa, like the famous "O Mian...," very full of ornaments?

Sultan Khan: Yes, the way they sing that. I have played it for a recording, on my CD from Germany.[13] But this does not mean that all musical lineages (*gharanas*) should follow this approach. I don't agree with that. My point is that everyone has his own way of doing things. Why do we have students recite *sargam* (singing the note names of a melodic passage)? Because it helps the hand gain an awareness of the notes. *He demonstrates by briskly reciting sargam of yaman, the raga usually taught to beginners.* This is sargam. Doing this helps the fingers gain a sense of the distance between the pitches. *He demonstrates the same raga on the fingerboard of the sarangi.* These are the "formulas" of our ancestors. Formulas to perfect the hand, to give a method for playing (andaz), and an approach to "charge the memory." It is one way of doing things.

    So master musicians each have their own way of thinking, I mean about the way they raise their children, and they turn out well. Their formulas turn them out well, and our formulas turn our children out well. The point is that there is no high and low in this respect. The real question is, how well does your mind work? That depends on each person. It is not necessary to bring in a 'degree,' or to have one or the other son become a graduate. We don't have graduates! Just this: if you have a good mind, a good hand, a good soul, and God is with you, then you will always perform well.

Regula: So in the beginning, how do you guide practicing?

Sultan Khan: Our education, the way I was taught to practice, I played three ragas: *bhairon* (*bhairav*), *yaman*, and *sarang*.

Regula: You mean, at their designated times of the day.

Sultan Khan: No, not at their times, just whenever I practiced. My father had me play these three ragas for at least *four* years. After four years, when my hand was set a bit and my fingers could run up and down the scale, and circle around every note, then he taught me additional ragas in this way: "If you add this extra note, it becomes so and so raga, if you take one note away, it becomes another one, and this is the way this raga goes (up the scale) and the way it comes back down." And he gave me all the small points that have to be taught.

Regula: What about sequence exercises, *palte* or *alankar*, which are taught a lot in colleges. Do you use them too?

Sultan Khan: Everyone has to be taught 2, 4, 5 alankar; after all, you need to learn the ABCs like in language, without that you won't recognize words. And once you recognize words, then you can be taught how to combine the few words you know, and how together they create different meanings. All these tasks are not so different from each other; in fact, they are one and the same. Ornamentation (*gamak*), too, they teach in the same way: make an ornament using two notes each, then between two and three notes, then between two and four notes. *He sings a demonstration.*

Regula: Well, on the sarangi is there a Rajasthani style, or a Sikhar way of playing (*ang*)?

Sultan Khan: No, no. The matter of style is like this, according to my philosophy: in our community we play the sarangi with three fingers. Some people also put on a few touches of four fingers; they do that in Panjab and also in Banaras. Now the way I do it, that's my own way of thinking. Their thinking is that two fingers do better than one, three better than two, and four better than three. Our thinking is, that to develop strength, that can be done only in three fingers, not in the fourth finger. No matter how much you work on it, its touch remains light because there isn't that much life in it. It's pursuing a useless art.

A *sadhu* (religious ascetic) practiced devout austerity (tapasiya) by sitting on a rock for 12 years. What did he gain from this? He could walk through water, even very deep water. Swami Vivekananda[14] came by, as he was walking from one village to another. He saw that the river (*nadi*) flowed high, so he stopped. There was no boatman in sight. Then the sadhu saw him and said: "Oh, this is Swami Vivekananda, a very famous man." He went to him and asked: "Are you Swami Vivekananda?" He said: "Yes, I am." The sadhu asked: "Where are you going?" He answered: "I have to go to that village, but the water is high; I can't go until it goes down." The sadhu said: "What is there to be afraid of? Come, I shall take you across." "How can you do that, without a boat or a boatman?" The sadhu took him by the hand and walked him across the water. Afterwards the sadhu said: "Did you see my spiritual accomplishment (*sadhna*)? I did 12 years of devout austerity for this." Swami Vivekananda replied: "That is fine, but a boatman can do this job for a few pennies."

Mrs. Pandit: In other words, what "value" does it have?

Sultan Khan: You attained an accomplishment worth pennies. If you had instead taken God's name for 12 years, then perhaps you would have come very close to divine favor.

Regula: Oh yes, this is profound.

"Mind and Hand"

Sultan Khan: And then we have this saying: "What if the rider is ready but the pony doesn't move!" (*Man chale aur tattu no chale.*) If your mind can create but your pony—your body—can't execute it, what's the point of exerting your mind? Both need to be in running order. Your brain must run, and your pony must run too. Pony means: your voice, your hands, fingers, whether on the tabla, the sarangi, or on the sitar. And if your pony is running but not your mind—that is, your "memory" is not working—then it's no good either. So until both are combined: your fingers are running nimbly, and your mind gives them direction, only then, my sister, does it all come together (*bat ban jati hai*).

But if one of them is lacking ... Let me add an additional point: suppose you have an extremely melodious hand, but you have no sense of rhythm. Now what will you do—what *will* you do? The Good Lord has given you all the qualities to make good music except for that one, and so the others also become useless.

And then the teacher can lose out too. You try to get a student to repeat sa (1)—while he keeps intoning the wrong note. *He demonstrates the clash very expressively by singing a tonic and adding a loud, false note to it.* Then you will say: "Brother, you offered me 100,000 rupees, take them back. I can't teach you!" Because it seems that all my efforts can't teach him my sa until the Good Lord opens his ears so that he can 'follow' my sa. One can lose out anywhere.

"I'll Tell You the Major Points in Your Playing"

At one point during our conversation I became the student and took out my sarangi to play for Sultan Khan to receive some comments and guidance from this master musician.

Regula: Alright, what should I play?

Sultan Khan: Whatever your heart desires.

Regula: Please show me the things I should know.

Sultan Khan: Sure, I will tell you the major points in your playing.

Regula: Alright, I will play something that my late ustad, Hamid Husain Khan, had taught me.

Sultan Khan: Yes, well done. *To Fazal:* Over there (in Pakistan) someone gave me a tape of Hamid Husain.[15]

Regula: *Briefly plays alap and a composition in raga jaijaivanti.* Enough, this is how it goes on.

Sultan Khan: Praise be to God, very good.

Fazal: It seems your playing is going very well *laughs.*

Sultan Khan: But now, sister Qureshi, there is the matter of 'movement': *He illustrates by saying the following English sentence, first in a rhythmically undifferentiated, almost slurred monotone.* "Sister-Qureshi-how-are-you-how-is-it-going-what-is-happening."

Then he repeats the sentence with appropriate rhythmic and tonal articulation. "Sister Quréshi; how are yóu; hów is it going; what is háppening?" Now this rhythmic articulation (*wazan*, literally "scansion"), this is a *very* important thing. In music too, as long as there is no rhythmic articulation in it, you continuously speak in the same 'mood,' and this reduces the effect of the music. And when you give it 'movement' ... *He demonstrates distinct three-note phrases of jaijaivanti.*

This is movement. When the music is imbued with movement (*rakhta hai*), that creates a distinct life within it. It is as if either a sick person is talking, or a very healthy person. It makes a big difference. *He again demonstrates both versions.* So this movement is extremely essential in making music; it's just a small point, but keep it in mind.

Regula: In fact it is a very major point!

Sultan Khan: Please keep it in your mind. God willing, you will enjoy your *own* work. That's all I wanted to tell you, nothing else. You have a very good hand; you understand everything; you can play, no question. Don't disturb or change this on any account, not under anyone's influence. Even if God Almighty comes down from heaven, tell him it's alright; you are Allah, I believe in you, but don't 'disturb' me in my playing.

Regula: True. Actually I haven't practiced, so I don't have the confidence, and before you even less *laughs*.

Sultan Khan: That's alright. Look, I am your brother, not some demon (*jinn*). But I am speaking openly in this matter. *Once again he demonstrates the difference, now using a sentence in Urdu, juxtaposing a monotone and rhythmically undifferentiated delivery with one of articulate pace, tone, and accent:* "Yeh-hone-se-aisa-ho-sakta-hai; yéh hóne se áisa ho sakta hái." This has one effect, that another.

Regula: I understand; I really understand!

Sultan Khan: And now a final point; I had told you that even at that time in Bombay. Don't learn from everyone. It will interfere with your playing. Whoever is your guru, keep his guiding principles (*niyatkar*) in mind, take the name of God and keep on playing. That's it!

As for 'technical' matters, sister, I cannot tell you what you can and cannot do. You have to find that out yourself. Play the bow so that you move it "down" on the string. Then your right hand becomes light. Now just give it some power, because the 'tone' is produced by that hand. And the 'notes' are produced by the left. If you want to play with a good tone, you have to make your right hand strong, and make it steady. And for playing 'notes,' make the left hand light. This is my own thinking, not something my father told me or my grandfather. You have to do your own thinking.

Mrs. Pandit: That makes sense, use your own mind!

Sultan Khan: *Addressing Ammi (Mrs. Pandit):* And I told her, "Put some plumpness in your hand, because plumpness is what generates resonance in each sympathetic metal string." *Turning to Regula:* A *little* more meat on your hand, that's what I mean. If you are so skinny, you get a "metallic" tone. If there is anything wrong with what I am saying, then tell me; try it for proof!

Fazal: *Chuckles.* Gain a bit of weight, that's what he means.

Sultan Khan: No, its not a matter of weight; just get some massaging done.

A Competitive Métier: What It Takes

Now Sultan Khan opens a window to the past for me when he tells me of the dangal—*a contest that used to provide the opportunity for masters and accomplished students to share their music and show their skill. Sultan Khan saw a dangal when he was very young.*

When Masters Competed: A Time of Real Music

Regula: Now at the courts, in Rajasthan, was sarangi played solo, with dance, with singers, with *ghazal, thumri,* or with everything?

Sultan Khan: The sarangi was played with everything, including solo. But let me tell you what the meaning of solo sarangi was. At one time our elders engaged in musical contests, dangal. In these contests, tabla, sarangi, and voice were most prominent. Yes, these three, they were most widely performed in Hindustan. If you look within history, you will find 50 to 100 tabla players of established excellence in each generation, and you'll find as many sarangi play-ers. But in comparison you will not find many sitar players nor sarod players, and not even a single *santur* player. Nor will you find any flutists. Therefore, the 'tradition' of music (*gana bajana*) resides in three musical lineages (gharana), the tabla, the sarangi, and voice. You will find many eminent sarangi players in all the cities of note—not one or two, but ten—and their 'influence' was in every place. Whether in the form of accompanying male singers (*gawayye*), female singers (*tawaif*), or in the form of worship, with *bhajan*, or with *qawwali*, sarangi music *was there*.

So, all this went on with the sarangi. Now as regards solo, I want to tell you about dangal. A dangal was like what we today call a (music) conference or concert, but dangal was also a contest of hereditary master musicians (khansahibs), of master teachers (ustads). Ustads from different places all got together. And in every major city there used to be a *juma* (Friday) event. After the midday prayer on Friday, there would be music making (*gana bajana*) in so and so's house—it had to be a large house. Now people would pre-pare all year long, practicing hard, to perform at a particular juma event. Small-fry (*chhote mote*) artists could not make it there. This was because the audience and those who sponsored the juma were themselves artists of such standing that they would not listen to any lightweight musicians. So they did not let anyone like that even attend the event. Here is what would happen. Say an ignorant or disrespectful person thought: "Let me be bold and play my sarangi here." As soon as he places his fingers on the string, the ustads would immediately recognize his level of competence. Believe me, they would curse and throw him out. "Hey, who is that boorish fel-low, get the bugger *out of here*."

Regula: *Laughs.*

Sultan Khan: So, I mean to say, a person did not *dare* to go and just do his thing among those great people. Only after 20, 25 years of com-plete practice and training, his ustad would approach them: "I have trained this boy; please call him before you and hear him play." It was like an exam for young players. So that was the old, proper way of doing things. *If* anyone committed an impropriety he would be stopped instantly, slam-bang on the spot. And then he'd get a beat-ing from his ustad and also from his family elders, for getting their noses cut off, and his ustad would say, "Who told you to go there and play?" The result was that after one such knock, a person would tread carefully.

Now Ammi (Mrs. Pandit) brings me lunch and offers dessert while Sultan Khan shares his own memory of a dangal.

"Those Khansahibs with Their Big Heads"

Regula: Did you yourself ever see a dangal?

Sultan Khan: I did, yes. It was in Ajmer (at the Shrine of India's greatest Sufi saint, Moinuddin Chishti). I was small, very small. But I did see it. In that dangal, during the day, there was sarangi playing, one after the other, each better, about five or six sarangi players. Only good ones were allowed to perform. On the next day, only tablas were played, with the sarangi playing only *lehra* to accompany the tablas. And on the third day there was only singing, nothing but singing, also with sarangi accompaniment. At those dangals, very great people participated, like Thirakwa Khan Sahib, Nathu Khan Sahib, and other khan sahibs of old times, and Ustad Allah Rakha Ji.

Now two dangals were most famous; they were held at two great Sufi shrines during the Saint's Day celebration (*urs mela*). One was at Ajmer, the other at Kaliar.[16] The people from Delhi and all around came to Kaliar, while those from Panjab and further out mostly went to Ajmer. In my childhood, my grandfather always used to say that anyone whose program was a success in this dangal also had his name made in the rest of India. Because that was before the days of newspapers, and there was no radio. So the musicians would spread their praise: "Brother, I have just been to Ajmer, and so and so youngster played *very* well."

This gave the person great fame. Something like today the Indian Padma Shri and Padma Bhushan Awards, or the Grammy Awards. But at that time it was not officials but the masters themselves who gave the praise, a recognition a thousand times higher, because those ustads did not easily give praise to anyone. If they could kick you off the stage for a poor performance, would they lavish their praise on you? But when they did praise then, God knows, it became like an official proclamation or a certification (*sanad*): "Brothers, this is excellent!" That was the weightiness of the dangal. Because the listeners were all ustads. And even if the occasional patron came to listen, he did *not* count. He would sit

God knows where in the back and nobody asked him to please come forward and sit in the front row (as is done in normal concerts). Here those great musicians were the ones in the front, the khansahibs with the big heads.

Regula: *Laughs.* Khansahibs with the big heads?

Sultan Khan: Yes, they sat in the front, with their big turbans (*paggar*) tied around their heads, or sporting their special caps. Yes, that was the *time!* The time of *real music.*

Mrs. Pandit: *Offering jelebi:* Here, have some.

Fazal: See, I am a "junior," that's why I am eating jelebi (a sweet considered less impressive than *laddu* and other rich varieties). *Everyone laughs.*

Sultan Khan: So this is the way it was. I have given you a small sketch of it.

The singers at the dangal performed with sarangi accompaniment. Sultan Khan now moves to what is involved in accompanying singers.

Accompaniment as Competition

Regula: I see that you have raised the sarangi to a high standard, in accompaniment too.

Sultan Khan: Nothing special. But yes, there is one thing: I never tried to impose myself on anyone whom I accompanied. Whatever I could play with ease and love, that I played. If I couldn't do that, I became silent. Anything beyond my capacity, I waited out silently. Because practicing, all that you do at home; don't do it in a performance (*mahfil*)!

Regula: But some people say that sarangi players would try to detract the singer from the tonic, or play a chromatic style to confuse a singer …

Sultan Khan: Now look, listen to this: the sarangi player is an imitation.

Mrs. Pandit: Of the voice.

Sultan Khan: Now in this process, who told you that when the singer goes "hihihi" you also go "hihihi," and when he goes (*high pitched*) "huuu-u," you also have to try the same thing? Of course, he may try to trip you up by singing something that you cannot play. Now this has been going on between sarangi player and singer, not from today, but from whenever the sarangi first appeared. And this has sometimes resulted in animosity. Because the sarangi player is the singer's "negative." The singer comes prepared, having practiced and thought out all the improvisational passage work (*tan*), while the sarangi player does everything 'on the spot,' whatever he does. He takes a 'photo,' and however well that photo is made, it has to be made clear. So this competition will go on, it has been going on, and it will keep going on.

Mrs. Pandit: Yes, competition is ongoing.

Playing Sarangi in a Global Context

Sultan Khan's global career has brought him back to rhythmic accompaniment through his enduring and highly successful association with global star Zakir Husain and his family of great tabla players (father Allah Rakha, brother Fazal Qureshi).

Joining Zakir Husain: The Art of Rhythmic Accompaniment

Regula: You now perform across the world with Zakir Husain. So what about the art of sarangi accompaniment for the rhythmic cycles of the tabla, I mean playing the cyclical melodies (lehra)?

Sultan Khan: Here is what it is … let me make a small point here. We have a team, Khan Sahib Allah Rakha, I, and Zakirbhayi (brother Zakir); we are 'just like family.'[17] What is his knowledge about me? That Sultan Khan is well regarded, plays well, and he plays a good *lehra*. He knows just this much about me.

Regula: What is a good lehra?

Sultan Khan: A good lehra is that I stick with the rhythm throughout; you understand that. And within that I also embellish the melody and add sweetness to it. You know about using jaggery (*gur*, "cane sugar crystals") to sweeten laddu (a ball-shaped sweet)[18]: the more sugar there is in it, the higher its value.

Now, consider the importance of good lehra playing: Zakirbhayi just had a 'program' in Jaipur. And I had a program in Ahmedabad, so I could not play in Zakirbhayi's concert in Jaipur. I tried very hard to arrange it, but it did not work out. Now Zakirbhayi did not get a single sarangi player for his program; they all ran scared of getting "out of tala" (*betala*) because Alla Rakha's lineage (*gharana*) is famous for its complex and polyrhythmic patterns. What they do is so subtle, it is like doing surgery to take off the skin of a tiny beetle. Ustad Allah Rakhaji, Ustad Zakir Husain, Ustad Fazal Qureshi, they do surgery on a tiny beetle. I am telling the truth, my sister! I don't speak uselessly. What I say is certainly blunt but never useless.

Regula: That's why it is so enjoyable to listen to!

Sultan Khan: Here is what these artists do. Rhythm for them means when they play in (a cycle of) seven, they make a cycle of ten and one-half out of it. This is what I call precision surgery on a tiny beetle, surgery so precise that the skin is separated and then sown into a tiny 'bag.' There is nothing more subtle than that. Now there are at least 15 sarangi players in Jaipur, some work at *kathak* (classical dance) academies, some in the radio. Not one of them wanted to accompany that concert. "Who is playing?" Zakir. "No, no, no"; they all made excuses; they were too scared to go, scared of having their reputations ruined.

Regula: But wasn't that a great opportunity for them?

Sultan Khan: Yes, but it also came with a heavy weight to lift. If a person is offered 500 rupees to lift a 200-kg weight, then he'd also be afraid that his neck might break!

Afterward, Zakirbhayi said to me: "This will make you very happy; I played a total of 41 minutes because you weren't there. How many times could I rescue that lehra player?" So he has to spend a lot on me for playing with him in India. But we both know that spending this money makes a good concert. I am also a good solo player. That gives me my applause, and when I accompany with him, then he gets his. So we are a group and have become 'used to' each other. We are one.

Otherwise, they could call for a lehra player anywhere, and someone would get up and play. *He sings the opening of the*

most famous 16-beat lehra in raga Chandrakauns: "na- na- na- na-
/ná - - -" (beats) 13 14 15 16 /1 - - -.

"Honor the Middleman and Trust in God"

Regula: Playing lehra for dance still gives sarangi players work,
doesn't it.

Sultan Khan: Yes, the dancers have preserved the 'traditional' way, and
that is very good: sarangi players are employed in dance schools,
etc. And most of all, All India Radio has preserved the sarangi
until now, by giving jobs to sarangi players. Even if their playing is
borderline, they pass their audition. So that's what it is now. Earlier, when all the singers used sarangi accompaniment, a lot of very
good sarangi players were produced. 'Life' was not a 'risk.' Alright,
study the sarangi well, and you are bound to get work. That's how
it was. Today there is the fear that, alright, I learned this work, but
can I survive on it or not?

Regula: Yes, it's a great 'problem.'

Sultan Khan: Now, I myself don't feel this 'problem' because I am
alright, I'm in business. But how difficult it is for younger people!
Someone just asked me what other sarangi players are coming to
play in Canada; well, whom can I name? Once someone has the
beginning of a career, I can identify them, but not if the poor musician remains sitting somewhere in a backwater. There are so many
sarangi players who are good, but they have stayed put where they
were and even retired there and became old. So who can I tell them
is up and coming?

Regula: True.

Sultan Khan: As for me, I give importance to those men who provide
an 'introduction' to others. Zakir Mian (affectionately respectful term of address) 'introduced' me, bringing me to this country. Ravi Shankarji introduced me and brought me to this country
for the very first time, in 1974.[19] I am grateful to both of them.
Lata Mangeshkar brought me to Bombay; I am grateful to her too.
Those who 'introduce,' or what they call the middleman, I honor

them as much as the Prophet, because it is through Him alone that we know God.

Mrs. Pandit: Yes, it is their graciousness, to lend their hand through which the work gets done.

Sultan Khan: From Lataji, I have never in my life taken a single penny outside my sarangi earnings. And not a single penny from Ustad Alla Rakhaji, nor from Zakir. And not a single *paisa* from Raviji (Ravi Shankar). I did my work for them, but I remain greatly indebted to them. Ravi Shankar brought me to this country for the very first time, on a tour in 1974. He was the first to include me in a touring group. Then, because of Zakir Husain, I have become famous, since he takes me along all over the world. So I will respect this until I die. I still keep up this inherited custom. And as for my own accomplishments, I leave that all to God. After all, it is written in the Qur'an that He can turn a speck into the moon. A speck is so insignificant, while we are humans, the children of Adam, He has made us in a very special way. Whether we succeed is all up to him: our death and life, our earnings and our well-being, it is all in His hands. So my faith is over there, not with people. If anybody squeezes me or pushes me down even a bit, then I won't give in to him, no matter who it may be!

Lucknow: Center of Tradition

CHAPTER 7

Mahmud Ali Lineage
College Ties

Introducing the Lineage

Lucknow stands out as a historical center of feudal patronage of the arts, particularly music and poetry, both marked by a unique fusion of local Hindi and cosmopolitan Urdu cultural forms. Despite the immense destruction of the city by the British in reprisal after the Great Uprising of 1857, and despite their banishment from the royal court at the same time,[1] musicians and connoisseurs continued to cultivate the traditional practice of music, dance, and sung poetry in the salons of landed patrons and of the cultivated courtesan singers who flourished in Lucknow until the early 1960s.[2]

Appropriately, Lucknow was chosen as the site of the first independent modern music college, founded in 1927. Funded by landed patrons, the college was conceived and established by the great musical reformer and scholar Pandit V.N. Bhatkhande, whose illustrious name it bears today. His vision of providing modern music education—founded in ancient musical theory and hereditary practice—was systematically implemented under the dedicated leadership of Bhatkhande's deputy and most learned disciple, Pandit Ratanjankar. I had the fortune of meeting him on my first visit to the college in 1965, shortly before his death. Under his leadership, the college disseminated music education to the growing professional and middle class of music lovers in Lucknow while also attracting feudal connoisseurs. For musicians, Bhatkhande College became the city's center of musical patronage, especially after the abolition of princely states in 1952 and of courtesan salons a decade later. Hereditary musicians, few of them from Lucknow, have been the mainstay of the college faculty, but they have had to adapt themselves to the college syllabus of classroom teaching and examinations.

When I found my first hereditary music teacher at Bhatkhande College, I was connecting with a musical institution familiar to a Westerner. Without knowing it, I also entered a major zone of contradiction between two systems of cultural knowledge and their musical representatives. A dialectic between college and heredity informed the discourse and teaching of my first teacher Maqsud Ali and even that of his aged father Mahmud Ali, despite the fact that he had been a founding member of the college staff. The dialectic extended to both Mahmud Ali's nephew Yaqub Husain and his grandson Munawwar, both of whom worked at the college as well.

Through their teaching and conversations, these four closely related musicians conveyed the challenge of joining the college system of teaching and learning while also retaining and transmitting inherited knowledge. They had other, related struggles at the college: mainly of being an isolated family surrounded by colleagues and competitors who were bound by solidarities that excluded them. They repeatedly mentioned the Misra musician community from Benares and the Maharashtrian music scholars, both Hindu, from whom they clearly differed. Furthermore, the two younger musicians, Yaqub and Munawwar, suffered from a limited capacity to sustain musical quality of performance and even to pass the examinations in "college knowledge."

On the other hand, these musicians were fortunate to retain their founder's college position within the family down to the youngest member, a rather standard employment practice in the college and, indeed, in other Indian institutions (see Chapter 9, Bhagvan Das). The unfortunate ending to this family's musical life was death: by 1983 both my teacher and his father had died, the former too early for his age. By 1992, Yaqub Husain had died in his fifties, broken because he could never find his long-missing son. Most shocking of all, in 1997, I learned that Munawwar Husain, the founder's grandson, had been killed over a debt dispute—a tragic end to their lineage.

The conversations in this chapter are marked by my rather formal relationship with each of these four musicians. What they chose to say and speak about clearly reflect my sometimes highly directed questions and their quest to match my expectations. Health was also a factor in their conversation: Mahmud Ali had become chronically unwell and bedridden, while his nephew Yaqub Husain suffered from a reduced state of health, which made it difficult for him to be articulate and focused. Substantively, the formal character of our relationship is reflected in the brief final discussion of that most touchy of subjects: remuneration.

The principal verbal sources for the Mahmud Ali family are conversations with the two youngest members recorded in 1983. In contrast, little of my encounters with the two senior members of the family was recorded on tape, a commodity then hard to come by, especially in India. I have therefore drawn on my notes of conversations, amplified by reminiscences from the two younger musicians.

A special mention must be made of the remarkably traditional Urdu spoken by all four family members when talking of music. Certainly expected from Mahmud Ali born in 1900, the same special terms derived from Persian reappear in the musical discussion of his son, nephew, and grandson. In other words, not only did they speak of the same musical subjects, they used the same archaic terminology and phrases that have clearly been archived within the family, while in the public musical sphere of the college they participated in the current use of a more Hindi-ized vocabulary. As a keen Urdu speaker and member of a cultivated Urdu speaking family, I found myself eliciting this largely defunct musical discourse, inadvertently becoming a successor to these musicians' Urdu-speaking patrons of the past. In the process, I likely missed out on the Hindi and Sanskritized terminology that these same musicians employed when speaking to their current Hindu and Hindi-speaking patrons.

My fragmentary but vivid engagement with the Mahmud Ali lineage poignantly expresses how four members of a family managed major change of patronage, both successfully mediated and tragically unsuccessful.

MIRZA MAHMUD ALI: THE FOUNDER

Introducing Mirza Mahmud Ali

Mirza Mahmud Ali has the distinction of being one of the founding musicians of Bhatkhande College, as is documented in an early photograph of the college staff.[3] Both his father, Wahid Jan, and his paternal uncle, Muhammad Jan, were accomplished sarangi players. But his father died when he was only five years old, so that Mahmud Ali was raised and trained by his uncle, Muhammad Jan, who in effect became his second father.

In 1933 Mahmud Ali was appointed to the regular teaching staff of Bhatkhande College as a teacher for sarangi as well as the other two bowed instruments, esraj and dilruba.[4] He also taught first-year vocal classes. His other important role was as accompanist in the vocal soirées of the college by the staff and visiting artists, since the blatantly Western harmonium has always been, and continues to be, scrupulously avoided in the college. In fact, Mahmud Ali was selected for the college as the best among four sarangi players who were hired to accompany a high-profile musical drama produced by college staff.

In her tribute to the music makers of the Bhatkhande College, Susheela Misra writes that "Mahmud Ali remained devoted to his work in the college, in spite of the fact that the college was too poor to afford a decent salary for its staff members. He was a regular and sincere teacher who worked inconspicuously throughout his long tenure on the staff."[5] Mirza Mahmud Ali died in the late 1970s. Ali had trained his son Mirza Maqsud Ali in sarangi and voice, but he also sent him to study voice at the college. Later, he imparted the same training to Yaqub Husain, the grandson of the uncle who raised him. He also gave initial teaching to his much younger grandson, Munawwar Husain. All three disciples gained successive employment at the college.

It is in Mahmud Ali's hands that I first saw and heard a sarangi. My father-in-law had taken me to Bhatkhande College to find a suitable Indian instrument for me to study. The classrooms were full of plucked instruments and drums, but I was a cellist. Finally, sitting in a corner apart, I saw an old man with wild white hair, drawing a bow across an upright type of fiddle. As soon as I saw the bow in his hand, my choice was made: this would become my instrument.

Mahmud Ali happened to be there because, even after retirement, he still came to the college occasionally to accompany; I might not have seen the sarangi otherwise, given that his son Maqsud Ali taught only vocal classes. But Mahmud Ali was not to become my teacher, for the principal, Pandit Ratanjankar, immediately called for Maqsud Ali, whose college training would make him a more suitable teacher, especially for a foreigner. I saw Mahmud Ali again briefly when I visited his house for my first lesson with his son, but his authority loomed in the background, to be invoked as needed.

That was in 1965. When I returned to Lucknow four years later, Mirza Mahmud Ali was ailing at home. I was determined to meet and listen to my teacher's father. Mirza Mahmud Ali was a stern father and a traditionally formal gentleman, but his son was kind enough to persuade him to meet me and perform for my tape recorder. I am grateful for his effort to put on record his precious music and his musical wisdom and priorities belonging to the feudal milieu of early 20th-century Lucknow.

The "Interview": Heritage Despite College[6]

The visit was arranged, the fee decided upon. Mirza Mahmud Ali would play and let me record two pieces of music, both vocal favorites in the feudal milieu of the region, especially the highly ornate genre of tappa. Since Mahmud Ali never left his house, I arrived there escorted by my father-in-law (Saeed Ahmad Qureshi) for an encounter that turned out to be highly formal, almost an audience. Despite his ill health, Mahmud Ali had dressed up in perfectly starched white clothes and a black vest, sitting very upright on his bed. His son, my teacher, set the tone by addressing Mahmud Ali with utmost respect and caution, having told us that his mood could be unpredictable.

Mahmud Ali in turn performed and spoke with the authority of a master. With his son playing the tabla for him, he began by playing two pieces of family repertoire, starting with raga gaur sarang, built around a pleasing and well-known song composition in the classical genre khayal. The second piece was a tappa in raga kafi, a light genre cultivated in the Lucknow and Benares region since at least the 19th century and once much favored among feudal patrons and connoisseurs.[7]

In the interview, Mirza Mahmud Ali spoke of a musical style that flourished in the private gatherings of landed patrons. He focused on style and refinement, not theoretical knowledge, classical rules, and structure. He also spoke of the quintessentially vocal style of tappa, where musical embellishment highlights and enriches textual meaning, even if the music is played on the sarangi. At the same time, he had a systematic notion of instrumental training and practice that is down to earth and technical. Though Mahmud Ali had spent his working life at Bhatkhande College, his discussion of sarangi training and practicing does not reflect the college's standardized approach to music. Rather, he identified two well-known legendary sarangi players as legitimizing figures for musical excellence and connects them to his person. He also discreetly pointed to the deterioration of musical standards with the amateur movement's continued expansion, lamenting the dwindling of traditional private patronage, and with it the genre tappa he considered central for musical knowledge and competence. He did not mention the college.

Maqsud Ali: *Respectfully addressing his father, he suggests that Regula should ask his advice on how a student should be taught according to his family tradition.*

Regula: You are a master teacher, the *ustad* of my ustad. Please give me some guidance about a student's training and practice.

Mahmud: There are four kinds of training (*tayyari*, literally "preparedness") for the hands of a sarangi player. The first kind is training in *alankar* (sequential patterns, i.e., *palta*), as many as possible. First the student must perfect sequential patterns in very slow tempo. After that, these same patterns should be combined into coherent passages, but he must practice them slowly and increase the pace gradually. Once they are well set in a slow tempo, the next step is to work on passages that go straight up and down. Any raga that goes straight up and down, he should take that raga and practice on it, moving very slowly, and progressing very gradually.

Then, once it is properly internalized, it will come out correctly and in tune.

Regula: Should this be done in all three octaves?

Mahmud: Yes, in all three octaves. But each octave should be managed separately at first. He should go up as well as down in the same manner. This is how the hand is brought under control. But going all the way up and down requires a lot of strength; this work is not for the weak. There must be strength in your fingers, in both hands: the hand that bows as well as the hand that makes the sounds with the fingers. Without strength, this work can't be done.

And now, the way to practice. *He now instructs Regula directly:* When you practice one sequential pattern, any pattern, you must play it at least 100 times. At the very least! It should really be played 1000 or 1200 times. But even if you do a minimum of practice, you must play it at least 100 times, so that you can at least know whether you have learned it or you haven't. Once you can say that, yes, every note of it has begun to resonate and sound in tune, then you have mastered it. This is the way to achieve preparedness.

One kind of training is for mastering sequences. Then there is the training in ornamenting single notes with rapid oscillation (*zamzama*), with mordents (*dana*), with slides or portamento (*sut mind*), and with heavy shaking (*gamak*).

Regula: I see. What kind of preparedness is that, for instance zamzama?

Mahmud: Just now I played for you a tappa in raga kafi with the many short passages that characterize tappa. These very passages contain all these four ways of ornamenting notes. Tappa is unique, because it is the only genre in which patterns of all four kinds can be heard. But to benefit from this, one has to learn tappa very well; tappa is something one must know to have finger control. Furthermore, all four compositional styles are present in this genre. Even free improvisational passages (*alap*) also occur in tappa, and the khayal style does as well. And the tappa style is of course there anyway!

But today, many people who have taken up singing or playing, they just perform tappa any way they feel like, based on whatever vocal ability they have. Nobody even knows any more what tappa is! Only those who have received special training in tappa, they know. But today this training is not given any value.

Regula: Oh yes, tappa has become very rare. Then who were the great sarangi players of the past generation, those who did have the right training? And could you tell something about your own training in tappa and sarangi?

Mahmud: Let me tell you about two great sarangi players I have known. They were Badal Khan and Mamman Khan. Badal Khan was the son of Mian Hyder Bakhsh of Panipat Karnal. Hyder Bakhsh was a great innovator of sarangi playing. And Hyder Bakhsh's brother, Hasan Bakhsh, was also a renowned sarangi player. They both established schools, or norms, of sarangi playing. I mean, you are either a follower of one or the other school. The two are distinguished principally by the way they use left-hand fingering. The school of Hasan Bakhsh uses four fingers, whereas the school of Hyder Bakhsh uses three fingers.

Regula: Did you learn from Badal Khan?

Mahmud: I learned at home; my first teacher was my father. Then, from age seven onward, my uncle forced me to practice many hours every day, until my training was complete. When I left home, then I went and became a disciple (*shagird*) of Badal Khan.

The second master, Mamman Khan, was from Delhi,[8] but he stayed in Calcutta, together with Imdad Khan, the famous sitar player.[9] Then some incident made Mamman Khan leave Calcutta. He went to Multan, to a Sufi shrine, and lived there as a mendicant devotee (*faqir*), renouncing everything. It is there that his mind matured and he became wise. He changed the sarangi, put metal strings on it, and played it with iron "fingernails." He called this new instrument "ocean of melody" (*sur sagar*).[10] When he returned to Calcutta, hardly anyone recognized him. Then he played sur sagar. At a musicians' gathering, he outdid even the great Imdad Khan. Imdad Khan played raga *puriya* best. Now Mamman Khan played the same raga. He could replicate each one of Imdad Khan's improvised passages and was able to add many more passages of his own. As a young person, I went to Patiala to meet Mamman Khan.

Saeed Qureshi: Master, we thank you very much. (*He offers an envelope with money to Mahmud Ali, and we take our leave.*)

MIRZA MAQSUD ALI: MY COLLEGE TEACHER

Introducing Mirza Maqsud Ali

Mirza Maqsud Ali was an active teacher at Bhatkhande College, occupying his father's position, as has been deemed proper in Indian social practice. Mirza Maqsud Ali (who used his full titled name, Mirza being a chiefly title of the Moguls) learned music from his father, and later studied at the college for several years, though his child's illness prevented him from completing his master's degree. Later, he became a disciple of the college principal Pandit Ratanjankar, who himself was the chief disciple and successor of Pandit Bhatkhande. Competence in singing is a standard result of sarangi training, since traditionally a sarangi player's principal role was teaching voice and vocal repertoire to professional women singers, a skill that was well transferable to the (mostly female) students at the college. Thus trained professionally as well as properly inducted into the repertoire, syllabus, and system of Bhatkhande College, Mirza Maqsud Ali gained a teaching position in the college even before his father was retired. He taught elementary vocal classes as well as sarangi, though there was hardly ever any student demand for the instrument.

However, this musician was not only a college teacher; he also had personal patrons. A landed and well-educated Shi'a gentleman (from whom I learned this years later) had retained him for several years to accompany his efforts at classical singing. He too was a disciple of Pandit Ratanjankar and may have facilitated Maqsud Ali's discipleship with this socially very highly placed teacher.

To arrange for my lessons, Maqsud Ali insisted on meeting at his home, not at the college, thus turning the arrangement into a patronage relationship between him and my family. Our contact with him was facilitated by my father-in-law, who urbanely dealt with the most unusual request for his young daughter-in-law to study the sarangi. He managed the relationship in all its aspects, especially fees and payments. He also set the tone for personal interaction, which included hospitality and conversation, even bantering. Maqsud Ali accepted and reciprocated, but he always maintained the distance of his professional status and the propriety of limiting this personal interaction entirely to the men of the family.

Once our daily teaching session started, Maqsud Ali's persona changed to that of an impersonal college teacher. He essentially took on the college sylla-

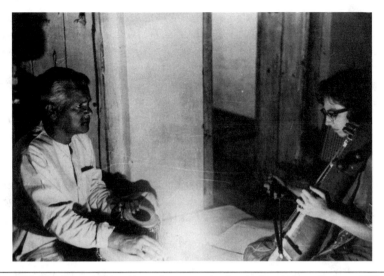

Figure 18 Mirza Maqsud Ali teaching and accompanying Regula, Qureshi home, Lucknow, 1965.

bus to teach me, and I immediately took to the familiar pedagogy of a music lesson with graded learning materials. Most striking about these sessions is a clear dichotomy between his music teaching and his personal interaction, as well as some efforts to harmonize them.

Maqsud Ali had married four times; one or two of his wives had died, as had most of his children. In 1960, his last wife bore him a son, Munawwar, the only one to become a musician. When Mirza Maqsud Ali died in the early 1970s, his son was too young to succeed him; but his college position stayed in the family, going to his junior cousin, Yaqub Husain Khan.

Personal Encounters

In 1965, Maqsud Ali was perhaps one of the last hereditary musicians whose conversation and demeanor reflected extended exposure to the company of landed gentry. At once submissive and bold, he spoke in few words, but always as a performance, and often with a self-deprecating underlying humor. In the following verbal cameos, Maqsud Ali enacts his hereditary musician's persona in the presence of patrons. Given my status as a daughter-in-law of the family, I was completely excluded from this all-male interaction, despite my presence throughout. Perhaps because I was a nonparticipating listener, these conversations have remained prominent in my memory.

The following conversations took place in the sitting room of our house in old Lucknow, usually upon the ustad's arrival around midmorning, or some-

times after our teaching session, which was held in an inside room. Also present are my father-in-law, S.A. Qureshi, and my husband, Saleem Qureshi.

Maqsud Ali had at first resisted teaching me because of the impending start of the mourning season during the month of Muharram, when hereditary musicians usually stop all music making (see Chapter 6, Sultan Khan). When he agreed to teach in our house, it was on condition that all shutters would be tightly closed to keep the sound from being heard outside, so that his teaching during this month should remain hidden. This was an obviously Shi'a concern, since Muharram mourning rites are the central tenet of the Shi'a practice. Furthermore, Mirza Maqsud Ali's name also suggested a Shi'a identity.[11] However, on the first day at our house, he said, addressing my father-in-law: "I venture to guess, Mr. Qureshi, that you must be a Sunni." (Qureshi is a patently Sunni name.)

"Yes, indeed, we are," was my father-in-law's reply.

"Well, you should know that I too am a Sunni," asserted Maqsud Ali.

"Oh, really?" replied my father-in-law.

Given the proverbial animosity between Shi'a and Sunni Muslims in Lucknow, my teacher's explicit harmonization of his religious identity with that of his genteel student's family was simply good form. On one morning, my husband Saleem, having heard of Maqsud Ali's four marriages, jokingly asked him, "Ustad, I have heard that you have made full use of the Islamic marriage laws (allowing up to four wives)."

Maqsud Ali answered with a hint of satire: "What can I tell you, Qureshi Sahib, they kept dying or I kept divorcing them." Marrying several times, an uncommon practice, could also be seen as a landlord's joie de vivre; hence, Maqsud Ali disclosed it with the expectation of being appreciated. Victorian middle-class sensibilities had not yet taken over his Lucknow milieu.

On yet another day, Saleem was smoking a cigar. The ustad, who smoked cigarettes, was intrigued and attracted to the cigar, since he hadn't seen one. He asked for one, and Saleem offered one to him. Maqsud Ali lit and smoked the cigar with relish. Sharing a cigar was a way of offering the ustad respect.

Being a woman, I was introduced to Maqsud Ali's wife on my first visit to his house. I asked my teacher, "Does your wife also know music?"[12]

"Not at all," was the reply. "She doesn't know anything. She came from her village and was so innocent, she did not even know what ice was. When she got a piece, she put it on a bread to eat it, and when it melted she cried." The ustad chuckled.

Teaching a Beginner

Mirza Maqsud Ali was a systematic teacher. He followed the college syllabus in its graduated form, as well as its use of written text. He himself wrote it all down for me in Urdu, since I did not know the Hindi script at the time.[13] *But his first concern was to correct my aesthetic, his next one to get correct intonation.*

In his test lesson, I had to learn a beginner's song from the syllabus. I played all the notes correctly, but he stopped me and asked me to add two very audible slides into the tune, the kind of slides I had practiced so hard to avoid on the cello. I resisted and asked him why? He looked at me intensely and said, "Because it is beautiful."

More than his words, his eyes and demeanor of controlled intensity conveyed an aesthetic truth that my ears were as yet unable to hear. But I played the slides. After an approving nod, he came to the most basic test of acceptability: "It's alright, but only if it is in tune."

In my last lesson, he had me sing and play through all the memorized raga material, when he suddenly said: "Now expand it! (barho)" I did not know what he meant. "Just move ahead, let it grow." He had moved beyond the syllabus. Helpless, I tried to play something, anything. Then I stopped. Maqsud Ali asked, "What's the difficulty? Just take the phrases I gave you and elaborate them." I could not improvise until years later, but this was the beginning.

Two Kinds of Training

Mirza Maqsud Ali's description of his early training used musical categories typical of the college syllabus and suggested that his father used that training on him. He also refers to his father as his guru, the term used in Hindi and Hinduism, adapting himself to the standard Hindi term used in college rather than the secular Urdu-Persian term "ustad."

"I learned at home in the beginning. From the age of seven my father forced me to practice every day."

In explanation of how he learned ragas, he stated: "First I learned the ascent and descent of a raga (arohi-avrohi). This is most important. I also learned the salient or central notes in a raga (vadi and samvadi). This would be done by singing the names of the scale degrees (i.e., solfège). Then came singing legato, without syllables. As for compositions, the first to be taught was the classical form khayal. Then came tappa and thumri, these two light forms are easy to do."

Mirza Maqsud Ali then entered the college program. He took classes and passed the exams up to the fifth year, the B.A. degree. Then he continued through years six and seven, but he did not take the exam for the master's degree because of the death of his child. He was unable to continue. "I entered the college program," he said, "but in class I acted as if I knew nothing. They teach differently, and don't appreciate what we do in our family. All the teachers don't have a family background of music, and so it is best to remain silent about that. My real learning came from my father. He is my guru."

He elucidated with one of the proverbial sayings that are an important tool of oral teaching, one that has a meaning specific to the community of musicians, as such sayings often do: "Blood and water are not the same," (khun aur pani ek nahin hota hai) meaning roughly: blood is thicker than water.

In the end, he identified a common platform across differences between college and family teaching: "The kind of knowledge is different, but in the end, teaching and learning are essentially by imitation, be it in my family or in college. Musicians have a saying for this: dikhiya (see), sikhiya (learn), parkihiya (assess). First you see, then you memorize, and only then do you have the discernment to create it yourself."

YAQUB HUSAIN KHAN: INHERITING A COLLEGE POST[14]

Introducing Yaqub Husain Khan

Successor to his uncle, Mirza Maqsud Ali, Yaqub Husain Khan belongs to a branch of the same extended family, but he is related to Mahmud and Maqsud Ali through his mother Siddiqunnisa, who was Mahmud Ali's sister. While he belongs to a different lineage through his father Mubarak Ali, Yaqub Husain Khan was raised and trained by his maternal grandfather, Ali Jan, a common practice among Muslim musicians, especially while his musician father was working and living elsewhere as a tabla player. He started learning the sarangi at age ten and also received training from Mahmud Ali, his maternal uncle. Later he learned from his paternal uncle, Chunnu Khan, who was also a sarangi player.

For some years, Yaqub Husain worked as a freelance musician in a market of mainly light and popular music, though he said little about it. It was upon Mirza Maqsud Ali's retirement from his teaching post that Yaqub Husain Khan was appointed to the college, replacing his uncle as a family breadwinner, though his position was limited to providing accompaniment for the dance classes that had become more popular in recent years. He was the only working musician among his siblings; three other brothers were tailors, including one who had a bad arm and could not play an instrument.

Like Maqsud Ali, Yaqub Husain suffered on account of the loss of a child. In 1983, he told me that his six-year-old son had disappeared and was never found. This grief further aggravated his already poor health. He died in the late 1980s, leaving no direct successor.

Figure 19 Yaqub Husain with Yavar Ali on tabla, Qureshi home, Lucknow, 1984.

I first met Yaqub Husain Khan in 1983, having wanted to revisit his senior cousin, Mirza Maqsud Ali, who had taught me 14 years ago. Someone identified him perchance and brought him to the music shop on Latouche Road, where I was looking for a new sarangi. We sat down to talk while the store manager offered helpful explanations and customers looked on. Hearing of Maqsud Ali's death was a shock; I felt an era had gone by. All the more, I was grateful for the chance to remain connected with the family of my first teacher and to help me with my inquiry into this family's special contribution to Bhatkhande Music College.

Yaqub Husain strikingly resembled his cousin Maqsud Ali, and in talking to him, I discovered many of Maqsud Ali's dry and somewhat stern expressions, opinions, and musical preferences, including repertoire. His presence really brought home to me the value of this special combination of musical and familial continuity. Sadly, I never saw him again.

Between Lineage and College

In summer 1983, Yaqub Husain Khan, then in his forties, visited our home for two mornings of music making and intense conversation. He brought along his nephew, Munawwar Ali Khan, who undertook to introduce and showcase Yaqub Husain's musical parentage by using formal address and titles. Khaliq Ahmad, a family friend with a landlord background, provided an easygoing but authoritative presence, occasionally punctuated by my husband and son looking in.

Regula: Yaqub Sahib, please tell about your family.

Munawwar: *Showcasing Yaqub's father:* Yaqub Ali Khan Sahib's father, Mubarak Ali Khan, was a tabla expert. He was the most "first class" of all; he used to go to the courts of maharajas and rajas, and his playing impressed everyone. Once even the great dancer Kanthe Maharaj was so pleased that he gave him a garland for his tabla playing.

Regula: So Mubarak Ali …

Munawwar: *Corrects, adding full title:* Mubarak Ali *Khan*. This is what I know about him. He sent his young son Yaqub Sahib to his grandfather, Ali Jan Sahib. Because he was Ali Jan Sahib's son-in-law, I mean Mubarak Ali Khan was. When Yaqub Sahib had gained knowledge of the basics of music, then his grandfather sent him to study with Chunnu Ustad, his paternal uncle, who was also a very fine sarangi player. His grandfather said: "I have taught you; now I've become old, so you learn from him."

Yaqub: *Amplifies:* My father found it convenient to place me with his father-in-law; I would learn from him, I would acquire knowledge and would also be looked after. My father was a free spirit—today he's in Calcutta, tomorrow in Bombay, and the day after somewhere else. He spent his life on the move. After two years he returned from Calcutta, after another year he came to Benares; he stayed one or two years in Benares, then he came back here again.

Regula: Did he send expenses?

Yaqub: Yes, but he was carefree, because he was reassured that the children and his wife were with her father. Hence he had no worry (*fikr*), whether he sent or didn't send anything. He didn't care much.

At home I was taught to practice patterns, each for two, three hours, four or five hours, as much as I can, working on this tan until the time is finished. However, playing it for three hours, it will pick up speed, won't it. Once this is set, then I am able to play everything: sequence patterns, ascending and descending, *sapat*, ornamentation, oscillation. *Here he switches momentarily to Brit-*

ish Army pidgin Urdu, still used by some older people to make for-eigners understand.

Songs I was simply taught to memorize: "See, these are the words and tunes of each section: *asthayi, antara, sanchai.*" I had to memorize them, and fit them into the rhythmic cycle. This is the way practice is done, so when this is properly practiced, then all the different patterns and embellishments will be ready to go. There is no practice of alap improvisation. But people do expand and improvise alap a bit, just to keep the habit, then catch the refrain phrase. This is the method.

Regula: Does the ustad give the student a prepared passage, like the small passage you mentioned, that fits into one rhythmic cycle?

Yaqub: That would be the training of the college. Our elders did not teach us like this; they taught us the composed song and the outline of the raga: "This is the way it goes, this is the design." Then they said, "Now you expand this out of your own mind. But the raga must not deviate; there must not be any 'difference' in it." Now on my own, when he is telling me, or when I have learned it, I must also make up faster passages on the same patterns. I must also do textless legato improvisation. For the raga not to be wrong, no other raga must touch it. It must stay correct.

Regula: What if I want to study accompaniment?

Yaqub: That's not something you study; it's a matter of your brain. A singer won't sing only what I have memorized. I have to know how to play whatever *she* knows.[15] The sarangi player who sits there, his hand should produce the song in this way: *He sings the opening line of a traditional song and then plays it, shwing exactly how each word is clearly articulated and separated with each bow stroke.* This is how the sarangi player "carves" the phrasing of the song. The phrases will always be shaped with the bow. This is part of our "idiom." Me, I have to be able to play everything. If I get an opportunity to play with a singer, then I have to play whatever she sings. Now if this string is tuned to the first note (sa) and the singer starts to sing from the third note (ga), then you have to play from ga. It creates a lot of difficulty.

Some time back, I was very keen on accompanying songs. I used to see a lot of films, and I memorized the songs and then played them myself. I had a passion for it. But now I gave up those habits, since I have employment at the college. Now I have to play cyclical melodies (*lehra*) for all rhythmic cycles, even those with 11, 13, 17, 18, 22 counts. A repertoire of two or four lehras in different ragas is necessary for each *tal*. Lehras are not taught at the college; you should simply remember them; otherwise you can't do the work. I learned them at home.

A Clash of Values

Yaqub: You know that this college started in 1927.

Regula: Yes, they recently had their 50th jubilee. Tell me how the artists lived at that time and how they came to join the college?

Yaqub: In the time of the *nawab*s, our sustenance came from the landed rajas (*ta'alluqdar*). There used to be soirées (*mahfils*) at their place; there were wedding celebrations; and we were also called just like that. They also employed us. My maternal grandfather, Ali Jan Sahib, he used to go to the Raja Sahib Mahmudabad—you must have heard of the Raja of Mahmudabad.[16]

Regula: Yes certainly, in fact I know the Rajkumar,[17] his younger brother.

Yaqub: That's where my grandfather Ali Jan mostly lived. He would go there, and when the Raja had the mood for it, he sat and listened for a short while. Then my grandfather would come back here, and for months he could live in leisure, eat, and enjoy himself without any worries.

Regula: But then your grandfather's brother Mahmud Ali and other musicians started teaching at the college.

Yaqub: Then the college was started in 1927. Bhatkhande-ji[18] was the first principal. Let me tell you what happened in the beginning. Nusrat Ali Khan, and Agha, and Munne Khan etc.,[19] all of them who were employed here in the Bhatkhande College, Bhatkhande-ji did the following (with them): These people came for their duty, sat down in their class, and started to sing and play. Then those compositions that they sang, Mr. Bhatkhande stood in the hallway and listened. He could do notation so fast that right there he took down the entire khayal composition they sang, the whole thing. Munne Khan, Agha Sahib, or Khurshid Ali Khan, whatever they sang, he took it down in notation.

Now once he had notated it, he sang it back to them. When those people heard him sing, they said, "How did you get to know this composition? And from where?" Well he replied: "What do you mean? You were singing, I transcribed it." Then they said: "What you did is very wrong." He said, "Why wrong?" They said, "This composition belongs to us; we are not about to teach it to outsiders. We haven't learned this to just give it away." He said, "I have employed you here for this very purpose, so that you should teach us nonmusicians, our children who will come to the college, you should teach them, instruct them. So how can this be that you say you won't teach anyone else!" Then the musicians said, "Well, we will not teach outsiders." Then he said, "If you won't teach outsiders, then turn in your resignation!" And they did resign, all of them. Bhatkhande said: "That's alright, you may go."

Yaqub: The reason I have told you these matters is that the people of earlier times taught only their own children.

Khaliq: Yes, well those were old timers. They did not teach outsiders.

Yaqub: Brother, they left such a great employment. They said, "Alright, we will resign," and that was the end of it. I have told you about this to show you that the things I have taught you, and had you write down, you might perhaps not get them from any other musician. You see, in those times, music making was not yet very widespread. That is, music had not become so widely practiced. Now it has expanded to enormous numbers. Earlier, the only musicians were the hereditary people, their offspring, their elders, or their relatives, grandchildren, nephews.

Today the entire world is full of singers. And now that music making has expanded so much, teaching has expanded, and also methods of teaching. And the styles have changed too. Who sings tappa now? Neither does anyone play it, nor are there any listeners for it. The music we have now is in cycles of 16 or 12 counts. People memorize solfège (*sargam*) and fast khayal compositions. Even slow khayal, no one sings the real thing any more.

Our Last Conversation: Fees

Regula: Now please tell me your fees.

Yaqub: The matter of fees is like this: What all I taught you and had you take down in notation, is this of value in your eyes?

Regula: Why would I come from so far to learn this from you, if I didn't consider it to have value? You have seen that I am not completely untutored.

Yaqub: No, no, absolutely.

Regula: So?

Yaqub: Therefore, I suggest to you that you give me 500 rupees.

Our meeting ended with an envelope of 501 rupees, a customary token gesture of offering more than the sum required, hence turning an obligatory payment into a voluntary offering.

MUNAWWAR HUSAIN: NEW SOUNDS AND TRAGEDY[20]

Introducing Munawwar Husain Khan

Youngest son of Mirza Maqsud Ali, Munawwar Husain Khan first came to my house along with his senior cousin Yaqub Khan. He recalled seeing me as a small boy when I first studied with his father in 1965. At this time he was in his early twenties and had learned some basics from his grandfather, Mirza Mahmud Ali, during his last years of life. Later, he tried to pursue a degree at Bhatkhande College, a sensible choice, given both his father's and grandfather's employment there. But despite a prize and a 50-rupee scholarship for learning the sarangi, he was unable to manage the subsequent courses and tried to pursue accompanying light music for a living.

After Yaqub Husain Khan's death Munawwar Husain did find employment at the college for accompanying dance classes, though his caliber for performance was very limited and he was isolated among his colleagues. Yaqub Khan had become his young cousin's mentor, and it is he who brought Munawwar Husain to my house in June 1983, when the conversations with both of them were recorded. Less than ten years later Munawwar was found murdered in a dispute over a debt that had made his life difficult for some time.

My last meeting with Munawwar was in 1992, when I encountered him in Bhatkhande College. On that visit, I inadvertently disappointed his expectations of more substantial patronage from his father's student, a memory that remains difficult. After some days I had finally met him at the college and asked him to come to the hotel where we were staying at the time. He became very angry and said he would not come to any hotel; he would meet me only in my house, like his father did. I tried to explain that we were ourselves staying at this (very fine) hotel and leaving the following day, but to him it was a rejection of our family ties since his grandfather's time, and he refused to come with me, while I did not understand his anger. I did not see him again and have deeply regretted this failure on my part ever since.[21] The violent demise of this young musician highlights the material and social deprivation that can befall hereditary families with little else to fall back on than training and excellence in music.

Claims to Family and Job

Munawwar Husain's words about his family and himself are embedded in the same multiple conversations during the visit of Munawwar Husain Khan and Yaqub Husain Khan to my Lucknow home. Because his uncle, Yaqub Husain was present throughout, Munawwar was clearly a secondary partner in the conversation and therefore did not say very much on his own, though he is quite eloquent, as the following brief excerpt shows.

While reconciling college and family figured in his discussion, he pragmatically focused most of all on the family and its musical assets, situating himself and his elders within the family lineage. Munawwar linked his family to royal Mogul ancestry and former court employment, placing his particular family lineage and its musical heritage apart from the major hereditary community of musicians.

Family History

Munawwar: You want to know about my family. This lineage, my grandfather has told me this thing about it. There was once a Husain Bakhsh; he was connected with the family of the Moguls; he belonged to one of the families of King Akbar Shah. Now Husain Bakhsh loved music so much that in his time he was a court musician (*Tanseni naukar*). But when the chaos of the Great Uprising (of 1857) came, all this was torn from their hands.

I mean, when the landed estates were taken away, we ourselves became servants of others. But we, I mean our elders, always had a passion for musical knowledge. We had such a passion that we ourselves acquired it from hereditary master musicians.

For instance, my paternal grandfather in his home learned from his senior father, that is his father's elder brother, Muhammad Jan Sahib. He and my great-grandfather Wahid Jan were real brothers, and they were both Husain Bakhsh's sons.

Regula: Was this a Shi'a family?

Munawwar: No, no. I'll tell you: it is over this very point that we had a court case with a Shi'a gentleman after the 1857 Uprising that lasted for 16 years. That is to say, because we were in the profession of music, the plaintiff said: "You do this work; I don't accept what you say you are." So we people, that is, our ancestors, started a lawsuit. Then there was a court case because they tagged us with the identity of the hereditary musician class. Our elders said, "That is no community of ours. We have acquired the knowledge of music through our own effort." So that Shi'a gentleman lost the case. And we could continue to attach "Mirza" to our name, like Mirza Mahmud Ali, Mirza Maqsud Ali.

My grandfather had died early. So his father's elder brother, Mirza Mahmud Ali, supported my father and taught him. He played sarangi very first class. Please consider that he came from the family of Husain Bakhsh, who was a Mogul court musician at the time of Akbar Shah (a minor 18th-century king often cited by musicians).

Regula: Where does your family live?

Munawwar: We both live in Khayali Ganj. It's a neighborhood behind Qaisar Bagh police station. That is our house, from the past. It was like this: since 1870, all the members of our extended family lived in the same place, in Khayali Ganj. That is our ancestral house since 1870. When the Great Uprising happened, in 1857, people went away; they left everything behind. When the Uprising was over, in 1870, they all came back here, and then all these houses and lands were given to them by the British rulers (*Bartania*, i.e., Britannia). That's when our forebears built their houses. They all resided there: my paternal grandfather, Yaqub's maternal grandfather, all of them. They lived wherever they got space, land, and a house. It all became theirs. Khayali Ganj was a center, all artists lived there: Ustad Bhure Khan, Ustad Alli Khan, and so on. The famous Ustad Rajab Ali Khan often used to visit. I have this much knowledge about this because my grandfather Mahmud Ali Sahib explained it to me.

Trying the College

Munawwar Husain studied at Bhatkhande College for one year, becoming a student there after I left in 1969. He received a scholarship for receiving a first-division mark in the subject "dictation," but then he did not pursue his studies the following year. I asked him why:

Munawwar: I couldn't figure out how to study there, so my grandfather, Mahmud Sahib, said: "Pull out from there. If you want to learn this music, then the degree and all that can be considered later, but first learn something from home. If you are not getting anything there at the college, I will teach you something." So I pulled out.

Now Mahmud Sahib was completely immersed in the college for many years, so he had all the knowledge. And here the system is that, in 'school,' you present the material of the 'school.' If you present something different, they will fail you. My father also studied at the 'college.' When Ratanjankar was principal, he even became his (Ratanjankar's) disciple with a formal *shagirdi* (discipleship) ceremony.[22] Then he got employment there.

Regula: He taught singing there, not sarangi. But at home you picked up the sarangi?

Munawwar: Yes, but playing the sarangi is a very difficult challenge. It's very beautiful to look at, and it has all other qualities but also some aspects that, because of them, people quit. I mean, for a man this is the right calling; to make the sarangi sing whatever the voice sings. But this is exactly what people are getting away from.[23]

Experimenting with "Sound"

Finally, uncle and nephew together discuss the sarangi as they get ready to play family repertoire for me to record. Yaqub Husain introduces the topic with an appropriately formal statement on a recording destined for Canada. Starting with traditional information about the sarangi, the discussion then takes a surprising turn into sound production and technology, reflecting their earlier involvement with studio music.

The conversation proceeds in an informal, dovetailed exchange between both musicians that vividly reflects their close association and background, in contrast with the more formal explanations of family, where seniority is acknowledged in titles and formal personal pronouns. To describe amplification, they used English terms adapted to Urdu/Hindi phonetics, e.g., "sound" and "fit" (pronounced "sohnd" and "phit"), reflecting a technology-specific vocabulary that I had not associated with these traditionally situated musicians.

Yaqub: There is, sir, no better instrument (than the sarangi). It is difficult and very fine, very tuneful. That is, it brings peace (*shanti*) to the spirit. There is, sir, none better. Though there are thousands of instruments, the sitar, et cetera, et cetera, whatever they are, but none can reach its heights.

Regula: Please tell me about the different sizes in sarangi.

Yaqub: There are different kinds of sarangi. A complete sarangi, a big one, is called double brained (*do-maghzi*), with extra pegs for more wire strings for resonance. That's what I'll play on for your taping tomorrow.

Munawwar: This instrument I have here is an *ek-maghzi*, a one-brained instrument. Then there is the one-and-a-half-rib sarangi (*derh-pasli*), the two-rib, and the two-and-a-half-rib sarangi.

Regula: What is a rib?

Munawwar: This! *He points to the right side extension holding a row of pegs for a separate set of resonating wire strings.* Extra strings are there to make sound.

Regula: I see. So what about sound holes? You did not make holes in the skin.

Yaqub: Why would I be making such holes?

Regula: *To Munawwar:* Your father also did not make them. I went to Pakistan; there they make them with a burning cigarette.

Munawwar: It's considered bad!

Yaqub: *Explains:* They make holes in the instrument because of the 'sound.' So that its breath, its 'sound' should come out.

Munawwar: *Speaking on behalf of his lineage:* And our way is to keep the skin closed. We find that more appropriate, because the air passes through the belly anyway, so you won't find any holes in any instruments here.

Yaqub: This is a matter of personal preference.

Munawwar: But many people put 'sound' into the instrument.

Both: *Seeing Regula's incomprehension:* 'Sound,' 'speaker,' 'pickup.'

Yaqub: The volume becomes bigger; that's why they put on the 'speaker,' a small one. They 'fit' it below. So when the instrument is played, then this makes the sound (*awaz*) loud. I tell you something: if you have a new 'note,' give it to me and I'll just make 'sound' for you.

Munawwar: *Seeing Regula's incomprehension, calls out:* Rupee, rupee.

Khaliq: *Helpfully produces a 20-rupee note, assuming the need for a special offering.*

Regula: Oh I see: money! You won't burn it, will you? *Laughs.*

Munawwar: It's to show you "sound."

Yaqub: *Weaves the banknote across the row of resonating wire strings of Munawwar's instrument while chuckling to Khaliq:* Now this poor lady is worried.

Munawwar: *Starts bowing across the main string, and the banknote vibrates against the wire strings.* You see, it has produced 'sound,' hasn't it! *He plays a scale, quite out of tune; the vibration of the paper is audible, adding some volume (as in a Kazoo).*

Yaqub: Actually, this is a large note; it should be smaller—a 1-rupee note.

Many people install sound because then the volume is louder. They use a 'mic.' I told you it is small; you put it here (on the skin side).

Regula: So what was the purpose of playing with the paper?

Yaqub: To show you sound, a louder sound. You could hear how with the note the sound was louder.

We drink tea; meanwhile Munawwar lights a cigarette.

Regula: *Teasing him:* Oh, so you smoke before your elders. In old times this wasn't done, was it?

Yaqub: Yes, yes, in old times. The point is, we are in each other's company 24 hours. Now he'll pay me respect once, twice, thrice. Then the elder himself gives him permission to do it.

Regula: I agree with this. Our children do everything before us. I like it; then we know what they are doing.

Yaqub: That is alright.

With this agreement, we conclude and enjoy our tea with biscuits.

CHAPTER 8

Bahadur Khan

A Freelance Past

Introducing Bahadur Khan

Bahadur Khan belongs to the last generation of freelance musicians who thrived in the North Indian region of princely states and courtesan culture. His family is part of the hereditary musician community of kalavant (artists) of Banda, a princely state south of Lucknow whose nawab (prince) invited these musicians to settle in the city at least as early as the 18th century. Banda's thriving musical culture is evidenced in the earliest Western account of musical practice written in 1834 by Augustus Willard.

Bahadur Khan was born and raised for a life under princely and salon patronage of music. He was refined and low-key in his manner, naturally polite, and clearly at ease with cultivated patrons. His playing revealed a flair for lively improvisation, unpredictable and spiced with accents. He could sport a dueling mode with the tabla player, and he liked to end his pieces dramatically with cadential flourish. The heyday of Bahadur Khan's professional life was as a freelance musician in the milieu of princely courts and, above all, in the courtesan milieu, with its special need for supporting and highlighting both singing and dancing, playing for the occasion, and creating the atmosphere of a contest by using the larant *(fighting) style of musical dueling.*

An important part of Bahadur Khan's freelance life was travel: from the hometown of Banda, where Bahadur Khan got introduced to the art of accompanying, to the regional capital Jabalpur, where he joined his father at

Figure 20 Bahadur Khan accompanies hereditary singer Zarina Parveen, her home, Lucknow, 1984.

a renowned singer's home to be taught the fine art of accompanying an inter-active performance engaging diversely reactive audiences. He then worked with singers in Jabbalpur, Nagpur, and Bombay, but finally returned to his own region, settling in Lucknow. Given the decay of courtesan performances, he obtained a government post as accompanist of classical dance classes, a secure living for 20 years until his retirement in the mid-'90s.

When I first met Bahadur Khan in 1984 he was well established at the Kathak Kendra (Kathak Center) of the Uttar Pradesh Sangeet Natak Aka-demi. He also continued to be engaged for performances on All India Radio and lately on TV. But he did not become a teacher, not even to train his son. This is because his community in Banda had decided collectively not to teach their children music any more, because of the total decline of court and courtesan patronage on which their well-being depended. Significantly, this is one of the first topics Bahadur Khan introduced into our very first con-versation. A more personal relationship developed, starting with a dynamic performance and teaching session.

Later that summer I was surprised to see Bahadur Khan playing a totally different musical role at the side of Lucknow's most renowned courtesan singer, whose private performance I was recording (see Figure 20). Eight years later (1992), I was privileged to hear his personal account of a young

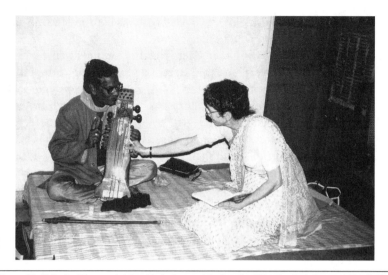

Figure 21 Bahadur Khan explaining his instrument to Regula, Uttar Pradesh Sangeet Natak Akademi, Lucknow, 1992.

musician's life in the courtesan era. I am deeply grateful to this gracious and thoughtful artist and only regret that he did not live to see this writing.

Life in the Courtesan Era[1]

After eight years I had returned to Lucknow. In the mid-afternoon I could always find Bahadur Khan in the dance section of the Academy, where he would sit watching over the class of young girl students and get them to do their warm-up exercises. Today he was to tell me about his early life as a bright young sarangi player. But Bahadur Khan liked the adjacent study area of the Sangeet Natak Akademi, where we could sit and talk. He had a scholarly bent and an interest in the past, including the history of Banda state and the origin of his own community of musicians. I enjoyed this special connection, and our friendship lasted until his untimely death in 2002.

From Schooling to Family Training

Bahadur: Our community are *kalavant* ("artists"), from Banda. We came to Banda because the Nawab liked music. He gave us a special neighborhood called Kalamatpura ("Kalavant place").

I was raised by my senior uncle (*taya*, father's elder brother) because he had no children. He was very harsh, that's how he could teach children. He used to have their heads shaved so they would stay home and practice. He broke his bow beating me many times.

When I was about seven or eight years old I went to school. I failed the first year, and in the second year I failed again. I didn't have much interest in studying. Well, my father (*bap*) said—actually it was my senior uncle, to be exact: "That's enough studying. Now let's see what you can learn at home. Leave the school." So I left. It was a government school, named "Khanqah School" because there is a Khanqah (a Sufi shrine) near where that school is located. Many saints are buried there, so they built that school there. It has become very large, but in my time it was very small.

I hadn't learned anything, just *alif be pe* (the Urdu alphabet). So my father stopped my reading and writing at school. Now the question was, what should I be taught? First I was started on the tabla *laughs*.

Regula: Really? Who taught you?

Bahadur: You must have heard the name of Nizamuddin Khan (an outstanding tabla player), in Bombay. It was his father. Banda is the home of Nizamuddin's mother's family, so at that time Azim Khan Sahib, his father, was staying in Banda, so he got me started on the tabla. After two months he left, saying: "That's it, I can't keep coming here just to teach you." After that I was taught sarangi. Once I was able to play, my father also engaged a tutor for me. He taught me Urdu, Arabic, that was the education. My father did that, now that I had started to play, because education is also very important. One should have some of it, at least.

Regula: Did your father know reading and writing?

Bahadur: Yes, a little bit. You know, in our community (*hamare han*) we don't pay too much attention to education. Not even today. Today, the boys who are not in the music 'line,' they are given different training. Otherwise, for those who are in music, it is difficult to get them schooling as well.

Regula: So why did you get it? You weren't even interested in reading and writing. Was the intent that you might change your 'line'?

Bahadur: No, no, nothing of the sort. The elders say that this young person will be moving away—if not today, tomorrow—then he can at least send us news of how he is doing and ask us how we are doing at home. That's how much I should learn. So I learned Urdu for that, and Arabic is of course very necessary.

Regula: Yes, to read the Qur'an … I understand. So for how many years did you study?

Bahadur: I think … about three to four years, 'master' came to the house and taught me.

Regula: That takes money.

Bahadur: Yes, well, whatever it took. At that time things were entirely different—life was much better. Those were the good times of the princely states in all of India, and they lasted until well after Independence. Now once they were finished off, the entire environment for music gradually changed and became something totally different. In contrast, the environment before that was very good for music in our country.

Training on the Job

Regula: I see, that is it. Okay. So first of all you had your training as well as education, then your practicing was complete. At what age did you leave Banda? Was there no work there?

Bahadur: Oh yes, there was work playing the sarangi in Banda, like in the bigger cites. There were *tawaif* (courtesan singers) here too. They had their salons and their own houses. In the city they had their neighborhoods, two of them: Mardannaka and Chaoni. Mardannaka is a very large area. So these singers lived in the upper part of the area and below them there is a road; that is where we kalavants lived. So whenever there was a need for accompanists, they could get somebody to come in time before starting the performance.

There was also work at wedding parties (*shadi-beah*), where courtesans danced and sang, the way it was done in earlier times. There was all kinds of work! My senior uncle occasionally went out of town. He had a disciple, Viddya Bai, and so he would leave me with her. Viddya Bai was a very good singer of her time. So she put me to work with her, although at the time I was still learning to do vocal accompaniment (*gale ki sangat*). But she taught me how to do it.

After that, at about age 15 to 16, I went with my father to Jabalpur. He mostly lived there, as did my younger uncle (chacha). My respected father (Pitaji, Walid Sahib)[2] was in the service of the Maharaja of Maihar[3] and played sarangi when the maharaja resided in town. There was his disciple, the well known singer Bibbo Bai, she used to teach me accompaniment of "light" genres—*thumri*, *dadra*, *ghazal*. So she sat me down to play with her, because knowing how to accompany well is very necessary. A solo player can play whatever he has practiced. But to accompany requires that I immerse myself into the process completely; only then can I provide accompaniment to whoever needs it. It is in fact a distinct art. So his effort was to train me for accompaniment. That is why I was staying there.

Regula: How did she instruct you?

Bahadur: I mean she is singing and has me play with her: "Whatever I am singing, you play it with me, whatever passage work (*tan*), whatever phrase variations I create (*bol banao*), or whatever slow improvisation (*alap*), you produce the same thing on the sarangi."

Regula: You mean, at that very time?

Bahadur: Yes, you have to do it together with her, just like wrestlers are made to fight together and push each other, that's what this training was all about: to get you prepared for action. Sure, you have been taught the right moves, but how will you apply them effectively? That too is a know-how you must have.

For instance, my father (senior uncle) used to serve the raja of Raigarh (Madhya Pradesh). Once the famous Akhtari Bai (Begum Akhtar) was invited there. This was when she was in her youthful prime. When Lallu Khan was challenged to accompany her, he exclaimed: "I am Lallu Khan, she better watch her notes." In the performance he played in fighting style (*larant*). He guided her further away from the tonic *sa* (1) in each interlude, moving it one step up to land on *re* (2), then up another step to land on *ga*, and the singer followed him each time. Then he put down his instrument, and now she was lost. Then he showed her the real tonic *sa* (1)—she was defeated. The Maharaja gave him a big reward!

Regula: How amazing! So these women singers, like Bibbo and Viddya Bai, what kinds of songs did these ladies sing?

Bahadur: Khayal *asthai* (classical compositions), thumri, dadra. That's what was in style then. Depending on the region, they also sang *bhajan* (Hindu devotional songs) and ghazal. In my region, in Bundelkhand, there were princely states with (Hindu) rajas. So obviously there you had an environment for bhajan (Hindu devotional songs), thumri, dadra, and the like. But Lucknow was full of (Muslim) Nawabs, so that meant an environment for (Urdu) ghazals.

Environment means: which kind of piece is more in demand (*kaunsi chiz zyada mangi jati hai*). Now if you sing a bhajan before the nawabs, they would not get it. And if you sing a ghazal before rajas, what would they understand? Nothing! Therefore, you keep separate repertoires for each region.

Measuring Competence: Juma and Audition

Regula: You mentioned how you went on to Nagpur and competed in a *juma.*

Bahadur: Juma (literally "Friday") was very popular among the khansahib community. Juma music making was generally arranged after Friday prayers (in the afternoon).[4] And whoever played well, if someone else was even a slight bit better, then it spurred him on to practice harder so that at the next juma he would play better than that person. That happened a lot. Children, too, played in the juma, and the eldest musician (chaudhri) would assess and comment on their playing, saying: "If you practice hard, you'll be able to play as well as so and so just did." The raga had to be flawless too; it wasn't enough to be technically accomplished while hitting inappropriate notes here and there in fast runs. The point is, along with virtuosity, there must not be any musical flaw (*aib*) either.

So when I first came to Nagpur, I attended a juma where one senior khansahib has control, Rahman Khan. He played *multani* in a special way—no one could do this raga better than he. My respected father told me about this. He advised me to practice and play this very raga multani at that juma. I did it, and it was a success. At first I startled the khansahib with my boldness: I was taking on his special raga. But then he and others present were astonished at my showing a new approach to the raga. Afterwards Rahman Khan Sahib embraced me, and from then on he took me under his wing, taking me along to play with him.

There is a proper standard (*mayar*) of playing sarangi. If you do something outside of that, the senior players will disapprove.... For instance, on bowing. The job of the bow is only to give sound, and if you lift it up and hit the string with it, then the sarangi will certainly resound with a clang (*jhanne se bolna*), but that is considered one of those flaws (aib). We call that "slapping down the bow" (*gaz ka dachka marna*).

Regula: Yes, so it's considered a flaw. But people do it.

Bahadur: No, not in those times. The person who introduced this is Ram Narayan. Before that, if anyone even accidentally struck the string, they would say: "Brother, look at this, he is slapping down the bow, really! Slapping the bow!" I mean, the "balance" of the bow should be even, both in going and coming back (pulling and pushing, downbow and upbow). Whatever (musical) activity you create should be done with the left hand—the fingers on the strings.

There are of course a few exceptions. For instance, when I have to accompany *tarana*.[5] In that I can use the right hand to mark the notes with separate bow strokes. And when the singer is singing *tarana* (a fast, strongly rhythmic genre), I am compelled to use the right hand to reproduce the syllabic and strongly rhythmic compositions. But for singing in general, the right hand is not doing any of this. Just the left. You have to provide "sound;" whatever you do, you do it with sound, whether it be fast patterns (*tanen*) or slow melody (*bilampat*). Only for syllabic tunes (*sargam*) and in tarana do you mark the tones with separate bow strokes, not for anything else.

All this is how we people were prepared to go before an audience. Then came the idea to play on the radio (All India Radio). You had to get "auditions" arranged *laughs*. Nowadays auditions have become very cheap (*sasta*). In my generation's time, auditions were very dangerous (*khatarnak*).

Regula: Dangerous, what do you mean?

Bahadur: I mean, at that time the situation was that you first gave a 'local audition.' There were 25 ragas to know. You played one of your own choice and one that they requested (*farmaish*). After that, if you got to go to Delhi for a 'recording,' then before you entered the studio, you were given an envelope at the gate. You were told to open it once you were inside. It had the names of two ragas written in it. You had to play one. If you played both, then it would be even better for you. And if you played one, it was alright too. Today you choose and prepare any two ragas that suit you. You go and play them, and leave. Then it wasn't like that.

I gave the first audition in Nagpur. First, when I gave the first audition, I played two ragas: *yaman*, and for a morning raga I think I played *todi—gujri* todi. And then, perchance, when my final came in Delhi, I was given the letter, and when I went inside and opened it, the raga I found was what they call "daytime *puriya*" or puriya *dhanasri*—they are both the same thing, whether you call it daytime puriya or dhanasri puriya. I also got the raga *mian ki* todi.[6] These were the two ragas. So I said: "I will play both ragas." And I did that. My result was "B high."

From Nagpur I went to live in Bombay; that was many years ago. After all, I have been in service here in Lucknow for 20 years. I have a very good friend there. You know Sultan Khan. He is not only a good player, he is also a good human being. He talks nicely to everyone, and he is a very good person. He is from Sikhar (see Chapter 6). He is like a brother to me. There is no kinship relation (*rishtedari*), although he belongs to our '*kasht*' (caste, professional community). But he is not a relative; no, there won't be any marriages between us.

Regula: So were you playing there?

Bahadur: There were a great many singers, all good. For instance Bari Shanti Allahabadwali and others. You got work! Just like that: I am sitting there, and "Mister (*miyan*), come on, get out, come on and play, let's go. Come on, there is a *mujra* (courtesan performance) in so and so place, please come and play. A man came from their house. And he would take you along.

Eventually I returned home and took a service position at the Dance Academy here in Lucknow. But times had changed in Banda, and our whole bradri decided to stop teaching music to our children.

Recognizing Banda

Much later, in 1997, in what turned out to be my last encounter with him, Bahadur Khan made sure to add his music historical perspective on Banda, to ensure that Banda's value would be recognized as it had been when Captain Augustus Willard lived there and wrote the first book on Indian musical practice:

Bahadur: Every musician considers himself a big shot (*top*, literally "canon"). But there is no *gharana* as old as Banda. In Banda there has been sangit (music) from times even before other gharanas like Jaipur. The evidence (*sanad*) is that Arjun, in the Mahabharata, was a very good fighter among the five Pandavas. His *shishya* (disciple) is Uttara, and Uttara was the son of the raja of Banda. Whatever the sangit of that time was, he learned it from Arjun. When he settled in Banda and lived there, he established sangit there. But we don't know what kind of sangit that was, since we don't even know the language they spoke.

The environment for music has been there in Banda, but that changed once the principalities (*ryasat*) were finished off after 1947. Musicians of that generation had no *rujhan* (inclination) toward 'service' (wage employment). My father served at the court of Maihar. After accession, the sons of the raja wanted to keep my father on for a monthly stipend. But he declined, since no more music was being made as before.

Now Bahadur Khan's dance class was ready to start, and he took leave quickly while I sat watching a dozen small girls start their dance drills to the drummed and melodic meter of tabla and of Khan Sahib's vitally charged sarangi. Later we would finish our talk over tea in my hotel.

CHAPTER **9**

Bhagvan Das

Sons and Disciples

Bhagvan Das Mishra

Introducing Bhagvan Das

Bhagvan Das Mishra is one of many musicians from Benares who live and work in Lucknow while their families remain in Benares and their children grow up there. Most belong to the kathak *community, whose members have histori-cally been dancers (of the classical North Indian dance form kathak) as well as instrumentalists and singers. In Bhagvan Das's family, sarangi and tabla play-ers predominate, and dancing has not been practiced for some generations.*

Unlike Benares, the state capital Lucknow has offered sarangi players a good number of positions as performers and teachers in government-spon-sored musical institutions, prominent among them Bhatkhande Music College, the Lucknow Kathak Kendra (dance academy), and of course the Lucknow radio and TV stations. Most desirable among these is the position of staff artist at All India Radio. Bhagvan Das held this position for years and is a very highly regarded musician, both as accompanist and soloist.

Bhagvan Das did not start his career as a sarangi player. His first instru-ment was the tabla, and he seriously studied the sarangi only later, adapting to changing opportunities, although he did not discuss this until he knew me better. His father was his first teacher on the sarangi, followed by his elder brother, both sarangi players. He then studied with, and also accompa-nied, Bade Ramdas, a renowned singer in Benares. Like many other Bena-

Figure 22 Bhagvan Das, immersed in music, Qureshi home, Lucknow, 1984.

res musicians, Bhagvan Das moved around as a freelance musician, living for a time in Delhi and then moving to Calcutta, working principally as an accompanist. In 1984 he was still working and focused on launching the careers of his two sarangi-playing sons in Lucknow, only one of whom had secured employment at Bhatkhande Music College. In 1992 his second son, Vinod, joined him at the college, and by 1997 Santosh had gained a post at Benares Hindu University. Bhagvan Das himself was retired from the radio but continued to live in his small flat in the center of old Lucknow.

Despite being quite settled in Lucknow, Bhagvan Das remains part of a joint family of three brothers and their family home in the musicians' quarter of Benares. This is where his six sons have received most of their musical training, under the guidance of his elder brother Narayan Mishra, who is also a sarangi player. But Bhagvan Das had only two of his sons trained as sarangi players—Santosh and Vinod; the next two were trained on the tabla, and the youngest two on the violin. Cognizant of the need for formal education, he has also sent his sons to college, making them more competitive for employment in government teaching institutions.

In Lucknow, Bhagvan Das has disciples outside his family. Omkar, a wealthy jeweler and patron of music, is an accomplished amateur disciple whom he visited and taught every evening for years. He plays the dilruba, a recently introduced bowed instrument derived from the sitar, which lacks the disreputable association of the sarangi with courtesans. Because that association is still so clearly remembered in Lucknow, the dilruba is a much more suitable instrument for a man of Omkar's status.

Soon after he was exposed to me and my playing in 1984, Bhagvan Das took the unprecedented step of teaching sarangi to a young girl, Archana Yadav, perhaps only the second young Indian woman to learn the sarangi professionally after Pandit Ram Narayan's daughter Aruna (see Chapter 4). Bhagvan Das took her along to the great government-sponsored Sarangi Mela (sarangi festival) held in the city of Bhopal, where she made a unique impact on the gathering, especially since the much more famous Aruna Narayan was not present. When a similar festival was organized in Lucknow, Bhagvan Das received a special award from the Uttar Pradesh (UP) state government for his contributions to music.

Bhagvan Das still plays the sarangi every day. He is satisfied that, with his help, his older sons have secure employment and families to raise. Santosh Kumar found employment at Benares Hindu University, while his younger brother Vinod was able to take over Santosh's position at Lucknow's Bhatkhande College. Even Archana is now employed at the Uttar Pradesh Kathak Kendra (State Dance Academy). Until recently he lived in Lucknow, but he has now returned to Banaras, where he teaches music to his grandchildren.

When I first sought out Bhagvan Das at All India Radio Lucknow in 1984, our only direct point of contact was the sarangi. My name and speech signaled me as a Muslim outsider to this member of a tightly knit Hindu community from Benares, and at first, he saw no need for an interview. Then he asked me to bring my sarangi to the radio station. When I did, he inspected the instrument and asked me to tune it, first showing me his tuning. I must have passed the intonation test, because he acceded to my request for a meeting at my home to talk and demonstrate. We met that same afternoon. In return, I agreed to join his evening session and play for his amateur student. (I had already met and recorded his son Santosh.) His reticence posed a challenge, and I was sorry for not being more generous and open to make him feel more comfortable. All this changed when I returned in 1992. Bhagvan Das was comfortably retired, and above all, he could show me a second female sarangi player whom he had started to train soon after our first encounter. Over the years, our relationship evolved from distance and cultural strangeness to neighborliness and a family-like familiarity.

Bhagvan Das—Risking a First Encounter[1]

After several visits to the radio station to contact Bhagvan Das Mishra, I was able to meet and invite him to our family's home in old Lucknow for a session of conversation and demonstration. He was reluctant to come and remained reserved throughout this first meeting with strangers not connected with any prior commonalities. I had, however, had a talk at Bhatkhande College with his eldest son, Santosh Mishra, who was an accompanist there. This was perhaps Bhagvan Das Ji's first visit to a middle-class Muslim house, although I later found out that he was almost our neighbor, living in the same predominantly Muslim neighborhood where I would later visit him. To begin with, he appeared guarded, reticent to speak, and hesitant to accept hospitality. In conversation he was assertive, even confrontational, to the point of suggesting that his dignified elderly host could accompany a courtesan. At the end, he tried to hide his devotional gesture to the goddess Sarasvati, perhaps expecting disapproval from these non-Hindu patrons.

Mahmud Raza, a senior uncle, was helpfully present as head of the house, and to diffuse any initial cross-gender awkwardness. Also present was Rehan, his young nephew and research assistant, who managed the video camera that was to record Bhagvan Das Mishra's sarangi demonstrations. Bhagvan Das arrived about 3 p.m., after his duty at the radio station was finished. He spoke softly and concisely, and often took a moment between sentences.

Bhagvan Das articulated a purism that resonates with the Hindu reform movement toward bringing the work of musical practitioners in line with classical principles of music and the meanings it derives from Hindu beliefs. He also very explicitly set his music off against the ways of the dominant Muslim fraternity of sarangi players, whom he refers to as "Khan Sahib people" in reference to their commonly used term of address: Khan (chief, a traditional title of Pathan origin) and Sahib (sir, gentleman).

Above all, this is a musician totally dedicated to his instrument and music. He was indifferent to being interviewed, and to my question about his fee, he pointed out that he had never mentioned money.

The Fish under the Grooves

Bhagvan: The sarangi is always with me, everywhere I go. *As Bhagvan takes the instrument, out, Regula asks him about a medicine jar in the case.* I get teased because of this can of Compline (a nutritional supplement). At the radio, they asked me to present it to Mrs. Kohli on staff, who just recovered from typhoid.

Regula: Is it for you? Are you not well?

Bhagvan: I need to be strong because I want to play the sarangi till I am 100 years old. I need strength in my arms to play, and my legs to place the sarangi on. I always prop the sarangi on my leg and against my chest; otherwise you can't use the necessary force to execute virtuoso passages. It won't do to just put the instrument in front of you, separate from your own body. The instrument will move and become dislodged. Mind you, for one or two hours I can also play sitting on a chair, by putting up one leg to place the sarangi on. *He now tunes the sympathetic strings, starting with the row of pegs along the side* pasli, *i.e.* "rib". These strings are tuned to the scale of the raga. And the rest are chromatic (across the instrument's belly).

Regula: What about the inlay on the fingerboard?

Bhagvan: All the friction of your fingers sliding creates grooves in the fingerboard; that's why they have to get this piece put on it. Otherwise your finger will get stuck in the groove.

Regula: And that fish (*under the second string*), what's the meaning?

Bhagvan: Here too you get grooves.

Regula: That's true. But why a fish shape?

Bhagvan: It is attractive.

Regula: To look at? You mean like they say "yogurt and fish" (*dahi machhli*). *He chuckles at Regula's knowing this expression,* A fish is a good thing?

Bhagvan: It is auspicious (*shubh*). Shubh means the journey will be good if you say this at the time of leaving. People consider it auspicious. That's it.

Regula: I see. In Lucknow, fish are found on so many buildings; so is that the meaning?

Bhagvan: Yes, there are fish. In our Benares, too, when someone starts to leave, people say it. Whatever work the person may need to do on their journey, it should be successful.

Tuning is completed and the video recording can start, but not without serving tea.

Regula: Please have some tea.

Bhagvan: Give me just a little; I have just had tea before coming— that's enough, enough!

Travel and Freelancing

The discussion begins with Bhagvan Das's professional life before becoming staff artist at All India Radio Lucknow.

Bhagvan: Before moving to Lucknow I was touring to different engagements for one to two months at a time. Before that, I stayed in Calcutta, for ten years.

Regula: What did you do there? There are many *mahfils* (concert performances) in Calcutta, and also in Muzaffarpur (a city north of Calcutta known for engaging sarangi players for its many courtesan singers).

Bhagvan: Yes. But I have never been in Mujaffarpur (local pronunciation). Nor did I stay there. I did go for a "program" once or twice, but I turned back right from the station. There are a lot of mosquitoes in that place ("mosquito" being a code word for "Muslims").

Regula: Mosquitoes? *Pauses, while the meaning of the statement sinks in.* But still, sarangi is still played there quite a bit, no?

Bhagvan: Well, people play there with courtesan singers. But there aren't any good players there. We played with male singers, not with courtesans. Our community has left that métier, it has nothing to do with us.

Regula: So with courtesans, did any particular people play, or anyone at all?

Bhagvan: Anyone. Whoever knows the job, only he can play *laughs.*

M. Raza: *Offers a helpful explanation to put our guest at ease.* They had their own special people who played with them.

Bhagvan: Well anyone may play. If *you* know how to play, then you can also play; if I know how to play, I can also play.

M. Raza: Mishraji, (*M. Raza is careful to use the appropriate Hindi honorific suffix for a Hindu name*) you see, some things are considered bad in society. Like if I go there and play, if I am fond of playing, then people think ill of me. Is it true or not?

Bhagvan: Absolutely.

M. Raza: Living in Indian society, if I go there and play ... if I sit with you, then it is a private concert and people won't talk.

Bhagvan: No they won't talk, but if you go to a courtesan's salon, they will talk. *He chuckles.*

M. Raza: I think that previously some of the courtesan's own people ...

Bhagvan: Their own fathers and brothers mostly stayed there. I have also heard this.

M. Raza: This is also my opinion, that their own fathers and brothers, they did all those jobs, this sarangi playing and other things. This is it. People from decent families did not go there.

Regula: Well, as an employment they could do it, if they could not get any job.

Bhagvan:　　　If they could not get a job, then … brother, for how long did I not have a job? I lived in Calcutta, and all I did was 'tuition.' I used to do tuitions all day.

M. Raza:　　　In tuition you can teach anybody.

Bhagvan:　　　Anyone who wants to learn from me, during the day, I can teach anyone, if I have free time. You agree that once I get free from the radio, after that I can teach anyone. Who is there to stop me? This is how I was doing my tuitions in Calcutta.

Regula:　　　You taught singing?

Bhagvan:　　　No. There, tuitions are like this: someone is singing, you play with them. Or someone is playing the tabla, and you play the *lehra* (metric tune) with him. There are so many from Bengali families who learn dancing: you provide lehra for them. That is the way tuition is there. So you do it for half an hour in some places, for an hour in others. That is how I did my tuitions.

Regula:　　　But earlier, didn't there used to be a bantering, even teasing between singer and sarangi player: he presents a *tan*, then the sarangi plays the same thing, or something different.

Bhagvan:　　　That we do even now! *Bhayi* (literally "brother"), it was like this: the singers of earlier times, in the *mujra* (courtesan recitals), singing with the sarangi was bliss for them. Now some sarangi players have come up who climb on top of the singer to show their mettle. The singer would go to the sa (1), and they'd go farther up the scale, to the *rikhab* (2), the *gandhar* (3). What happened then is the singers did not like this; that's why they stopped using the sarangi. So now many singers don't use sarangi accompaniment.

　　　　　The second point is that the singer (*ganewala*) will get 5000 rupees for a performance, and for the sarangi even 500 is too much. So I refuse to play in a lot of 'programs.' Look, you are giving the singer 5000, at least give me 500! Because it is I who will provide the singer with melodic support; the tabla player won't be doing it! The tabla player just plays *tirakita dhin* (metric syllables); he just marks the rhythmic cycle. Yet they pay him more.

Regula:　　　Was it any different earlier?

Bhagvan: With male singers, it was the same from the beginning: he gets his fee, while sarangi players do their own negotiating. Whatever the sarangi player negotiates, that's what he will get. Right here, so many programs have come up, but I have turned them down. I have said, "Brother, I won't play for that amount; you can pick up anyone else. You give me this much, then I will play."

Regula: Were they prepared to give you more?

Bhagvan: No they weren't. If they really need you, they will give more.

Regula: So then, is this why the sarangi is dying out?

Bhagvan: That is why it is dying out! Bhayi, who will teach his children sarangi? You give the singer 5000 and it is a burden on you to give me 500? So why should I impose the distress on my son that when he misses reproducing just one phrase of the singer, the singer will criticize him publicly: "The sarangi couldn't do the job." Well, singers say these things! Then, why should I teach him sarangi only for him always to play tagging behind a singer? Why should I not teach him an instrument that he can play alone before an audience?

Launching Six Sons in Music

Regula: Absolutely. But you did teach two of your children sarangi.

Bhagvan: Yes, I taught them myself. But I have six boys. Two of them I taught sarangi, two of them tabla, and the last two I will teach something different. At this time they are still studying, all of them. My oldest son is Kishore. I taught him the tabla. When he started to play better than me, I entrusted him to Sharda (Sahai) Maharaj, who is in England now. He is related to me, like a brother. I entrusted my son to him in discipleship. His house is in Benares. My son used to go there and learn.

I already got one boy to pick up the violin; so now he is playing the violin. And for the other, I am still thinking what to teach him. Whatever strikes my fancy, that's what I will teach him. But it won't be sarangi.

Regula: So these boys, Santosh Kumar and Vinod Kumar: I noticed that their style of playing is a little different.

Bhagvan: Look, I taught them in a particular way. After that, they do their practice (*riyaz*). I have taught them how to do it in my way. Then they are responsible for their styles in their careers. I taught them in the exact manner in which I play. Now they create the art in their fashion.

Regula: So you got your sons an education too.

Bhagvan: Yes. My boys are all B.A. or Inter (intermediate). Bhayi, what are my earnings for? If I don't educate my children, then my earnings go wasted *laughs*. That is what I earn for.

Regula: Well, I have noted that most children often do not learn from their father, in the beginning, because the father is working, playing somewhere else.

Bhagvan: When I lived in Delhi, my eldest boy, Santosh, played on a sarangi this small. *Gestures the length of a foot.* That sarangi is still there. It was in our family, and it sounded very well. So he went to Delhi with his mother. That sarangi of his impressed whoever heard it; it was very beautiful. First of all, such a small sarangi, but sounding very loud, and a small boy too (*laughs*)! He had great enthusiasm to play the sarangi, right from childhood. I said, let him play. So my elder brother taught him. I started teaching him once he came to Lucknow. I still teach him now. When he needs something, then he sits down with me and I tell him.

Regula: Yes, he told me, you practice together.

Bhagvan: Do I ever practice? See my hand; there is no mark of practicing anywhere. I only teach him. Where do I have time to practice? At the radio I get no time for practicing. Like today, I left the radio only at 2:30. At 3 o'clock I ate lunch; after that it was coming to your house. And then I have to go there (to his wealthy student's house). So how can I practice? Sometimes, when I am in the mood, I sit down for an hour or half an hour and play.

Regula: But your playing is in top shape. You did your practicing earlier?

Bhagvan: Yes, there was a time when I practiced for 14 hours a day. Now I don't practice. That same practice is still working for me. *Drinks tea as snacks are being offered.*

The Training of Bhagvan Das: A Family Model

Regula: So how did you yourself learn the sarangi?

Bhagvan: My father used to play the sarangi. So he placed my hand on the instrument.

Regula: Was your father your teacher?

Bhagvan: Yes, he taught me how to place my (left) hand. He lived in Benares. So he got my hand set on the sarangi. Then, after that, I became the disciple of Bare Ramdas Ji. He was like my grandfather. He sang very well; that is where I started my accompanying, with his singing. Along with that I did my practice. Then two years later he passed away. After that I, did a bit with Gopal Ji (Gopal Misra). He was related to me through marriage. So he also taught me a bit. After that, my elder brother, Narayan Das Ji, has been teaching me; he still guides me. We are three brothers. Narayan Das Ji is in Benares, I in Lucknow, and one brother is in England. He plays the tabla. He has been inviting me to visit.

Regula: Do go; people there like the sarangi too.

Bhagvan: They may like it, but I have to get there first *laughs*! For now I am still stuck here, and he is hanging around there *laughs again*. Brother, if I go abroad, then who will get these boys ahead? Yes, it's a very great responsibility. Bhayi, who will get the children launched? Someone had to be there to get Santosh to Lucknow (where he found employment). And now the same thing has to be done for the younger boy who plays sarangi. Only the oldest one is employed, the others have not yet got any jobs. Once they are all employed, then I myself won't need to keep working at the radio. Then I can live anywhere. Also, my elder brother has become very old and he hardly plays. That is why if I also leave, then who will look after all of the children and their music?

Regula: You mean you also look after his house.

Bhagvan: We all live jointly, in Benares. Everyone, lives together in a joint family, all three brothers. *His tone is astonished, as this is clearly a matter of course.* The children also all live there. Only Santosh stays with me here in Lucknow, and his wife and his two children.

Building the Benares Gharana

Regula: So you told me your father set your hand. After that, you started to accompany. But before that, your fingers have to learn the notes. How is that taught? Suppose you are a child, what is taught first?

Bhagvan: At first, they get you to practice sargam (*sargam ka riyaz karvate hain*) using all the notes: sa re ga ma pa dha ni sa. They put the bow on the sarangi and teach him. But first of all, they teach how to sit. Then comes the method (*hisab*) of holding the bow in your hand and drawing it across the string. *He draws a smooth bow across the open string.*

M. Raza: *Shouts to curious children peeping in through the open French doors:* Get away from here, get lost. *Some kid shouts back.*

Regula: I see that your bow stick is tilted downward.

Bhagvan: This way all the hair touches the string, and that way half do, half don't. *He continues playing to show Regula.* That is why we have been taught this way. *Plays again.* Okay, now many people, like the khansahibs, break off their bow strokes. *Demonstrates short bows but moving faster, hence louder and more intense.* But the way we draw the sound will create ease, a relaxed feeling. Also, their finger trembles; you please take note of any khansahib's playing. *Demonstrates vibrato on pa (5).* Our tone *sur* does not tremble. *Demonstrates smooth tone, also on pa.* Should a tone tremble? Brother, in classical music it certainly does not tremble. It only does so in light music. Our tone stays firmly on one pitch, and these people's hand, I don't know why they make it tremble. Bhayi, it must sound good to them; to me it does not sound good.

Regula: At first, which raga will you use for teaching: raga *yaman*, or also *bilaval*, as in the Bhatkhande College?

Bhagvan: No. Ragas will be taught according to the time of day. If a child is taught early in the morning, then what raga will you decide to teach him? Will you teach him yaman, (an evening raga)? Or will you teach him bilaval? Yes, it's a daytime raga, but still, at seven in the morning, you can't teach it. *Bhairav*, that's what we will teach. If I taught at 9 or 10 o'clock, then I would teach bilaval. If I taught in the evening, then I would teach *puriya dhanashri*. And if I taught at 8, 9 at night, or at 10 o'clock, then I would teach yaman.

Regula: So you would teach that many ragas at one time?

Bhagvan: No, I will teach one raga. But at whatever time—it won't be that I tell all the ragas in one day. I teach today, then you practice this. Some days later, if this one gets to sound good, then at a different time I take a second raga: That raga you play in the morning, this raga you can play at this time. This is the way we teach. It can't be that all the ragas are taught at the same time. Well, the person I told you about earlier (his student Omkar, the jeweler), so far I have only started to teach him puriya dhanashri. I reach there in the evening. At first, I used to go in the morning; then I had started him on bhairon (bhairav). And when I go there at 5 to 6 in the evening, then I teach *multani*, etc., *bhimpalasi*, etc. Even if I have to provide a lehra (a cyclical tune to accompany tabla), I will choose a raga that fits that particular time, not another time. *He strikes up raga pradip, an afternoon raga, to exemplify the point—it being afternoon.*

Regula: Ah, pradip. *Starts to tune her strings to his instrument and wonders.* When there is no time to tune the sarangi, do you sometimes put a cloth across the (37) sympathetic strings to dampen them so that they don't give false resonance?

Bhagvan: I never do that. Others may do it, but when in the radio people do this to me, saying "just play like this" (without tuning), then I say, "brother, I won't play." If you give me time to tune, then I can play; otherwise, I don't play an out-of-tune sarangi. If my instrument does not sound good even to my ear, then how can it sound good to others?

Regula: Please show me how you do practice sequences (*palte*).

Bhagvan: *Plays sa re ga (1 2 3), re ga ma (2 3 4), sa re ga (1 2 3), re ga ma (2 3 4), ga ma pa (3 4 5), all with separate bow strokes, and very fast.*

Regula: The way you use your bow is like the Western detaché style (middle of bow, downbow starts), unlike other sarangi players I have seen (starting near the tip of bow, with upbow starts).

Bhagvan: See. *He repeats it again, showing virtuosity.*

Regula: I have not seen this rapid (detaché) bowing much among sarangi players.

Bhagvan: And see this. *Now he plays tremolo.* Our Gopal Ji in Benares (Gopal Misra), his playing was extremely virtuosic, and he was my guruji. His principle was: "Son, as much as your tan (legato bowing) must be perfect, your sargam (separated bowing) must be equally perfect. Every singer sings tan (legato), but suppose a singer starts singing sargam (syllabic passages), what will you do then?" If a fast-paced *tarana* starts, or a *palta* (sequence) is turned into a fast turn, then what will I do? At that point, I would have to stop and put down my sarangi! Unless I have practiced both these bowing styles.

Regula: Some people just play what the singer sings in one long bow, like a tan.

Bhagvan: Like a tan? The singer is singing separate syllables and I should play it legato, will that sound good *laughs*?

Regula: No, but it does happen. I have seen it.

Bhagvan: Yes, you've seen it correctly; I've seen it too.

Regula: Could you show the trembling style once more, for the recording, even though you don't do it for real?

Bhagvan: No. What I don't do—why should you look at what I don't do? What I do, that's what you should look at. Besides, to bring anyone's flaw to light is not a good thing, in my understanding.

Conclusion

Bhagvan: Enough?

Regula: Enough. Thank you.

Bhagvan: *Pauses, bows, and then begins to pack his instrument after a quick salutation toward the small medallion of Goddess Sarasvati that is affixed above the fingerboard of his instrument.*

Regula: *Intrigued:* What did you just do—this gesture, what does it mean?

Bhagvan: This means, this is my art; it is Sarasvati. It is because of her blessing that I have become well known. So first I offer her …

M. Raza: *Showing familiarity with Hindu ritual:* Offering, your *pranam* (salutation).

Regula: Show me again how you do it, please.

Bhagvan: *Laughs.* This is not something for showing to anyone *laughs again.* I am offering a salutation to my art. What should I be showing this to the world for *laughs more*?

Regula: This is not the world; it is only me. I like this a lot.

Having packed the instrument, Bhagvan lights a cigarette. I quickly find an ashtray.

M. Raza/Regula: *Both realizing their faux pas:* Why did you not say so before, we would have ordered cigarettes.

Bhagvan: Well, the conversation had started; otherwise, after tea, I don't start anything without first having a cigarette.

M. Raza: Well, if you had only said so. Which one do you smoke?

Rehan quickly goes to bring a packet of his favorite brand, and our meeting is over. An envelope had already been presented with the agreed reward enclosed.

SANTOSH KUMAR MISHRA: ACCOMPLISHED VIRTUOSO

Introducing Santosh Kumar

Santosh Kumar Mishra is the most virtuosic (tayyar) young sarangi player I have encountered during my studies. He clearly has had years of intense technical training and has now emerged as a young artist of note. In Western shop talk, he "gets around" on the instrument and has the "chops" to produce improvisational patterns of considerable speed and complexity. A particular strength of Benares players is their rapid-fire passages played with separate bow strokes (sargam), made famous by the late Pandit Gopal Mishra, elder brother of Hanuman Prasad Mishra (see Chapter 10). These "chops" also enable him to embellish song melodies with rapid turns, mordents, and slides (mind).

Figure 23 Santosh Kumar plays tappa, Bhatkhande College, Lucknow, 1984.

*I first encountered Santosh Kumar through the then-principal of Bhat-
khande College, S.S. Awasthi, who was introducing me to the college and its
musicians while also testing my knowledge, particularly of Hindu musical
culture. He highly recommended Santosh Kumar and then had him called
to his office so that I could interview him. This attractive young man was
clearly the special protégé of the principal, who playfully asked him to issue
instruments to accompanists over the head of the senior sarangi player, K.K.
Mishra. He was then already known as a young player who is in top shape,
though at the college he principally accompanied dance and tabla classes.
But he also received invitations to accompany touring singers. He generously
agreed to let me record his playing informally, since there was no time to
arrange a proper concert.*

*The performance took place in an empty classroom, followed by the con-
versation presented here. When he showed me his instrument, I noticed an
image of Goddess Sarasvati affixed above the strings, something I had seen
only on Pandit Ram Narayan's sarangi when I studied with him. "Yes, I have
received blessings from Panditji," Santosh told me proudly. It turned out that
he, too, had once had the opportunity to play for Ram Narayan, who praised
him and suggested an adjustment to his instrument. Santosh also told me
that he listened to Ram Narayan's recordings, clearly taking inspiration from
this most famous Hindu sarangi player. However, this in no way affected his
total personal and musical identification with his family, his gharana, or his
home city of Benares.*

*Santosh Kumar has since moved back to Benares to become the first
sarangi player ever employed at Benares Hindu University (BHU), and he is
now a member of one of the country's premier music departments. In Lucknow, his brother Vinod has inherited his position at Bhatkhande College.*

Santosh Kumar Mishra—Triumph of the Joint Family Model[2]

*After his impressive performance, Santosh moved into our conversation in
a confident and professional way, conveying the certainty and support of a
strong professional family environment. His language as well as his message
conveyed a total respect for his elders (using the suffix "ji" for respect), who
remain his teachers, regardless of his own high standard of accomplishment.
Above all, Santosh speaks always as a member of a group that is both musical and familial: his guru brothers are also his real brothers; his gurus are his
father, his father's brother, and other relatives of his father's or grandfather's
generation; and even other musical partners in Benares are relatives in the
widest sense of belonging to the hereditary kathak community of Mishras.
The core of this group identity is the extended family, extended not only in
membership, but also in extending beyond the boundary of the household*

to include members who reside elsewhere. For master musicians, who must earn their living away from home, their extended family provides the necessary continuity to maintain the model of musical training that produces the next generation of master musicians.

Learning to Sing God's Name

Regula: Your father trained you, but he was away a lot. So when did you start learning sarangi?

Santosh: When I was eight. At that time, our *tauji* (senior uncle, i.e., father's elder brother) instructed all of us in singing. So the first four to five years, I learned to sing: classical—the way one learns from the beginning. First the scale, then more and more difficult sequence patterns up and down the scale. *Demonstrates, using sargam, i.e., using note names or solfège.* We usually practiced in the evenings, and so we mostly sang in the scale of raga yaman (an evening raga with a raised fourth scale degree—ma), but it could be done in any raga scale. After that, I was given instruction on the sarangi.

   We all learned this one composition in puriya dhanashri (another evening raga).

Santosh intones the raga with notation syllables: pa pa ma ga ma re ga ma ga re sa ni re ga ma pa dha sa (5 5 4 3 4 2 3 4 3 2 1 7 2 3 4 5 6 1), then sings the song in an attractively lyrical voice and a style of devotional simplicity.

Sumiran karo man Ram nam ko,[3]
Aur nahin jag koi kam ko,
Jo chahta man ichcha puran,
Ramdas bhajo Radhe Shyam ko,
Sumiran karo man Ram nam ko,

Remember the name of Rama (an incarnation of Krishna),
Nothing else in the world is more important,
Your heart's desires will come true,
Keep reciting Radha, Shyam, says Ramdas,
Remember the name of Rama,

Santosh: Two of my brothers played the tabla: an older and a younger brother. We would practice together. When I practiced, they would play the tabla. And then when they practiced, I would give the basic beat pattern (*theka*) on the tabla. I learned these just by listening to the others practice.

Regula: That means that all the brothers have some basic knowledge of singing as well as tabla playing?

Santosh: Yes, everyone knows the tabla and singing. Only two brothers know the sarangi. One is younger than me. We are six brothers in all. The oldest brother plays the tabla. I am next on the sarangi; the one after me plays the tabla again. The one after that, Vinod, plays the sarangi. The two youngest brothers are learning the violin.

Regula: So tell us, how was the decision made that you would play the sarangi? Did you decide, or your father, or your senior uncle (*tauji*), or your grandfather?

Santosh: I never had a chance even to see my grandfather; he passed away before I was born. But sarangi playing has been in our family for three generations. My grandfather, Shri Madhav Prasad Mishra, used to play it. After that, my senior uncle, Pandit Narayan Misra, and my father, Pandit Bhagvan Das Mishra became sarangi players. Now my brother Vinod and I play it.

My starting the sarangi happened when I was learning to sing…. We had a very small sarangi in our home, about a foot long. As children, we treated it like a toy. It had all the right strings fixed on it. I started playing on it for fun. Almost in play. When our father saw that I was keen on it, he gradually guided me toward it. He put marks on the fingerboard where I was to place my fingers. As he saw my interest increase, he gradually began to teach me. He taught me how to hold the bow and then how to position the left hand and fingers.

Regula: So you press the base of your fingernails against the strings?

Santosh: No, I press and slide with the finger (just below the nail). My father's hand position and fingering is the same. He and my uncle showed me how to place my fingers on the instrument in this very way. Everyone in our place plays like this. *He demonstrates and shows me his left fingers, marked with deep calloused grooves.*

Regula: I have to take a photograph of your hand!

Santosh: *Laughs while Regula takes the photo.*

Regula: And both your father and you play so fabulously! I cannot imagine how you slide so fast on your skin. Doesn't it hurt? I use my nails to play and hate to think how quickly your skin would get rubbed off.

Santosh: As you practice, your skin gets hard. Then you can play for a long stretch and it won't hurt. But when you practice excessively, the calluses get embedded deeper into your skin. That is when it hurts, and you can feel it while playing.

Regula: So when you were being taught by your tauji, would you practice in the early morning?

Santosh: When I began, my tauji would have to come and wake me up, because we were just kids and used to sleeping late. If we did not practice waking up early, we would never get accustomed to it. Then after a few days of being woken up, we got into the habit. So we would wake up promptly at 5 o'clock.

  We all sat together and practiced for three to four hours. First came singing and then playing the sarangi. We all played the same raga. If I was working on a sequential pattern (*palta*), the others would also play or else sing that pattern. The tabla player would give the beat, either in a rhythmic cycle (*tala*) or just with a practice pattern like "*dha tirakita, dha tirakita*" (verbal drum stroke syllables). Since we all practiced together, we also concentrated because we were enjoying it.

  And we were egged on by mutual competition: whether I could play better than he or he could sing better than I.... We would place bets as to who would last the longest. If someone broke off first or stopped while singing, our elder father (*bare bap*, i.e., father's brother) would also hit us, with the bow of his sarangi. But only if we made mistakes. No music can be learnt without beatings.

Regula: In Delhi I have heard from a musician who gave up the sarangi because his older brother hit him so hard that the bow broke.

Santosh: *Chuckles:* No, we did not get hit that way. If you hit a child that much, there can be grave consequences. We were beaten only to correct a wrong note.

After paltas (sequential patterns), we were taught the *asthai-antaras* (two-part song compositions in different ragas), to set them into our memory. My senior uncle (*taoji*) was a really good singer. His tone and intonation (sur) were excellent. Even now he sings beautifully. First he would demonstrate by playing and then, if we did not understand, he would sing naming the notes (*sargam*). Then he taught us how the notes fit with the words of the text.

Regula: So you would always know the words to the song as well as how to play the notes! We in the West do not sing if we are instrumentalists. My cello teacher never opened his mouth to sing; he would demonstrate by playing. Then I would play.

Santosh: We believe that it is better to teach by singing than by playing. It is easier to pick up music that way. The student can really understand quickly if you sing. After singing a passage, you can place the fingers on the string and show them how to play it on the instrument. Singing really imprints the music into the brain of the student. For example, when we were taught our first song in raga bhairav, we learned to sing the tune with note names (*sargam*), and then with the song text.

He sings both versions. intoning the two opening lines of the song, with notation syllables:

pa ma pa ga ma re sa sa re ga ma dha pa
ma pa dha ni dha pa pa dha pa ga ma re sa

Then he sings the song, with attractive vocal embellishments:

Dhan dhan murat Krishna Murari,
Sura chara Girdhaari,
tava sundar lage ati pyari,
Bansidhar man mohan suhave,
Ban ban jaun more man bhave,
Sab Ras gyan bichari.

Loud praise be to the countenance of Krishna,
My mind is full of Girdhari (Krishna),
You are most beautiful and most beloved,
My heart belongs to the flute player (Krishna) and his charms,

I will sacrifice myself for you,
Sab Ras (poet's signature) is your humble devotee.

Regula: *Wah wah* (bravo)! This is really good. It is not easy, though. And I notice that the songs you have sung so far have been devotional or religious; all their words refer to Krishanji (Krishna). Were they commonly used for practice?

Santosh: Yes, these songs are dedicated to the Gods. They are for the morning hour when one is supposed to invoke the name of God. Like this song we were taught in *ahir bhairav*; it too contains the name of God. *He sings:*

Utho Gopaal, utho Gopaal.
Ban ki chiraiyan bolan lagi.
Dwar khade sab karat pukar.

Wake up, young Krishna, wake up, young Krishna.
The birds in the forest have started to sing.
Everybody is at your doorstep calling for you.

There are some songs for the evening, too. This would ensure that we took the name of God morning and evening. All these are very old compositions. But we also learned to compose a new setting for a devotional song (*bhajan*) on the spot. You create the *mukhra* (refrain) for the first line, and the two complementary parts (asthayi, antara) for each verse, and you are ready to play the song right then. But that's after a lot of study. Depending on how hard a student works, it can take as long as ten years just to learn *khayal* (the basic genre); I took around two to three years.

Regula: So you learned fast. Did your brother pick it up so soon too?

Santosh: Yes. Our senior uncle taught children of the neighborhood to sing khayal and *thumri*, etc. He does this even now. He taught the children to sing while playing on the sarangi. The children sang, and we played along with them on the sarangi, as accompanists. So our uncle would play and we would play with him. This gave us a very clear idea on how accompaniment is done. He would make up his own tunes and challenge us to play them with him as a practice.

Regula: So you learned music through playing with others and accompaniment. Would all this have been possible if you did not have such a large joint family? And if you did not all work together?

Santosh: Then we would have to go to other musicians' houses. For example, we would have to search for a khayal singer to practice accompaniment. Or else look for a thumri singer.

Once we mastered thumri, we were in the market and started out on our own. This gave us an opportunity to spend productive time in the company of many musicians. Gradually, we refined our ideas about how to accompany. For example, when Sulochnaji[4] came here about a couple of years ago for the Bhatkhande Birthday Jubilee, I provided the accompaniment for her singing. I have accompanied many musicians since coming to Lucknow: Savitaji, Tambeji. And when Hafiz Khan Sahib came here, I played with him too.[5]

Regula: I have heard both Sulochnaji and Savitaji. And I recently spoke with Hafiz Khan.

Santosh: He was very happy with my playing and called me to two other programs. If you meet him, you can ask him about me. He is our elder (*buzurg*). We need all blessings we can get from revered people like him.

Regula: Your sound is very resonant. When did you learn tuning all those 37 resonating strings on the sarangi?

Santosh: Initially, our elders would tune them for us. After we had attained a full knowledge of intonation and could distinguish one note from another, we were taught how to tune the instrument, for instance, how to tune the gamut of all the notes above a particular ground note (sur). This enables us to play any raga, no matter what modal scale it uses. If we tune to only one particular modal scale, we will have to retune it when we are accompanying someone else. If we keep that tuning fixed, we don't have to tune the strings again and again, because all 12 (semi)tones are included in the tuning. So we just follow the model that we were instructed in.

Practicing for a Lifetime

Regula: Do you ever play with your father?

Santosh: Yes. Every day after finishing with my college work here, I go home and practice with him. He sits to play every night. I practice together with him at night, and by myself every morning. He goes on duty daily in the mornings.

Regula: So you get double practice. How do you practice at night?

Santosh: Usually with khayal. He teaches me how to play solo.

Regula: Have you ever performed *jugalbandi* (interactive duo) between the two of you?

Santosh: No, how can I have a jugalbandi with him? Jugalbandi is possible only if there is someone young or my peer, not my father and teacher. I accompany him as he plays. I follow behind (note by note) as he practices.

For myself, I practice in the mornings, with a tabla accompanist. He comes every morning, and I help him with his practice. He lives right next door to our house. He comes every day and can manage a basic 16-beat cycle (*tintal*). He doesn't know more than that. I usually start with a raga improvisation (alap) in the morning. For example, the bhairav mode (*that*) or maybe even some composition (*bandish*) based on that raga. I may practice a few khayal songs and then some sequential patterns (palta). As I come to a close of the session, I practice in a light classical style like thumri.

But my father does not need such a regimen. He has had a lifetime of palta and all that (*laughs*). The age for practicing is over for him. I try to learn from his vast experience.

Regula: I would really like to hear a practice session of yours. In the West we have our own methods of practice and rehearsal, but I can see that this is a very different way of learning and practicing that has awesome results.

Santosh: I just follow the model!

MR. OMKAR: THE PATRON-DISCIPLE

Introducing Mr. Omkar

Mr. Omkar is a wealthy jeweler and connoisseur of music. In addition to a comparatively opulent villa, his compound also houses a temple; Mr. Omkar had it built for his wife. In the music room off the front veranda is where Mr. Omkar sits, playing his fretted, bowed dilruba. Bhagvan Das sits to his right and at a right angle, playing the sarangi. I join them at the invitation of Bhagvan Das, who wanted me to meet him at the house of his most out-standing amateur student, so that I could see what Bhagvan Das has taught him. An amiable and sophisticated host, Omkar inserts English phrases into our Hindi conversation, communicating to me his fluency in that language. Omkar is an accomplished player who knows ragas. In fact, according to Bhagvan Das, Omkar knows so much that he can give an audition at All India Radio; Bhagvan Das just hasn't asked him to do so yet. Bhagvan Das is comfortable in his dual role as guru of a student who is also his patron. He easily enacts his musical authority together with social subordination, observing a self-effacing reticence as a general stance. My visit gives him the chance to impress his wealthy patron with his new Western student and vice versa, thereby raising his own stature.

Figure 24 Bhagvan Das guiding Omkar on dilruba, Omkar's house, Lucknow, 1984.

An Evening Session at the Villa[6]

As I had promised Bhagvan Das that afternoon, I made my way to the pleasant new neighborhood near the Gomti river where Omkar has built his villa. I follow the soft sounds of bowed strings through the garden and suddenly find myself in front of the wide-open door of a veranda where Omkar and Bhagvan Das are immersed in their music. Bhagvan Das looks up briefly; I enter and quietly sit down facing Omkar. They are playing alap and some passage work in raga jaijaivanti. Bhagvan Das is leading; Omkar follows him, echoing the same phrases in an intimately expressive musical conversation. Bhagvan Das is visibly pleased with my visit and has surprised me by choosing to play my favorite raga, Jaijaivanti.

Regula: How come you played Jaijaivanti; it's my favorite raga *laughs.*

Bhagvan: That is why!

Omkar: *Addressing his guru:* Is this why you played it? Jaijaivanti, you knew that?

Bhagvan: *Nods, indicating that he must have heard Regula state her preference on a radio program a few days earlier.*

Omkar: I see! After months, we have played jaijaivanti today!

Bhagvan: *Resumes the raga, now in a light classical thumri style, using more ornamentation. Omkar plays after him, and at the end Bhagvan Das lets him play alone.*

Regula: *To Omkar:* You play very well.

Bhagvan: *Chuckles.*

Omkar: One or one and a half hours, every day, in the morning, with Pandit Sahib. *Adapting his speech to Regula's use of Urdu, he adds the culturally Muslim honorific "sahib" to the Hindu title "pandit," rather than the suffix "ji" appropriate to Hindu names (Pandit-ji).*

Regula: *Noticing the picture of a sarod player:* Ah, a famous sarod player!

Omkar: I played the sitar, but when I heard him play sarod, I liked sarod very much, so I said this, too, is a good instrument. Then I switched to sarod. So I learned sarod too. But after a while I got tired of it, that "dum dum dum dum"—is this (strumming) anything nice? So I turned to this bowed instrument (*esraj*). I heard it first from a goldsmith of mine, Mr. Handa, he was from Panjab. He came down from Panjab after the partition of India and all that. I myself "belong" to Shahjahanpur.

Bhagvan: *Explains softly:* Near Bareilly.

Omkar: And there he played at night one day, after dinner. Then I thought, this is a very good instrument, it has very good "continuity." So I said, let me study this one. Since then I have played this. I had two or three sitars and *tanpuras*. I gave all of them to the music college; now they are in bad shape—not taken care of. They were of superior quality. I had one very fine sarod; it was an instrument from the hand of Allauddin Khan Sahib, Maiharwale, the father of Ali Akbar Khan, guru of Ravi Shankarji, and his father-in-law.

Regula: Yes, his daughter played too.

Omkar: Annapurna. He was a very great man—not a Hindu— very fine (*barhia*).

Regula: So do you play tans (passage work) as well?

Omkar: I play a few, but can't do much; on this instrument, slides (*mindkari*) are played most of all.

Regula: But you can't do slides like on the sitar, pulling the string sideways.

Omkar: No, no, we slide along the string, the same way as on the sarangi. *Demonstrates.* This instrument has thin (wire) strings, not thick ones (of gut) like the sarangi.

A servant offers soft drinks to Omkar and me; Omkar refuses and takes a betel leaf (pan) instead. He demonstrates more slides, intoning raga megh (a raga for the rainy season).

Bhagvan: *Starts playing along and soon starts leading.*

Regula: Now you are playing for the rainy season (*barsat*) (which has in fact just started).

Omkar: Raga megh.

Both play, first in slow improvisation (alap) then adding a pulse with separate bow strokes (jor). In the end, Omkar falls behind and Bhagvan Das continues solo.

Omkar: *Interrupts:* There is someone from Madras, "I don't know his name and all that." He plays the violin—I have heard this, not seen it—for the last four or five years he has been playing, practicing, this same rag on the violin; he keeps at this—well, it's a 'historical fact' that playing megh will make it rain.

Regula: It must have rained since then.

Omkar: I don't know; he is still working at it.

Bhagvan/Regula: *Laughter.*

Omkar: Well, it is a 'historical fact' that when Tansen[7] played raga *dipak* (a raga to produce fire) and lamps started burning, then there was trouble; five, six hundred years ago, so many have written it, so that it can't be wrong. Then there was fire everywhere and he sang megh to make it rain to extinguish it. So that fellow from Madras is practicing megh. Let us hope so; otherwise he may do it … but it is a fact.

Bhagvan: *To Regula:* Play a little bit for him.

Regula: Certainly, if you say so.

After playing a bit, the visit becomes social. Omkar shows me his house and the newly built white temple in his compound, and I meet Omkar's wife. After this he offers scotch and requests that I bring him fancy wine glasses from Paris. Bhagvan Das is comfortably included, but stays in the background. Later he tells me that Omkar knows so much that he could give an audition at All India Radio, though he hasn't initiated the process yet.

ARCHANA YADAV: BREAKING THE GENDER BARRIER

Introducing Archana

Open and trusting, tuned into tradition but not fettered by it, Archana Yadav is a remarkable young musician. Trained by a master, she is perhaps the first woman to find professional employment as a sarangi player. Originally from Benares, she does not come from a hereditary background but was given early training in classical dance (kathak) as well as voice and tabla. She began her training on the sarangi in 1984 and at age 16 had a chance to participate in the Sarangi Mela, a festive assembly of 200 sarangi players invited to Bhopal (capital of Madhya Pradesh State) for performance and discussion (Bharat Bhavan 1989). After school and college education, she obtained a Government of India youth scholarship to continue intensive study with her guru from 1991 to 1994. Soon thereafter she was employed at the Provincial Dance Academy Kathak Kendra, where she provides accompaniment for dance classes.

When revisiting Lucknow in 1992, I heard about Bhagvan Das teaching a female student and sought him out at his residence, since he was now retired from the radio. To my surprise, I found him living in an apartment building very near my family's home. Now retired, he was taking his afternoon rest when I knocked at his door, and he told me to visit in the evening. It turned out that Archana lived with her family in the same building, and had been receiving daily instruction from her guru while she also went to college and

Figure 25 Archana playing for her guru, Archana's home, Lucknow, 1992.

did housework. Archana was strikingly outgoing and articulate, and so was her mother, who had two graduate degrees and worked as a government social worker. Intensely proactive in furthering her children's education, she came to visit me with a gift, brought me Archana's music certificates, and appealed for my support for her career.

When we met in 1992, Archana was already married, and by 1997 Bhagvan Das played grandfather to her little boy, playfully teaching him sarangi. Since then, she has moved into her own house with her journalist husband, and her son concentrates on his schooling, having left the sarangi behind. Her mother is no more, and Bhagvan Das has returned to his home in Benares.

Archana and Her Guru[8]

I find my way up the narrow stairs and into the dark hallway when Shirish, Archana's younger brother, meets us, and we enter the family's one-room apartment. The room is dominated by the guru, Bhagvan Das, who reclines against the wall smoking a cigarette. He is pleased to have our visit, especially because Saleem has come to meet him for the first time. I want to reconnect with Bhagvan Das as well as learn about Archana and his teaching her. I also ask permission to make a video recording of her playing. While Archana makes sure that we are comfortably seated on the floor covered with white sheets, her mother comes in to greet us and offer tea. Now Archana sits down at a right angle to Bhagvan Das, so that she can face the video camera, and the recording begins. Archana feels insecure and wants her guru to play along with her. First he plays a passage while Archana plays it after him. Then they play together, and eventually he stops playing and she

Figure 26 Archana, Saleem Qureshi, and Bhagvan Das, Archana's home, Lucknow, 1992.

continues on her own. The atmosphere is relaxed and familylike: Archana calls Bhagvan Das "uncle" (chacha, i.e., father's brother), and he treats her like a daughter.

Focus on Performance

Regula: *Addressing Bhagvan Das after Archana puts her bow down:* Wow. That was wonderful. You have taught her a lot in these years.

Bhagvan: She played the entire song well, didn't she?

Archana: No ... My hands went absolutely cold. Wouldn't you be, playing in front of someone else?

Regula: What is there to be scared of when you are in the presence of your guruji?

Archana: *Giggles.*

Regula: *To Bhagvan Das:* I notice that you have molded her completely in your own style. Where to place the finger, and which finger to place on which note. Totally.

Bhagvan: Yes, it is my way of playing.

Regula: Do you still play? Or do you just teach? Do you perform at programs?

Bhagvan: I perform at programs. And I play by myself an hour, a couple of hours every day. Alone. I played till two, then ate and had just retired for a rest when you came yesterday. At that time I never expect anyone. But I can expect you in the evenings. From 8 till 10:30.

Archana: That is the time we practice every day.

Bhagvan: I teach her in the evenings. And mornings are for my practice.

Archana: Now I have even got a human resources scholarship: the Young Workers and Culture Department Scholarship. Under it, I am getting 600 rupees a month ($20 at the time). The program is for two years, and I have got the opportunity to learn under him. It began in September 1991. So I got some inspiration for *riyaz* (practicing). Due to this support, I felt like going ahead with my lessons. And then at the big Sarangi Mela in Bhopal (the first great reunion/convention of sarangi players) I received so much love.

Regula: So people appreciated your music?

Archana: Oh yes! As if they have found something incredible! I really liked that. I really enjoyed myself there. I cannot forget those days. I am in touch with so many musicians I met there: in contact by letters, etc.

And Uncle Bhagvan Das ji got an award last year too. From the Uttar Pradesh government. An Academy Award. The governor felicitated him with the gift of a shawl. A plaque and money too. Quite a good sum of money. But the respect gained was the most important thing. At the Academy Samman Samaroh, held at the 25th-year celebration of the Uttar Pradesh Academy.

Bhagvan: And there was a solo performance at the academy, for an hour and a quarter.

Regula: *Excited:* Where did they hold it?

Archana: Here at the Uttar Pradesh Sangeet Natak Academy. Next to the Bhatkhande College. They organized a two-hour item for him. There is also a video recording of it. A tape recording too.

Bhagvan: So I play solo. On the radio, the television. At the same time I rest too.

Regula: That's right. You have worked so hard for so long now. So now is the time to relax. Isn't it?

Bhagvan: Even so, I continue with the work. What else is there to do?

Focus on Teaching

Regula: So please tell me if there have been any special problems in teaching Archana. What did you find most difficult? Did you face any difficulty or was everything smooth and easy?

Bhagvan: The main difficulty is that I have to repeatedly explain the same thing to her. Instruct by playing with my hands. Demonstrate again and again the correct way to hold the fingers on the strings. Place it this way, not that way. And if she doesn't get it even then, I have to sing to instruct her.

Regula: And when you sing, she gets to learn the words of the composition as well?

Bhagvan: Yes. If she does not understand the notes that go with the words, I have to tell her by singing the names of the notes (sargam). So that she can grasp them. And the tala, I demonstrate it with my own fingers.

Regula: So you have to instruct again and again. This is the same problem that we face. In our environment, we don't develop a good memory system. We are not accustomed to learning things orally. We are used to writing everything down.

Archana: No, with me the problem is that I used to do kathak dance. So I only had to work with rhythm. In addition, there was no conducive atmosphere at home. And for music, you need the right environment. It is essential. Until and unless you hear the master musicians at least for 10 to 15 years, follow stage shows, attend public performances, you cannot really learn anything yourself.

Regula: That is so true!

Archana: So without the environment ... Now, when Sukhdev was here, Bhagvan Das's youngest son, he used to practice on the violin. So we would have a healthy bit of competition between us. How long can you play? And how long can I last out? It was enjoyable to practice that way. And then there was Pramod Bhai (his son next in age), who played the tabla. So there was a routine and continuity. And then Chacha would instruct us meanwhile. First he would teach us and then we would practice.

But problems can arise when that atmosphere disappears. And then there is no such space at home. Everybody in my house is into studies. And so when I came to him (Bhagvan Das), I would run into trouble trying to understand intonation and rhythm (*sur* and *laya*). Everything seemed new.

Regula: So do your melodies get out of tune (*besura*)?

Bhagvan: Yes, they do. And then I have to explain again. I say, my daughter (*bitiya*), you are getting out of tune. Try to play in tune.

Archana: It feels very difficult. In the beginning I found it very hard. But I couldn't understand. Gradually I began to concentrate on what was being played on his instrument and what sound was emerging out of mine. So when I myself made the effort I felt a little difference. "Chacha, should I go up or down?" Chacha says, "Take it up." So I take it up. Then a little more, then some more. So on and forth, and now I feel I understand the nuances a little bit. I can hear it when my instrument is playing on a different note. When I go off tune, I cry, "Chaccha, I went wrong. Let us do it again." So that is how it is with me. But I am adamant too that until I can master the piece, I won't let it go. I keep on practicing till the right notes emerge, even if that is the only piece I learn that day.

Regula: *Addressing Bhagvan Das:* What about your sons? Don't you have to tell them again and again?

Bhagvan: No. I don't have to instruct them repeatedly because they have been singing. They have received lessons in singing since their childhood.

Regula: So they knew the ragas from the beginning?

Bhagvan: No, I have to instruct them in the ragas.

Regula: What about memorizing?

Bhagvan: Well, they have learnt to sing, so if I tell them something a couple of times, they grasp it.

Archana: Because their ears are accustomed to catch the sur.

Regula: That is true.

Archana: Since childhood, they have been listening to music. For example, Santosh Bhaiyya tells his son to start a bhajan. So everyone is sitting around and they begin singing a bhajan. Come on, listen and then sing. So the child begins to sing. In this manner his ear has been absorbing the sounds for the past six or seven years. So by the time he is ten, he is ready and prepared. His ear is attuned and trained to sur. And then when his hand is set, he needs to be instructed only two or three times. Not like us who have to be told 10 or 15 times. The crucial difference is that they have a strong pick-up power.

Bhagvan: *Turning to Regula:* So, is my method of instruction correct?

Regula: *Amazed:* Are you asking me? You are the guru, the master!

Bhagvan: No, no. You have listened to a lot (of musicians). What do you think about what I have taught?

Regula: I admire your teaching. *To Archana*: And when you play alone?

Becoming a Player

Archana: I play according to my style. I pay careful attention to the way Chacha plays. When we are picking up a raga, we will practice it at least for 15, 20, 30 days. For a whole month sometimes. Till I have it strongly memorized. Till I understand its nature completely. Only then will I feel free to add a bit here and a bit there. I don't add too much. I try to play like Chacha does and just add a few little things.

Regula: Do you make her play by herself?

Bhagvan: Yes. She has played alone on stage too. I have got her to play on the television too.

Archana: I have a television recording.

Regula: *Interest sparked.* Really?

Archana: *Coyly:* Yes.

Bhagvan: I had to make her play within the metric cycle of the tabla (*theke se*).

Archana: And two or three performances on the stage, too. I went for a competition too, the youth category at the Sangeet Natak Akademi (State Music and Dance Academy). I got second position. There were ten ragas to be fulfilled. Puriya dhanashri, bhairav, *kalyan*, yaman, *todi*, all of these. When I sit to play in the mornings, I play bhairav. If I practice in the afternoons, then it's todi. And puriya dhanashri in the evenings. So I have been playing all these varieties. Any time I play whatever Chacha is in the mood for. I don't say a word in front of him.

Regula: And you shouldn't. That is just as it should be. So when are we going to hear you play a little piece with the tabla? Should I come tomorrow morning?

Archana: I realize you have come for this. But I feel slightly scared because I am picking up the instrument after ages. So my hand is not back in shape yet. I wouldn't want to fall below my own standard, at least. I want that if there is a recording, it should not be too bad.

Shirish: *Archana's brother, who has kept in the background until now:)* She is well taught, and the other thing is that girls' hands are much better than men's. And they produce quite a good tone. And then there are not too many girls who play this instrument.

Archana/Shirish: *Together:* The only other female player is Aruna-ji (Ram Narayan's daughter, see Chapter 4).

Archana: And when there was the sarangi assembly in Bhopal, she was not here. She couldn't come from Canada. Chacha does not want me to go on the stage now. I don't want to either. I don't want to appear publicly before any audience. Because this is the age for serious practice (riyaz). And it is ideal if I get well-practiced now. Who knows later on how much time I will get to practice.

Shirish: It is a matter of encouragement. She needs someone to force her. Teach her something well and let the good results appear. Someone should tell her that she has to move forward and do well in the field. For example, this scholarship now that she has received. That has inspired her a lot. She had actually dropped out ...

Archana: I got depressed. You must know about this experience in the line of music. You have seen it yourself. So I was depressed. It was the easy and quick depression of youth. But the moment I got the slightest bit of encouragement from the Government of India, I was inspired to move forward. I was convinced that I had work to do. The world may say whatever it wants to. I have to accomplish something.

Actually, it is because of my mother that I am learning this!

Shirish: Our mother has a big hand in making us whatever we are today!

Epilogue: A Working Mother[9]

On a brief return visit five years later, I find the door to Archana's room locked, but then go upstairs to Bhagvan Das's room and find him with his sarangi playing softly. Archana and her younger brother Shirish are there with little Samarth. The toddler is lively, laughs, and when Bhagvan Das strikes up a tune he heads for the sarangi. The guru seats him on his lap and takes his little hand in his to hold the bow, playing on and smiling. Then Baba (Samarth) is asked to dance, and Bhagvan Das intones a lively synco- pated tune on the sarangi with everyone else clapping the beat for encourage- ment; the baby laughs and trips around with outstretched arms.

After this warm welcome, we talk about looking after a baby while also working and doing housework.

Archana: Since the baby I could not really practice. There is too much work; until 11 A.M. I am busy with housework, cooking. Then going to work.

Regula: You are the first woman instrumentalist/sarangi player at the UP Sangeet Natak Akademi. How do the other musicians, all men, relate to you?

Archana: The staff treats me normally, as a person. They know me from being a dance student there earlier and are therefore familiar with me. They still think of me as a child (*bachchi*), a student, and tell me how to do things. They take me along and find me a place.

Outsiders are surprised, but don't react in any extreme way. She is there, so she is there. No one gives me any special lift. People also have come to know about me since quite a bit has been published about me in the paper. And since I have a regular post ('service'), no one can do anything to me.

Regula: Who now makes decisions regarding your progress?

Archana: It's my mother who guides me. She is a double M.A., in English and in sociology. But Bhagvan Das Ji does a lot for me, even when there hasn't been any payment.

I say good bye, leaving an offering to Bhagvan Das as well as little Samarth and feeling very privileged to have seen, and perhaps had a small part in, the breaking of social limits that have been imposed on women and on economically disadvantaged people generally.

Benares: Center of Indian Culture

CHAPTER 10

Hanuman Prasad Mishra
Make Your Mark!

Introducing Hanuman Prasad Mishra

Hanuman Prasad Mishra is the doyen of Banaras sarangi players and of the Benares Gharana represented by his two sons, the world-renowned singers Rajan and Sajan Misra. First of all, he has long carried on the heritage of his famed brother, Gopal Misra, who until his death in 1972 had established a distinct style for the instrument suited to rhythmic articulation in the archaic genre of dhrupad. Second, he has trained his two sons to become the premier vocal duo of their generation under the name of Rajan Sajan Misra. Most important for the sarangi, Hanuman Prasad Misra has been the chosen guru for a number of foreign students studying his instrument. After initial training by his father, Suraj Sahayji, he became the disciple of his father's elder brother, the revered Bade (Elder) Ramdasji, a singer who imparted a strong vocal foundation to Hanuman's training on the sarangi.

Hanumanji accompanied singers all over India, but he never travelled abroad. Yet many foreign students have sought him out, some of considerable caliber, like Nicholas Magriel and Joep Bor. Despite the success of his sons and their move to Delhi, he remained in the traditional family home in Kabir Chaura, the old-established musicians' quarter of Benares, named after the famous Kabir Math, a monastery and temple for followers of Kabir, a great 16th century poet and singer of devotional Hinduism or Bhakti.[1]

For me, visiting Hanuman Prasad Misra in Benares was a musical pilgrimage to the center of North India's prime community of hereditary Hindu

Figure 27 Hanuman Prasad Mishra, performing at the Sarangi Mela, Bhopal, 1989.

*musicians whose common last name, Mishra (also Misra or Mishr) identi-
fies them as Brahmans, while their community name, Kathak, associates
them with the dance and musical representations of Lord Krishna. I had
heard much about this Benares community from its numerous musicians,
especially sarangi players, who were employed in Lucknow (see ch 9, Bhagvan Das) while their families continued to be based in Benares, living quite
closely together in a neighbourhood of singers, instrumentalists, and dancers. "Just go to Kabir Chaura," said my Lucknow Kathak colleagues, "and
you will find Hanumanji near the Kabir Math."*

*Accompanied by Saleem, I reached the impressive Kabir Math in the
evening where everyone knew the house of Gopal and Hanuman Mishra.
Located in a small lane, its outside wall was adorned with attractive painted
figures from the Hindu pantheon. Inside, a clean inner courtyard extended
to a spacious and well appointed house. Hanumanji was expecting us, having been informed of my visit by his relatives in Lucknow who had shared
their knowledge with me. Clearly accustomed to Westerners and interviews,*

he appreciated my connection with some of his Western disciples, especially Nicholas Magriel whom I got to know in London that year. He appreciated my desire for recording his knowledge of the Benares sarangi and we negotiated a frame and remuneration for two days of discussion and demonstration. But he questioned whether I was really foreign, or simply from Lucknow, as suggested by my language (Urdu-Hindi instead of English) and demeanor. Connecting like insiders despite being foreign is what became the real personal link between us during these unforgettable two days.

Hanumanji created a compelling picture of his and his family's preeminent artistic identity, achieved within his kinship network of the Benares musical community, and marked by the greater identity of Benares as a center of music and of Hinduism in practice. Hanumanji showed a strong pride in his family and in his close ties with other renowned musicians within the Kathak community: He married his daughter to the son of the famous tabla player Sharda Sahai whose house is next door. And while his family does not practice or teach dance, his son Rajan is married to the daughter of the legendary master of Kathak dance, Briju Maharaj (Maharaj is the standard form of address for a master of Kathak).

Locality, from house to neighbourhood, became real the next morning, when Hanumanji, together with his young grandson, took me up to the roof terrace of his house, past the family quarters on the second floor and past the fragrance of frying fennel seed from the kitchen where his daughter and daughter-in-law were preparing lunch. But first he introduced me to his wife as "the ruler of the house." The view from the terrace revealed a panorama of roof terraces in this closely knit neighborhood. Hanumanji pointed out two more houses he owns just across the Kabir Temple and also mentioned land which the family still owns in his ancestral village. Across the other side of the terrace a deep male voice resounded in an ascending scale of powerful vibrato patterns. Seated on the adjacent roof terrace, a corpulent older man was intoning Todi, a raga that perfectly matched the morning time, while a young boy was massaging his back with oil that glistened in the sun. Hanumanji's grandson explained that this was a maternal relative doing his daily vocal practice.

I had asked Hanumanji to demonstrate his performance style and play something for my video camera. To use the natural light for the camera, the terrace was transformed into a sitting space for Hanumanji and now his smooth-sounding sarangi took over from the next roof terrace, filling the air with another morning raga. Discussing his performance, he conveyed a strong sense of a distinct "Benares style" represented by his sarangi playing, and contrasting with the playing style of the Muslim community of sarangi players whom he referred to collectively as Khan Sahib, their common form of address (Khan=chief). Above all, he took pride in his two sons' pre-emi-

nence as vocal artists, even though this meant the likely demise of his family's instrumental lineage, since both Rajan and Sajan had become the voice of Benares as singers, not sarangi players.

Spread Your Fame by Staying Home

For our first conversation, Hanumanji took us through the veranda into the music room. A large wooden sitting platform took up much of the room, with a sofa and chairs in a row facing it. Pictures of deities and musicians adorned the walls, most striking among them a hugely enlarged portrait photo of Hanumanji's famous brother, the late Gopal Misra, adorned with a garland. He seated himself on the platform, the image of his brother towering above. As we were getting acquainted,

Also present is a young boy introduced as Sharad, a student and neighbor's son. He calls Hanuman Prasad 'uncle' and has just announced a letter from abroad.

An 'Artist Colony'

Hanuman: There was a letter this morning? Go, boy, and get that letter. That disciple of mine who lives in England, he sends me letters. At this time I teach an American disciple who lives in Delhi, and this boy Sharad learns from me. Sharda Sahai (a famous tabla player) is his uncle. He lives next door. In fact, you may consider this neighborhood to be an 'artist colony.' Many 'artists'—Kishan Maharaj, Uday Maharaj—live here.

Regula: So you and Sharda Sahai are related!

Hanuman: No, we just live in the same neighborhood. We belong to the same *bradri* (community). Sharda Sahai lives just next to us; it is like the same house. There is interaction, dialogue; the children call me '*chacha, chacha.*' ('paternal uncle,' i.e., father's brother.)

I was born in a family (*ghar*) of artists. My grandfather, great grandfather, and father all were sarangi players. They were very good at playing the sarangi. They were 'first class' artists of their time. Then Gopal and I came onto the scene. Gopal and I served the people with sarangi as much as we could. From 5 years to 20 years we studied singing. And along with singing we learned to play sarangi. Our father was a hard taskmaster. All the time he used to push us to practice sarangi. We did not go to films, exhibitions, nor play any games until age 20!

After my father's death, my senior uncle Ram Dasji, became my Guruji. Look, this is my father's sarangi. And that is my Guruji's photograph. Bade Ramdas Ji. And this is my father's photograph.

Regula: So you did not learn from your maternal uncle or grandfather? No one from your mother's side?

Hanuman: I learned from my father and then from Bade Ramdas Ji, who is also a relative on my father's side. Many ragas and talas I learned from him. He taught me the fine differences between different ragas and between rhythmic cycles. He taught me a large number of ragas. I can explain ragas in detail, if I get the chance—how many kinds of raga *shri* there are, how many kinds of *nat* and how many of *bilawal*. Shri Ramji, our guru, taught us about all these things. He was a great singer as well. A champion of India. He lives in the house next door.

Regula: So have any of your sons learned the sarangi?

Hanuman: I have two sons, Rajan and Sajan. I made them both into singers. Sarangi is a really outdated instrument. But it is absolutely unique, really "first class." There is no better instrument than this in instrumental music, I tell you. But there should be someone to play it well. After all, sarangi means *sau rangi*—hued in a hundred colors. You can play music of any color you want on this instrument. You can play *alap, jor, jhala* styles; you can play *thumri, khayal, dadra, ghazal,* and *geet* genres. Listen, there is no song in this world that you cannot draw out from the sarangi. Only, the player should be skilled! Do you get my point? That is the thing: you have to have skill. You need a lot of hard work; it is a very cerebral instrument. At this moment I am running in my 72nd year, and still working on it.

Regula: Really?

Hanuman: Absolutely. So you understand me! Your Hindi is really good; that pleases me a lot. I have a disciple, Mike, who also came from Canada—or was it Holland, where Joep is from? The first time he came to study with me for two months and left. And now he is here again; he comes on Wednesdays.

People build their fame by going abroad. I became famous abroad while sitting at home—because I have trained students who live all over the world: in Russia, France, Italy, America, England, Holland, everywhere. And a few of my students are so good that I would love to have them play sarangi for you. You understand what I am saying! I just stay at home, and those who want come and study with me. That's the way things work.

The first to come was Nicholas, then James, and Luke. Sometimes they would stay in this house, especially if they were going to be here only for a few days. Nicholas lived in my house for a year. Initially he would come here for his tuition. Then when his money ran out, he said, "Guruji, I have spent too much, I cannot stay any longer." So I told him to come and stay with us.

Regula: Did you teach Rajan and Sajan the sarangi too?

Hanuman: *Emphatically:* No. Why should I? It was singing right from the start. And see where they have reached through their singing? How much money they have made; how much they are respected. They charge 10,000 [rupees] for their performance[s] these days. And there is not a single person to pay me even 1,000. They are willing to give 5,000 to a singer at a function, but not even 1,000 to the accompanist, the sarangi player. "Five hundred, four hundred … because after all the harmonium player also has to be paid, the tabla player has to be paid…."

Regula: But for solo performances?

Hanuman: The sarangi is such a great instrument that for a solo performance, we charge 2,000, 4,000. Now I am going to Jhansi, where I will give a "program," a solo performance! And in Bhopal, when they had the Festival of Musical Instruments (Vadhya-Vrindh), there were about 30 instrumentalists. That festival had three or four workshops, and all the artists had a chance to perform. I played on the last day (when the most renowned performers are featured). They sent me a huge cutting and a photograph, because the sarangi was judged to be the winner. Knowledgeable people were in charge! And in Gwalior, too, there are experts; they put on a very good event. It is on the 7th and 8th this time, isn't that so, Sharad? They have set my performance on the last day. So I'll leave on the 6th, reach there on the 7th, rest for the day in Gwalior and meet the artists there. We'll converse about things. After my program on the 8th I'll leave for Delhi.

Regula: What will you play?

Hanuman: Depends on the mood of the moment ... the time, the atmosphere. You have to take everything into consideration. For example: time, if it is night. Say I am asked to play at 12 in the night, then I cannot determine beforehand what I will play. I will have to play something that is appropriate for that hour. Only then will I earn the respect due to a real master, someone who is knowledgeable about the appropriate time for all ragas. But if I begin playing something that is appropriate only for the evening or morning, then there is no way I can maintain my reputation.

Sarangi Playing: Benares Perspectives

Regula: I am very interested in knowing how the sarangi was used in earlier times. Was it predominantly used to accompany the female voice, for example?

Hanuman: Actually, the sarangi ran its course mainly as an accompanist's instrument, which is why it came to be completely devalued. In ancient times, there was a *mahatma*, (spiritual master, literally "great soul"), called Jogiraj. He was a king but became an ascetic. He began singing *bhajans* on the sarangi. Ravan, the great achiever, created the sarangi.

Saleem: Ravan in the Ramayana?

Hanuman: The king of Lanka (Sri Lanka)—haven't you heard of him? He was meditating on Mount Kailash, to convince Lord Shankar (Lord Shiva) that he should remove his abode from Kailash to Ravan's territory. Now it so happened that there was an old dry palm gourd hanging on a tree. When a bird brushed against it in flight, a sound emerged. Ravan was an extremely intelligent man. He had been meditating with folded hands at Sundari jal, a place ten miles beyond Nepal in the Himalayas. He brought the palm gourd down and tried to produce sound by running a little cane over it. And that is how, in appeasing Lord Shankar (Shiva), the sarangi was created.

Initially, the sarangi used to be a tiny instrument, with three or four strings strung over it. You might have seen the wandering mendicants who tour about carrying a sling bag around their necks, begging for alms. The sarangi became a convenient instrument for them to carry around and sing their bhajans on, whereby they could eke out a living. Just fling it round your neck and sing on. Music (*sangit*), as you know, is for us mainly a means of singing to the Lord, but after that need has been met, it also helps us for our upkeep, to fill our stomachs. Whatever lies within your means you could donate to the singers. And so, ages passed. Seekers (*sadhak*), who had no connection with worldly matters or material aspirations, roamed around singing hymns to the gods, earning a livelihood, filling their stomachs somehow, maintaining even their spiritual guides in the bargain.

Regula: So that is how the sarangi evolved?

Hanuman: The sarangi was tied to the singer's body, and in this way the sarangi reached our family. The fact is that we were singers to begin with. My ancestors would sing in the *dhrupadgah* (where *dhrupad* hymns were performed), and they had jobs in princely states. And then my great-grandfathers lost their hearts to the sarangi. The pleasure that a sarangi can give to a singer is unparalleled. So that was when the sarangi earned its first fame. There was no TV in those days, no radio, nor any records. They used to have *mahfils* (private concerts) in those days; "functions" were organized for weddings. Artists were called to perform at these functions. And that is how my ancestors earned fame during such occasions. In Calcutta, in Delhi—after all, these were cities, and so their art became specialized through such intimate gatherings.

Regula: Did you perform at such functions in the old days?

Hanuman: Yes, we would perform at mahfils. Brother, you need money at all times. We had to earn a living in whatever way we could. When we had adopted this as our profession, then whether we played in salon gatherings, on the stage, or on the radio or TV, we were concerned only with the money. But we certainly did not take to singing on the sidewalk, nor did we play the sarangi roaming from one street to another *laughs*.

Regula: *Laughs too.* Naturally. You performed for good listeners.

Hanuman: I will tell you an interesting story. Once, when Nicholas had left Benares, he came back in just two months. He would keep on returning periodically. But this time he came back very quickly. Now when these Western students go back, they do not shirk from any kind of work. They can feed themselves through any kind of work. In India we are full of shame about things like that. And there they work in hotels, even wash plates, or mow gardens. Whatever they do, it has to be work. They are only concerned with the dollars. So then I said, "How come you came back so soon, son?" He answered, "Guruji, this time I made 50,000 rupees." So I asked, "How so?" The boy began saying, "Guruji, in the park, the parks that they have at all the four corners of our England. So I stood there and tied the sarangi to my waist and began practicing. And I would keep my hat in front of me. As people passed by while I was practicing, they would stand there for a minute or two, and drop a dollar or two, or five dollars. And so my hat would fill up every day. And then you see, I would end up with $100 or $200 every day. I did this for two whole months, Guruji. I made so much money that in Indian currency it was 50,000 rupees. That's how I came back to you." If I told you everything about Nicholas, it would fill a book.

Should I tell you another story? Nicholas kept on going to England and returning to study with me. About 88 miles from here, there is a new colony, Nagwa, on the banks of Ganga ji (River Ganges). It is a very deserted spot and there is a monastery there. Mahatmas lived there. So he began to live there. So one day I told him, "So, Nicholas, show us where you live. Where is it?" He said, "Guruji, come any time." "Okay, we'll come, *bhai*." So, with four or five friends of ours we decided to go. It would be like a picnic, and we would visit him as well. Peas were out those days, so we bought some. Loaded with stuff, we landed up at his house. His 'lady' made *pakoras*. Nicholas bought some sweets. And we brought this dish made of peas; we made that. And then we had a grand time eating and drinking. Then we made some music, singing and playing. And then I said, "So you like the peace and quiet, Nicholas. Just the fields ahead and the holy Ganges below. This place is absolutely still." I advised him, "Son, you don't know Benares as yet. There are lots of ruffians around. If they arrive, what will you do? Do you keep any pistols?" "No Guruji, nothing. If they come, I'll just hit them with my sarangi bow."

Regula: Just now you were saying that the sarangi used to be a very small instrument.

Hanuman: Yes. There are sarangis with as few as five strings too. They are carried on the chest, or even tucked in the armpit. And as time went on, as knowledgeable people improved upon the instrument, the sarangi became better and better. Now what is this *sarod*? It is a matter of class. In Afghanistan, they dance around with small sarods and sing along. Understood? And from that, the instrument spread and gained renown. And now there are such excellent players of the sarod; even highly placed people have started playing it.

Regula: Now, some people say that in the old times the sarangi was not played along with singers of khayal. They believe that it was played more with dance music.

Hanuman: To the contrary, it is now that the sarangi is not allowed to accompany singing artists. They want the instrument to remain inside their throats, that is what singers of today believe. Earlier there would be such accomplished singers who would refuse to sing without the sarangi: Pandit Omkarnath Ji, Fayyaz Khan, Ghulam Ali Khan, Bhayya Sahib Poonchwale. Is there a singer of the past with whom I have not played? They were the real masters, accomplished artists. They would keep singing and then pause for a rest, and then the sarangi players were given space to perform on their own too.

Those who sing dhrupad and *dhamal*, we sarangi players were sometimes at war with them, but I tried to beat them through my *sur* (musical tones). A district collector (high government official) who was very pleased with my performance, he said: "Kishan Maharaj (the famous tabla player), keeps rifle bullets and a gun with him, so why don't you also keep these things? After all, you are a famous sarangi player." I replied that I have a rifle and gun for which I do not need a license. I have a small sarangi and a big sarangi. For me, the sarangi is everything. I use sound to defeat other musicians—do I need bullets? Am I a hunter who hunts wildlife? You understand my meaning! We are simple folks who stay at home in peace and pursue our music, day and night.

But now the situation is such that we are forced to be only accompanists. And that is what caused the complete destruction of this art. Through accompaniment, its value plummeted. The money became less and less, and people became convinced that it was the singer who was the primary artist. The fact is that the way a sarangi can 'follow' a singer's voice; no other instrument in the world can. No instrument; neither the harmonium nor the *sitar*.

Does the sitar have such versatility? Whatever the singer does, all the sitar can do is dir dir, dar dar (plectrum stroke syllables). How can a sarod player create an ornamental turn? How can a harmonium do a slide? *Passionately:* Isn't this true? That is why I say that the sarangi is a very great instrument. But as great as it was, the masters of the instrument have given up on it and have guided their progeny to follow other roads, toward more lucrative means of livelihood.

Regula: Yes, they are putting an end to the sarangi.

Hanuman: Of course they are putting an end to it, when there is no money in it, no 'value,' and no employment in this line. Whatever 'service' you might get is restricted to accompanying dance. "Yes, maharaj (term of address for dancers), just play the *lehra* (cyclical time-keeping tune)."

Regula: Yes, I have noticed in the music colleges in India that the emphasis is on the lehra.

Hanuman: Yes, wherever there is dance, you will get the sarangi. Because the harmonium players cannot create enough appropriate music to fit the dances. And the sarangi's bowing is much more rhythmic.

Regula: I have heard that in the music college in Benares, there are no positions for the sarangi.

Hanuman: Take Benares University. I wrote to Pandid Onkarnath Ji repeatedly when he was the principal. Then when the next person came, Deodhar, I asked him to engage a sarangi player. Then the people now: Prem Lata Sharma. Yes, they all respect me, appreciate my contribution, invite me to functions. But I charge my fee from them as well. I won't let anyone get by without that. I told them, look, you fellows earn 2000 rupees a month, so for the one program that I get in a year, I need to be paid something. After all, I have to make a living too. They plead that they are heading schools or colleges. So I tell them, then you too should not be earning the salary that you do. Why don't you use the same logic for yourselves, that schools and colleges cannot afford to pay too much and take a cut in your paycheck? Say that you will take home only 1000 or 500 rupees. Then I will accept your argument and understand that you truly serve the college and have its best interests at heart. So this is what happens. And then, the principals do not stay long enough to finish their tenure of three years. One year, two years and they are transferred.

Regula: So would you conclude that the sarangi was used mostly as an accompanying instrument with dances, like kathak, or with songs in temples?

Hanuman: The fact is that in earlier times we didn't have that thing, the harmonium, so the sarangi would play with all the dance compositions and with the singers. In the temples as well, the sarangi would be played with the bhajans (devotional hymns) and *kirtans* (chants). In Bombay there are still a number of temples where sarangi playing is still done. I also have a disciple in Brindavan, the region of Krishna. He really plays well and is a prominent exponent of Ras Lila, the devotional music for Krishna celebrations. He is associated with the radio station there. And when he comes, I teach him.

Whoever comes here to learn, I teach him. But I don't go to other people's houses to provide instruction.

Regula: We'll come here as well then tomorrow.

Hanuman: You are coming to conduct an interview. Are you coming to learn music? *Laughs, then turns toward the guests:* And you people are not even drinking tea, that is another great problem.

Regula: We had tea just before we came.

Hanuman: Have something. I will ask them to make some savory snacks, some sweets. *Instructing a boy:* Go ask them to make some tea. We have gas to cook; it will take only a few minutes. This is a matter of Indian etiquette, after all.

Saleem: You make a valid point.

Hanuman: Well, brother, if you have good people dropping in—your brothers, your guests—you have to do something. Whoever comes to meet me. *Impersonating a conscientious host:* Will you have *pan* (betel leaf) or not? Now you people from abroad don't even take betel leaf.

A child enters the room and is introduced as Rajan's son. Tea is offered.

Hanuman: No, I won't drink any tea. I just had some.

Regula: But so had we.

Hanuman: But I have a routine: one cup in the morning and one small one in the evening. That's all. Not more than this limit. There should be a limit in everything you do. That is how you see me in the shape I am at 72. My health is fine. I can play the sarangi for you for two hours at a stretch. I wake up at dawn and practice from 4 to 6 A.M. Every day. Then I have to take care of business at home, tell people to do this or that.

As the saying goes, *"Nami male nam ko, petu male pet ko"* (the famous person polishes his fame, the glutton polishes (rubs) his stomach). You get my point? Of course, one can make a living selling potatoes and eggplants. One can earn money through labor, but who knows about such people? If you are born into this world, then you should wake up at least a few people and really announce your arrival. So that is how I serve you all through my music.

Have you heard Rajan and Sajan sing? I have taught them to be first-class singers. Most important of all, the two brothers are together. If I had trained them differently, then one brother would be in Assam, the other in Bombay. They would have been on some radio station in different parts of the country if I had taught them the sarangi. Now they do everything together: live in the same house, eat meals together, sing together. If you heard them sing, you'd realize…. If you ever heard them live, you'd be really impressed. Now what more can I say in their praise, being their father after all. Very skilled, very good boys. Highly educated too; they've studied up to M.A., B.A.

Regula: Yes, I have heard that. Kanhaiya Lal told me. They both sing, while you and your brother both played the sarangi, didn't you?

Hanuman: Yes, we both played the sarangi. Now one of us is gone. One of us is left. When this one goes, the sarangi, too, will go. Look, this is my father's sarangi. And that is my guruji's photograph—Bade Ramdas Ji. And this is my father's photograph. And my brother (Gopal Misra). *He points to the hugely enlarged photograph that covers one wall of the living room.*

Regula: So did you learn to sing as well?

Hanuman: Yes, but I began sarangi in earnest at age nine.

Regula: The tabla?

Hanuman: No, the tabla is different. Sarangi and singing have a different relationship, the connection between the throat and the hands. The good player has to have deep knowledge of music. When you have internalized all the forms and rules of singing, then you will be able to accompany the songs that much better. Only one who has received parallel training in singing can be a truly excellent sarangi player. There are so many excellent sarangi players who received parallel training in singing. And all of them can sing to a certain degree. There is no sarangi player who does not have some knowledge of singing. As for myself, I can sing for you for two hours at a stretch.

About Women Musicians

Regula: But do you teach singing too?

Hanuman: Yes. So many people have come to learn from me.

Regula: Any big artists like Siddheshwari Devi of Benares?

Hanuman: No, I did not teach her. I taught others. I have accompanied them vocally, sung on the radio. What is his name, that high-caliber singer? Lakshmi Shankar. Then there is Girija Devi, Kesar Bai, Lila Bai, Gangu Bai. There is no woman singer of my generation with whom I have not sat to play. As for the others, nowadays I have decreased the number of accompaniments I do. Solo performances are another matter, though; I'll play those. The connoisseurs will listen.

Regula: So can a woman ever be a sarangi player?

Hanuman: Yes, I have a few female disciples. But they are not able to be popular.

Regula: I mean all over India?

Hanuman: Aruna, Ramnarayan's daughter.

Regula: Yes, she plays. Have women played in the past too?

Hanuman: No. In the old times, they might have played for pleasure. For, example if someone didn't have children, they might teach their wives how to play. But marriage put an end to everything. Women were not allowed to move out of the house. No one was aware of the work they were doing?

Regula: But it was possible?

Hanuman: Why wouldn't it be possible? For example, take Chote Ramdas Ji. His maternal grandfather, Thakur Prasad Ji, had only one daughter, Maina, who was brought up with a lot of love and pampering. She was taught to play as she was sitting around idle in the house. It was a hobby. She was a first-class sarangi player. She was of course never allowed to perform in public, so she never became 'popular' (i.e., famous). She would play at home, and then she got married. When she had children, all music stopped. Where could she play now? It wasn't a profession for her, after all. Since she had never played before an outsider, no one knew anything about her. We know because we are members of the family. Then her son, Chote Ramdas Ji, was born. He was a first-class singer in his time. So he never performed on the sarangi. He learned from his maternal grandfather, Thakur Prasadji, who was both a sarangi player and also a singer.

Regula: In old times, Benares was famous for its women singers and mahfils. Are they still around?

Hanuman: No, everything is finished. There is no one left. When the English (British) government was in power, it restricted those things. Forced the women to get married. Even the good ones like Girija Devi, Siddheshwari Devi. So now they perform on the radio, for films. Some of them run schools, like Girija Devi, who teaches young children.

Regula: But Benares is still famous for its community of sarangi players. What makes their music distinct?

Hanuman: It's the training! The Khan Sahibs (hereditary Muslim musicians) belong mostly to places outside Benares, you understand. So these people can only play whatever they have been taught. But the sarangi players of Benares get their training in Benares itself. The difference is that, in Benares, all four parts of vocal music are practiced, and therefore all four parts of instrumental music as well. So Benares sarangi players can play together with singers of dhrupad, they can play with dhamal too, and they can play with *tarana* (in addition to khayal that everyone plays). Sarangi players from outside Benares cannot play a single bow stroke of tarana (which is highly syllabic), because they have only practiced *tan* (legato patterns). That is the difference.

A child enters the room and is introduced as Rajan's son, Hanuman's grandson, who announces two visitors.

Hanuman: Oh what a great coincidence that you all could meet each other. *Addressing Saleem:* These are really famous people. The *shahnai* (North Indian oboe) is in their hands now. He is Bismillah Khan's son. Lives in Delhi. He has really important people as his disciples. As for the other gentleman, there is no comparable flute player today.

We exchange greetings with the visitors who represent another important musical lineage in Benares. It is time to leave; we agree to meet the next day and make sure to settle the rate of payment for next morning's music session on Hanuman's Benares rooftop.

Karachi: Center of Émigrés

CHAPTER 11

Hamid Husain

An Indian Past Remembered

Introducing Ustad Hamid Husain

Hamid Husain Khan was my first ritually bonded master teacher, and I remained his disciple to the end of his life. On an extended visit to Karachi in 1968, I became his formal disciple; our relationship ended with his death in 1979. Ustad Hamid Husain taught me with a love and dedication that I can never forget. It was both his deep knowledge and his love for music that he extended to his students. His greatest concern was to transmit that love to them and have it suffuse their music as well. Time and again I found my unthinking drive toward accomplishment, correctness, and virtuosity derailed by his simple question: but is this beautiful?

I was always struck by the repose with which he drew his bow across the string. Hamid Husain's ability to savor beautiful sound and to create it himself stayed with him through momentous changes in a life that spanned three distinct eras of rapidly changing musical environments, from the patronage of a princely state, to the nationalist expansion across Indian cities, and then to the newly settled metropolis of Karachi.

Hamid Husain grew up in unusually privileged circumstances, surrounded by the personal patronage and cultural environment of a princely court. Through his grandfather, who had spent years as a court musician in Rampur State,[1] he gained comprehensive musical training, a basic education, and exposure to the era's great musicians, which is considered the best training of all.

Figure 28 Hamid Husain, portrait, Bombay, late 1940s.

At age 14, Hamid Husain auditioned and was accepted at the newly established Delhi Radio Station, where his singing and dramatic declamation were a success before his sarangi playing was discovered. He also built and played on a new instrument from a broken violin, naming it "Hamidi." From the start, the attractive and versatile young musician enjoyed the personal patronage of the station director and twice followed him to establish new radio stations: first to Bombay in 1939 and, after India's independence in 1947, to Karachi, the first capital of Pakistan.

During his Bombay years, Hamid Husain's world expanded as he visited musical centers like Calcutta, Madras, and other cities in southern India,

Figure 29 Hamid Husain recites Regula's first shagirdi ritual, Karachi, 1965.

performing at new radio stations and gaining considerable acclaim. Remarkably, he was also invited to perform in Europe (London and the Netherlands) and the United States, where he played in New York and Washington. But his tour—and a Hollywood film project—was cut short by the upheavals in the wake of India's partition that were endangering his family in Bombay. Reluctantly, Hamid Husain decided to move to Pakistan, but only after making an emotional farewell tour to the South, perhaps in the hope of employment in a safer city.

In Karachi, musical life had to be built from scratch. Hamid Husain soon became a prominent radio artist and teacher of elite music lovers. As a teacher, he was prized for his phenomenal memorized treasure of traditional compositions and for delineating the subtle flavor of the raga, especially in the slow alap *portion of the classical genre* khayal. *On the other hand, he also improvised in a jazz group with American diplomats in 1956. I connected with Hamid Husain through a radio producer who hailed from Delhi and was soon included in his daily teaching circuit to the homes of his affluent students. Unforgettable, too, was joining the brotherhood between codisciples. All migrants from India, they hosted music evenings and joined our ustad in re-creating traditionally interactive performances of intensely shared affect. No one visited his modest home, however, nor would he have expected it.*

Broad support for music and musicians was lacking in Pakistan. Encouraged by Radio Station director, Z. A. Bukhari who was also a writer, Hamid Husain turned to writing down what he had lost in a compelling memoir of

*his musical life in pre-Independence India. And true to his courtly upbring-
ing, he dedicated the work to his patron. I am privileged to be able to present
his story in this chapter.[2]*

A Memoir from the Court of Rampur[3]

*Unlike all other voices in this book, Hamid Husain speaks here on music and
life through his own writing. Written with the aim of sharing his personal
knowledge of a rich musical life now past, this precious Urdu text was, however, not published, and the present whereabouts of the original are uncer-
tain. Including a selection of his words in this book is the beginning of what
will eventually be a complete publication; I only regret not being able to
honor his intention during his lifetime.*

*I first discovered the existence of this unusual text when I saw Hamid
Husain writing into a large and well-worn black notebook, his hand trac-
ing the words slowly and deliberately. He carried the book in an old leather
briefcase along with his daily supply of betel leaf paraphernalia.[4] A journalist had asked him to write something on Pakistani music. Then he told me
about the book: "I have written down how music was before Pakistan, in the
time of my grandfather and when I was young." He added, "I have written
a book about my musical training and experiences in India until I came to
Pakistan." He also told me that people were trying to get his book published.
I told him then that I wanted people in the West to read it one day in English,
and in the absence of copying facilities at the time, he was happy to give me
permission to make a recording of the text on tape.[5]*

*The book is really a personal memoir, but a totally unassuming one,
focused entirely on the musical priorities that constitute the essence of hereditary musicianship and its practice during the last phase of a flourishing
musical scene in undivided India. In the process, Hamid Husain emerges
as an unusually talented and appealing musician whose courtly upbringing
enabled him to find appreciative patrons everywhere, even in the uprooted
milieu of Karachi.*

My Grandfather Was a Court Musician

My maternal grandfather's name was Haider Baksh. He belonged to the
district Bilaspur, which was then part of the princely state of Rampur. In
the period of Emperor Jehangir, the players and singers who belonged to
the imperial court of Akbar the Great dispersed to different states of India.
The grandfather of my *nana* (maternal grandfather) had settled in Lucknow. He stayed there for a couple of years and then brought his entire
family to Bilaspur. He started farming, but his love for music did not desert him. He kept his treasure of knowledge close to his heart and continued

to teach his children and grandchildren. At times he was summoned by *nawabs* and rajas. He would perform for them and bring home prizes and gifts worth thousands of rupees, and he would then sit at home and live off these rewards.

When Haider Baksh's grandson—my nana—grew up and his art reached its pinnacle, he came to Rampur and became the guest of the Rampur Darbar (grand court assembly). Nawab Kalb-e-Ali Khan Sahib was ruling at that time. Nawab Sahib had occasion to listen to my grandfather's music at his *darbar*. My grandfather said when he reached Rampur, the darbar was full of singers and instrumentalists. He would tell me stories about them, and I listened to him very attentively. This is how he described his first court performance:

> The grandeur and pomp of the darbar was indescribable. It looked like the legendary Raja Inder's court. Singers and instrumentalists were wearing different and colorful clothes, and all of them were sitting in a very nice and orderly way. Some were wearing dresses made of expensive silk, glittering caps and *churidar* (tight trousers), ornaments on their wrists, and rings that had rubies as the stone. Some wore traditional coats and trousers (*achkan*, churidar) of patterned silk (*poth*), and they had tied turbans on their heads. Some were seen wearing an older style of coat (*angarkha*) in velvet, with brocade shawls draped over them and embroidered caps on their heads.

> A *sarod* player sat wearing a long velvet coat and a necklace made of rubies, and he wore a slim cap worn in such a way that half the head was left uncovered and the parting could be seen. I was wearing a pink gown that had sequins and tight green churidar trousers made of richly woven cloth and a cap that had embroidery of gold and silver threads. All were seated properly according to courtly etiquette when we heard the royal announcer say, "Your respectful attention, please! His Majesty the Shadow of God, His Highness the Exalted and Enlightened Ruler of Rampur is conveying his presence." Upon hearing the announcement, the assembled court rose in respect.

> The assembly hall was glittering with chandeliers bearing hundreds of lights. Pure white sheets were spread everywhere, covered with velvet carpets and bolsters for guests to recline on. There was fragrance everywhere. A sudden breeze was bringing with it the fragrance of henna, rose, sweet grass, and *shamamat-*

ul-amber.[6] Now the entire court assembly bowed low in reverence as if starting to bow in prayer. The nawab entered and ascended his throne. On either side of the throne two servants had peacock fans in their hands, and they were fanning him. Two servants were standing; one held a container of rose water and the other a container of betel leaf. Everyone performed three salutations and sat down respectfully.

It was then ordered that the musical performance should start. First Kalka Bande Binda Din Maharaj showed his dance.[7] He danced so beautifully that the entire hall was awestruck. His Highness bestowed 200 gold coins (*asharfi*), and the dancer bowed before offering three *salams* (salutations); then he stepped backward and sat down in his place. Next Kale Nazir Khan Sahib was summoned. He sang very well and was similarly rewarded. After him, the announcer raised his voice, calling on Ustad Hyder Baksh Bilaspur to entertain the audience with his art. As soon as I heard my name, I immediately stood up and, with a low bow, offered three salams to His Majesty. Then I sat down with my sarangi and carefully checked its tuning. Kallan Khan Nagori was to accompany me on the tabla. Taking the name of God, I started intoning raga *malkauns*. By the time my improvisation had reached the tonal center of malkauns, there was total silence in the room, and it seemed as if I was playing in a deep forest, all alone. Once I finished malkauns, people were shouting "Wah! Wah!" from all over the darbar. That made my heart pound.

His Majesty praised me and asked me to present the Hindu genre *hori dhamar.*[8] Again I stood up and offered three salams; then I sat down to play hori dhamar, starting with both parts of a composition (*antara asthayi*) in raga *hindol.* Now for this genre, Baldev accompanied me on the *pakhavaj* (barrel drum). As I started rhythmic improvisations (*boltan*) in heavy vibrato style (*gamak*), Baldev showed his hand at complex cross rhythms. I more than matched his rhythms in my raga, and soon Baldev was sweating. When I ended this section with a resounding triple cadence (*tihai*), the entire palace burst into sounds of "Wah! Wah!" Altogether I dueled with the pakhavaj for one and a half hours; then I concluded hindol, and there was much applause from all directions. I saluted the king and then raised my hands, offering salutations in all four directions. Finally His Majesty asked me to play a *tappa*. I again offered three salams and started, while Pathan Kallan Khan intoned the rhythmic cycle. After playing tappa for nearly an hour I ended my performance. His Majesty gave me 500 gold coins and said, "Haider Baksh, you have the twittering of the nightingale in your fingers." I took the pouch of money and offered three salams while retreating backward to my seat. Afterward, Khan Sahib Rahmat[9] came to sing. He was accompanied on the sarangi by the famous Badal Khan. They continued until daybreak and were given 5000 rupees. After that, His Majesty retired to the private wing of the palace.

I went back to the guest house and fell asleep. My food came from the royal kitchen. I got up when my lunch arrived, had my bath, and began eating my lunch. I was about to finish it when Furqan Sahib arrived. He said, "You really played well. Everyone has your name and your wonderful music on their lips. You have stamped your name in the hearts of the connoisseurs and musicians at court. His Majesty is very happy with you. He has retained you in his darbar on a salary of 150 rupees." I thanked him and I offered profuse thanks to my Creator.

My grandfather concluded: "I took employment at the court and started living in Rampur. A few months later I brought my entire family to live with me."

I Was Educated with Love

My mother was married to her paternal aunt's son[10] in Muradabad. When I was born, my maternal grandfather rejoiced and celebrated my birth. I was one of 14 children, but now only five are still alive: a brother and three sisters. I am the oldest brother. When I was two years old, my grandfather took me to live with him and to train me in music. My entire upbringing took place in Rampur. He pampered me and gave me the highest education in music.

My grandfather used to wake me up very early in the morning when it was still dark, and I was taught God knows how many raga compositions.[11] I learned on a small sarangi, a good instrument, probably 500 years old. This sarangi had been in the family for a long time. My grandfather would tell me about ragas, teach me the notes, and how to sing them. He would make ragas understandable to me by describing them in ways suitable to me. For example, one morning a servant boy walked into the room. My grandfather called him rag *bhairon* (bhairav) and said, "Look how he steps in at this time, because morning is the right time for him. See him place his foot as he takes the second step (of the scale), *rikhab*, with special enjoyment, and this is how the different *surs* appear one after the other in bhairon."[12]

I was educated with a lot of love and affection. If I threw any tantrum while learning a particular raga, my maternal grandfather would give me four or five rupees and say, "My dear son, keep this and memorize this khayal composition and recite it to me." I would happily take the money and learn the khayal and sing it to him. Very early in the morning, when it would still be dark, I would get up and I would memorize many compositions. At breakfast my grandfather would explain the khayal to me, and during the entire day I would play with friends singing songs and playing the sarangi. I played no other games except this game. The school and foundation of my education was my *gharana* (musical lineage).

I also did a lot of informal learning, being around musicians all the time. One musician lived next door. His name was Nanhe Sufi Khan, and he wore the garments of a devotee (*jogi*). He had so much melodiousness in his playing, you can't imagine. We shared a neem tree and its shade—and he practiced all night. As a boy I used to listen to him at night. His music moved people to tears.

Formal training tends to start between 12 to 14 years of age. Practicing for "real" is called *riyaz*. I did six years of riyaz, while some do 12 years. During riyaz you do nothing but music. Your nourishment—that is, eating, sleeping—it was all music. In this way you do about 14 hours daily of music, practicing, playing, often until you get into a transported state (*sama*). You can't stop. When dinner is ready, you think, "Just two more *tan*s," and by the time you have played them, an hour has passed. You delve deeply into the raga and you forget everything. I often would get called for dinner while I was practicing, then my meal would be brought up before me, but only four hours later would I see the food and remember to eat. I never got bored. Often I would kiss my fingers and embrace my instrument for the wonderful, great gift they are and the happiness they give. Once the practice period is over, then you start getting invitations to play. You get invited and entertained; that makes you feel good, and you practice less, eventually. Instead you sit and play with singers for hours.

My Introduction to the Darbar—20 Years Later

One day, when I was still small, I told my grandfather that I too wanted to go to see the darbar. My grandfather said, "Alright son." I accompanied him that night. Abba (grandfather) sat in the performance hall (*gunikhana*), and I began playing all around. The previous Nawab, Hamid Ali Khan, had brought an electric generator from abroad. The Nawab had electrified the entire city. The palace was brightly illuminated. Every nook and corner was lit up. Trees and branches were all lit up, and there were five trees made entirely of glass that were lit up and shone all over. It was a sight to behold. Even fountains and springs had bulbs around them. Wandering in the palace, I reached that part where His Majesty was sitting. Its illumination had to be seen to be believed. The Nawab was entertaining his guests of the day: the Maharaja of Gwalior, the Maharaja of Patiala, the Nawab of Tonk, the Maharaja of Jaipur, and the Nawab of Junagadh. The nawab sahib of Rampur was sitting surrounded by his guests, and they were busy eating. Asrar Khan Sahib, wearing a flowing velvet gown embroidered with silver thread and sequined cap, was playing music and was circulating among the guests. The sounds of his instrument were so resonant that they seemed to be oozing from the walls of the palace. The way he was moving about everywhere gave the impression that an angel had descended from paradise and filled the atmosphere with its music. Now the nawab spoke, and it seemed that a lion was roaring. The Nawab asked him to present raga *hamir*. Asrar Khan bowed in acceptance. He started to play, and the hall resounded with its music. Sometimes one could discern the lionlike voice of the Nawab among the applause of the assembled guests. Asrar Khan Sahib bowed again and saluted.

I was watching all this from a window. When dinner was over, Nawab Sahib took his guests to the main darbar, where the rest of the musicians were sitting. First on the list was Gauhar Jan from Calcutta. She had a very beautiful and resounding voice. After her was Zohra Bai Agrewali. Her singing was such that no singer had the courage to sing with her. She was the disciple of Khan Sahib Makhdum Bakhsh, who was a sarangi player of Agra. When she sang, there was pin-drop silence in the entire palace. After her, my grandfather played the sarangi, and then Wazir Khan Sahib entertained the guests (with his sarod) until dawn broke. Then everyone dispersed.

After the death of the previous Nawab, Hamid Ali Khan, his successor Raza Ali Khan had dismissed all the court's singers and musicians and given my grandfather a pension of 10,000 rupees. Only when there was an occasion to rejoice would he then call singers and musicians from outside the estate. But the Nawab still looked after his artists. My grandfather had sent me to a madrasa to learn Persian in addition to teaching me Urdu and Arabic to read the Holy Qur'an. But soon my Persian teacher's beatings left me very ill. My grandfather reported this to the Nawab, who became so angry that he had the teacher dismissed, though with a two-year salary payment.

Facing the World of Work

When I was 13 years old, my father requested that I leave my maternal grandfather to live with him. Upon hearing this, my grandfather started crying. I hugged him lovingly and tried to console him as if he were a child. I consoled him by saying that I would keep coming to visit off and on. Since he was crying so much, we stayed back for another day, and the next day we went to Muradabad. My grandfather was deeply hurt by my absence. In a short time I started loving my father and felt less and less attached to my grandfather. Slowly, my father started introducing me to his circle of friends and colleagues. They would request me to sing for them. When I used to sing and play, they encouraged me and blessed me. However, my father did not give me as much of his attention as my grandfather had. My grandfather used to teach me even during breaks or during meals. He was always giving me tips.

I had gone to Delhi for some work, and after a few days I received a telegram from my mother that grandfather had been seriously ill for some time and that he was longing to see his beloved Hamid Husain. "Please bring him along with you to Rampur." Before we even boarded the train, we got a telegram that my grandfather had died. My heart broke and I cried a lot. My whole world changed. But I had to bow my head to God's will.

I came back to stay with my father. His economic condition was not as good as my grandfather's. I was very worried and prayed to God to give me a decent job. For this purpose, I moved to Delhi and stayed with my uncle. My eldest paternal uncle, Talib Husain Sahib, used to play the sarangi, and my younger uncle Ghulam Ahmed Sahib was a tabla maestro. Both gave me a lot of affection. But my remaining education was completed under my maternal uncle Ali Jan Khan Sahib. My father and my younger uncle would take me to meet different people—for example, people who worked at the Gramophone Company.

During this time, the Delhi station of All India Radio was inaugurated. My younger uncle took me to the radio station to get me an audition. He took me to Mr. Zulfiqar Ali Bukhari, who was the station director, and to Sajjad Sarwat Niazi, who was in charge of music. I passed my audition, but he only called me for a program after quite some time. My program was a success. Since I did not have any knowledge of how to sing on the radio, I sang without any fear. In my first program I sang a *na't* (hymn in praise of Prophet Muhammad), which became very popular. After ten days I was called and told, "We are employing you as a singer. Besides singing, do you know any other work?" I gave a flat denial, thinking that they would not like my being a sarangi player and would refuse to give me the job of a singer. Niazi Sahib took me to Bukhari Sahib. Bukhari Sahib asked, "My dear son, if you are taken here as an employee, what salary will you take?" I vividly remember that I replied very proudly that I would take 50 rupees. Bukhari Sahib said, "I cannot give you this much." I replied, "Then give me leave to go." As I got up to take leave he said, "Please wait," and turning to Niazi Sahib he said, "Niazi, this boy is very clever." Turning toward me he said, "You are young. You will get 30 rupees." After a lot of arguing I relented and agreed to stay.

My colleagues were the singers Asad Ali Khan and Afzal Khan from Nagina, who now are well-known singers. I would go at 7 A.M. and return at 11 P.M. Zulfiqar Ali Bukhari's love showed me the right way to progress. He taught me the art of dialogue delivery in drama and made me deliver such dialogues that made me famous. I even got letters of praise from fans. When Bukhari Sahib was happy with my work, he would give some money to me. It was my daily routine that I would practice my sarangi after returning home and in the afternoon when nobody would be in the studio. One day I was practicing my sarangi in the studio when Niazi Sahib entered. I was unaware of his presence. He stood behind me and listened to my sarangi. Suddenly I heard a voice from behind me: "Beautiful." I was caught unaware. I turned around, got up, and quietly kept my sarangi aside. I was frightened. I said, "Sir, I do not know how to play the sarangi." He said, "How can it be?" In spite of my not wanting it, Niazi Sahib asked permission from Bukhari Sahib to put me on duty in the orchestra and also playing along with the singers. In this way I got a lot of opportunity to practice; I played all day in the studio and then practiced at home at night. My salary was increased from 30 to 35 rupees. My job was now six months old.

Inventing a New Instrument

One day I went to the Jama Masjid area[13] for a walk. I was walking, and then my eyes fell on a shop belonging to a scrap dealer. I saw a broken violin that had only its body intact. I gave four *annas*[14] to the scrap dealer and bought the violin. I came back home and put two pegs and copper wires on it. I played. There was sound, but the notes for which my soul was searching were not there. I was a bit disturbed because of this. One day, when I was roaming at Qazi Hauz, I came near a house. I went inside and could not take my mind from the notes of which I was in search. Suddenly I saw a small bottle. I placed it on the strings, sliding it to make a melody and used a plectrum to pluck the strings. The sound that came from it was so exhilarating that my mind freshened and my soul got excited. I continued playing. The music was so sonorous that I slowly started to fall asleep. I took this instrument and changed it into the shape of a *tanpura* and changed the strings from copper to some ferrous metal.

Now I started thoroughly enjoying this instrument. I loved playing. It gave me the music that I was looking for. I practiced day and night on it. I started to take it to the radio station. In afternoons, after my practice on the sarangi, I spent some time on it also. One afternoon I was sitting in the studio and practicing on this instrument. There was darkness, and I was so engrossed in its practice that I was totally unaware of my surroundings. Suddenly I heard a snoring sound near me. My hands stopped abruptly and I opened my eyes. There was light in the studio. Bukhari Sahib and Niazi Sahib were sitting on the chairs, and Baba Malang Khan and Haider Husain Khan were standing around me. As my hands stopped they said, "Don't stop; carry on; *shabash* (praise). Beautiful. How well you play." I started playing again, finishing raga *multani*, and everyone appreciated it. Bukhari Sahib got up and said: "My dear boy, tell me, what is the name of this instrument?" I said, "I have not picked any name." He replied, "I will name it after you. I will call it 'hamidi.'" On that evening after his speech, he broadcast a program of hamidi. From that very evening, hamidi with its lovely music became famous and listeners enjoyed it. I had a command over this instrument. I used to love playing this instrument, usually in slow tempo (*vilambit*) and especially the strongly rhythmic patterns (*jor*). My salary was raised to 50 rupees per month.

Hindu and Muslim Musicians: Religion and Music

In the beginning of 1939, Bukhari Sahib was transferred to establish the Bombay radio station, and he summoned me to Bombay the same year. I stayed at his residence. Here Allah Rakha—who was a disciple of Mian Qadir Baksh of Lahore—entertained me thoroughly and took me sightseeing. Most of the time I was with him. He was a great tabla player. When he played, it was like honey dripping. He treated me like a younger brother and took great care of me.

My solo recitals were broadcast from Bombay radio station. We were given a lot of time to play. I put a lot of hard work into my performances. Listeners were full of praise of my performance. This proved to be a great incentive for me. In a few months, people had started to know me. By God's grace, I was now being called to play at big music concerts and music conferences. I would play the sarangi before a crowd of 1000 people and get applause for my effort. Among those who applauded me were former musicians who were already well known in the field of music. The great khansahib Alladia Khan Sahib invited me to his house and inquired about my lineage. When I told him about my family he was very happy and blessed me. He praised me for the night's program.

I also had the opportunity to play along with Rehmat Khan. Vishnu Digambar is the disciple of Rehmat Khan Sahib, and he learnt his singing after serving his teacher with great devotion. After 30 years he sang only because he wanted me to play along with him. There was a huge audience. He sang as if he were singing 30 years ago. He sang for four hours. The four hours seemed as if only some moments had passed. I praised Khan Sahib and he said, "My dear son, I am now old. I have nothing much to give to singing. It is now your turn." His younger brother, Nanhe Khan, was also a great singer and belonged to the Mysore darbar. His disciple was Shankar Rao, who made people cry with his singing. He served Khan Sahib with sincere devotion. He cooked food for him, looked after him day and night, and in return worked hard to learn music from him.

The incomparable Ustad Fayyaz Husain, whose title was "moon (on the firmament) of music," (*aftab-e-musiqi*) used to give many concerts. When he sang alap his voice would boom. Pandit Ratanjhankar, the principal of the music school, was his disciple, as was Pandit Dilip Chand Vedi. Another disciple was the singer Swami Biswas, who served Ustad Fayyaz Husain with devotion. Swami Vallabh Das gained musical knowledge from these disciples. He was a good friend of mine. I vividly remember how at the Baroda conference he took me to the temple where not even the breath of a Muslim could reach. He invited me for tea. He very courteously asked me to sit and offered me tea he had poured himself. I said, "You should not have taken such great pains for me." He said, "Khan Sahib, this is no pain at all. You play with my teachers. It is my duty to honor you."

The Hindu community claims that music is their heritage. The ragas also belong to them because the ragas have names that are based on Hindu names. There is absolute truth in it, but all the Hindu singers and pandits have learnt their music under Muslim ustads (master teachers). In return, the Hindu students served them with much love and care as if they were their sons. The Hindu community consists of connoisseurs of music. They took music so close to their hearts that they made it a form of devotion to God. The Muslim artists have attained the status of masters. The Hindus therefore respect the Muslim masters; they showered gifts and praise on Muslim artists, and in return the Muslim masters imparted knowledge to them and accepted their praise with all humility.

Muslims did not incorporate music into their daily life because they thought that it was prohibited in their religion. But music has nothing to do with religion. Those who tried to keep music away from the lives of Muslims were those who had no love for music. They did not understand it and were narrow-minded. Since they could not sing, they said that music was prohibited in Islam. In fact, the Muslims have given birth to music. A shining example of this is the Prophet (peace be upon him), who would ask Hazrat Bilal to recite the *azan* (*adhan*, Muslim call to prayer). His azan was so melodious that people would leave their work and start thinking of God and would come running to immerse themselves in prayer. In the Hindu religion, devotional music can be heard only two times a day, but in Islam the call to prayer, which is music to the ears, can be heard five times. Music is the thing that inspires people to pray. The yearning to pray increases two- and fourfold. For example, if the imam of a masjid reads the Holy Qur'an with a certain melody, one would always like to go to that particular masjid for prayers. If reading of the Qur'an is melodious, you feel calm and relaxed. Music has played a vital role in bringing people together. Those who do not want to patronize music have made it a very low profession. On the contrary, there are some who have given respect to music and musicians. They enjoy happiness. The English say that "music is divine." If you are truly in love with music, then you will have happiness in your life.

A Rising Career Cut Short: Travels and Migration

In 1945 I was transferred to the Calcutta radio station. Haider Husain Khan, a sitarist, and Muhammad Tufail Khan, a tabla player, were there with me. I was not happy in Calcutta. No doubt the city was very beautiful. Calcutta was one of the main centers of music conferences. I became a sensation there. I performed at public concerts. All India Radio Calcutta put a ban on my performing outside the radio, but my solo sarangi recitals were broadcast on the radio for two to three hours at a stretch. Everyone stayed glued to the radio. My reputation in Calcutta grew within two months. I became very popular. Then the ban on my private concerts was lifted.

In Calcutta there is a music hall where, every year, two music conferences are held. Concerts are held for three days continuously, and top musicians and singers take part in them. I was also invited. I played the sarangi for one hour and earned applause. Here the musicians were grilled on ragas in every minute detail. When I finished my performance and was coming down from the stage, the audience applauded me. They said, "You have clarity and you play the ragas very distinctly." The All Bengal Music Association had also invited me. Muslim ustads and Hindu pandits participated in this concert. After the conference, Mr. Bose, the organizer of the conference, took us on a round of his palace. He had a collection of rare photographs of musicians and singers who played 100 years ago. He held a tea party at his palace for all the musicians and music lovers at the conference. His palace was a museum of photographs. After looking at them, one could visualize the various scenes of music at the darbars. Huge photographs adorned his wall. Also there were paintings of the darbar scene at that time. Each painting must have been about 10,000 to 15,000 rupees in value. The paintings were of nawabs, princes attired in royal dress wearing royal ornaments. They were all rare paintings. Among them were portraits of Zakiruddin, Allah Bande Khan Sahib, Bahadur Khan Sahib Binkar, Badal Khan, and of Hyder Baksh, my maternal grandfather. The photographs of the musicians and instrumentalists from the darbar of Rampur whom I have discussed have also been found extant in this palace. We musicians thoroughly enjoyed viewing this museum of a grand musical gathering.

After this conference I returned to Bombay and proceeded toward the South of India. My first stay was in Hyderabad (Dakan). Here, my sarangi performances were broadcast on the radio. And I received praise and approbation from Nawab Zahir Yar Jung Bahadur. This nawab is extremely fond of music. His Highness also knows music and is an expert in this art. He does not eat a meal without listening to music first. He has given thousands of rupees to musicians and does so repeatedly.

From Hyderabad I went to Madras. There, I took part in many concerts and celebrations. I also broadcast programs on the radio. Here I met Sultan Husain Sahib, the judge. He gave me a very fine invitation and had me play for him. He was most pleased with my playing and also invited some other artist friends of his to perform. How remarkable! When I heard these artists, I realized for the first time that truly the musical art of the Hindus must have taken birth here.

Now I went on to Mysore. The vocalists here sing their ragas with real purity. But their singing style and rhythm is quite different from our music. I got absorbed in their performances. They would invite me to their homes and would listen to me and would have me listen to their art.

Whenever I sit down to play the sarangi, I invariably shut my eyes; this is my special habit. By doing so, the light of my heart is directed toward the mercy of God. In Mysore I was playing at a concert and, as usual, I had my eyes closed. People were listening to me in peace and silence. When I opened my eyes, it seemed that all these people who were my audience looked to me like dark serpents who were swaying with their eyes closed, completely entranced by the music. Often when I finished a performance, my listeners touched my feet and said: "Ustad Sahib, hearing you has created peace in my heart." At many such performances people gave me money, saying that they wanted to offer me their service. My journey ended with stops in Tiruchirapalli, Coimbatore, and other places where I heard many more artists.

Thereafter I embarked upon a journey to foreign countries. I had settled my entire family in Bombay, and my younger brother Zahid Husain was taking care of them. Across the ocean I had stays in London, Holland, New York, Washington, Hollywood, etc. That was the time when political tensions in India were intensifying.[15] I would inquire about my family by telegram. My brother replied that political activity was heating up in Bombay. Conflict was rife, and the family might have to move away, to Hyderabad in the Deccan, within a few days. I got very upset when I heard this and felt the ground slip away from under my feet. I told my disciples that I could not stay for even a minute longer. They came to see me off on my journey back. I had performed some concerts in Europe and canceled some others. Unfortunately, I had to cancel a film project in Hollywood.

When I reached Bombay, I saw that the situation was really tense and that my family was in a state of extreme distress. I moved them to safety in Rampur and stayed back in Bombay for my work. But in a few months, some unbearable events[16] made me change my mind, and I too bid farewell to Bombay. I traveled once again to Madras, and then to Mysore. There I was invited to perform on the radio with honor. Mysore had a studio called Gazette Hall, a three-walled room with a glass partition on the fourth side. Seated in front was the maharaja surrounded by many officers and city elites. I was accompanied by a couple of tanpura and tabla players and really invested a lot of energy into my performance here, more so than in any other place before. I was feted and venerated here. When I left Mysore, a huge crowd came to bid me farewell. Their eyes were moist.

My train passed Calcutta and continued to Dacca (then East Pakistan). There I performed many a program on the sarangi. I met Bukhari Sahib again, and he invited me to join the newly established radio station in Karachi.

Bringing Music to a New World

Once I came to Karachi, I tried to popularize the art that I had acquired so painstakingly from my teachers. That quest is still on. Janab Syed Bukhari, who can be considered my patron, made me realize that I would have to learn some new ways of courtesy and literary skills in Karachi. He is not only a great admirer and patron of music and the arts, but an extremely cultured man as well. He has a refined and highly evolved sense of literature. Not only does he compose fine poetry himself, he also teaches others how to create good verses. With his dedication he has bestowed adornment on the refined body of Urdu and its poetry.

Apart from Bukhari Sahib, Janab Shahid Ahmad Dehlvi (of Delhi) has been my special patron. He is an old and respected name in literature as well. His has maintained his literary journal for the past 25 years. I have gained much from being in Shahid Sahib's company. Apart from being a benefactor, he is also a musician of high standard. Having a deep interest in music in addition to literature has raised his level of culture to the highest level. Bukhari Sahib's personality has bestowed renown to the media form of the radio. He is a man of deep insight. He has adorned Radio Pakistan with the choicest buds and flowers in its artists and performers.

By the grace of God I am now in Karachi, and this is Pakistan. If I am alive, I will in the future write about the condition of music in Karachi. I pray that the all-merciful God may make Pakistan's prosperity and progress double by day and quadruple by night. Goodbye, and long live Pakistan. "Good afternoon."

Hamid Husain
15 November 1952

Teaching Regula: Let Music Be Beautiful and Personal[17]

Every few days, the noise of a motorcycle rickshaw broke the lull of the early afternoon heat. Ustad Hamid Husain had arrived to teach me; he was making the rounds of his students' homes after finishing his duty at Radio Pakistan. Often he had his regular tabla player with him, so that we amateurs could learn to keep within the tala cycle. But his first concern was the careful teaching of ragas, not as systematized structures, but in the form of inherited compositions. To have me learn a song completely, he played the complex melody beautifully on the sarangi, but he also sang the song in his now creaky voice to make sure I learned the words. Only upon reading his memoirs did I realize that these songs were the repositories of raga melodies his grandfather had him memorize when he was a child.

Ustad Hamid Husain Khan's lessons consisted mainly of playing the music without explanation, as he had been taught himself—something that I took time to adjust to. Whether listening to his own playing or to my attempts at it, Ustad Hamid Husain savored every distinctive raga phrase, even if incompetently rendered. If he found me wanting in expressiveness, he asked for it. Like his grandfather, he was teaching me how to feel as well as play his music. He wanted his students to take his music forward in a world of change and progress, as he had taken forward the courtly music of his grandfather.

Sonic Beauty

To show the beauty of tones is the most important thing in music. And to savor it. Alap, to draw the face of the raga, is the real essence of music. After that, is it necessary to show one's own artistry? It's all right to show what you can do, but it should be done well. What's the sense in virtuosity, just running up and down the scale, aimlessly? The essence lies in bringing out the beauty of the single note, of the raga.

One day I asked Ustad Sahib how he had acquired the refined melodic ornaments and how these were to be learned. I demonstrated to identify the ornaments and he replied, "These jerky movements you are making, I don't go for them. I do my work with subtle gestures, not with big jolts. You have to practice each ornamentation for a long time, to make it finer and finer. Don't rely on writing. If you just practice only what you wrote down, the result is coarse. The main thing is to savor the sound."

Power of Music

You know, the praise, Regula, that you get for your playing and I get for my teaching, that is not the praise I want. It is very good, but that's not the real thing. What the real thing is: someone dying of heat and thirst comes to you, and you give him a glass of good cold water; their relief and gratitude (*ustad heaves a sigh of contentment and relief*), that is the real praise. Am I right? Is it a correct example? Of course, I mean praise from those who know music, not the general public. For them it is enough to show virtuosity, speed, and they break into applause (*Wah! Wah!*). But that doesn't count.

For music is nourishment for the soul. Real ecstasy comes only a few times, when you are able to touch a tone (*sur*) in such a beautiful way as to make the audience shed tears. Twice I have brought a gathering (*mahfil*) to tears with my playing. Once they were a few hundred, once more than a thousand in India. Then I myself also wept. That is possible only after very much practice, and even then it is an exceptional thing. And it does not come from running around doing passage work or playing fast, but only from savoring the slow, profound, beautiful tones you create in the alap.

Only when the heart has been really hurt can one play most beautifully. My first wife, who died in Hyderabad long ago,[18] I loved her without bounds. I met her in Bombay, and once we had such a quarrel that I left Bombay to go to Calcutta—that was before our marriage. But I was restless and unhappy all the time I was away from her, and she was too—she wrote to me from Bombay. I wrote to her. But that time in Calcutta I made people cry with my playing several times.

The sound of music has such power. You can't explain it, but it just takes you in.

Taking Music Forward

Every musician has his own style, once he is accomplished. For example, I have mine, Natthu Khan[19] his, and you can tell the difference between our playing immediately. There are certain tans which I play, and they will appear in every raga. But the raga is different. (*Hamid Husain explains further:*) The individual style stays, it is the mark of distinction; the raga varies, and the more ragas a musician knows, the more it shows his knowledge, his insight into music!

You make progress through learning. The world has made so much progress. Just think, about 50 or say 75 years ago, what was India, even what was London or any of those places in the West? Since then, so much progress has been made: paved streets, *pakka* (brick and concrete) houses, electricity, etc. Music has of course also made progress. I could do more than my teacher, and you can learn more than I.

Tragically, Hamid Husain did not live to take part in the progress of music in his new country, but his legacy lives on, now in Canada, among many enthusiastic students of his foreign disciple.

Epilogue
Memoir of an Era for the Future

This book spans an era and a generation that has shaped it. Together, the master musicians who have authored this book have shown us not an episode or an ethnographic present but a series of both, comprising the changing musical world from before Independence to the new India of an open economy. In their own words — albeit in translation and edited into a text — these hereditary masters have created an entirely personal work of awesome reach and depth. It is their memoir of an era. It is also a musical-historical canvas of the second half of the 20th century. On this canvas, these sarangi players have brought to life a musical and social world that connects them in a dynamic of mutuality, of never-ending give and take, of collaboration and competition, of retention and innovation, and much more. It is an enormously rich offering of discourse and practice, rendering separate concerns with context superfluous because context is integral to all their words, regardless of speaker. Their enactment is marked by the lived moments of music making and conversation that I was so immensely fortunate to experience and learn from.

Sharing the unprecedented impact of those moments without taking over the role of spokesperson has been my goal in this volume, so that my teachers' own words situated in their own musical world should establish a new validity for oral knowledge and a new way of representing their knowledge directly and contextually situated, as it is learned, taught, and practiced by these hereditary masters of Indian music. Access to this knowledge in published form will be a step toward according their orally based authority its rightful place within the world of musical knowledge — Indian, Western, and global.

What stands out in this oral text is the wealth of particular and individually diverse knowledge presented by each musician in an associational
rather than linear style. Though the texture of these portraits is admittedly
challenging, the shared general premises that emerge from their diversity,
with a strong message of difference from dominant (Western) notions
about music, offer invaluable personal narratives anchored in lived experience. Making the otherness of these premises understood in practice is
a central legacy of *Master Musicians of India*. Heredity is clearly central.
And if this book has succeeded in establishing heredity as the primary
source of authority for these sarangi players, then it will have also opened
up the centrality and significance of the family as the primary locus where
inherited knowledge is managed and transmitted orally. Musicality itself
is hereditary and is therefore presumed to be present in children, to be
channeled by elders, though not inflexibly so.

Hereditary families cultivate oral milieux unfettered by written can-
ons; they bypass the institutional split between theory and practice in art
music. Oral tradition is solid and shared, but it is not unchanging, and
musical authority is strict, but it is not rigid, only functional. Being rooted
in received knowledge or tradition through heredity produces self-con-
tained competence. It also creates a secure takeoff into the challenge of
change, at home as well as abroad. Furthermore, extended family ties are
not only local and intimate, they are also far flung and capable of being
mobilized to recreating the local away from home

Families, then, are the solid core for life, both musical and personal, and
filiation is the foundation for musical as well as social identity. It is in this
sense that musicality is heredity, because father to son and guru to shishya
or ustad to shagird are interchangeable concepts, not only as concepts but
also as practice. Above all, as this book shows, learning music is never
separate from family life and its practice of hospitality, acceptance, and
generosity — even extended to outsiders, foreign students included. Taken
together, these musical masters and their musical families can expand
Western-dominated understandings of the family's role, of genius, mastery,
style, and transmission, bypassing the literary, historical, and philosophical foundation of music and going directly to practice. From a global perspective, these chapters are bound to broaden the notion of the family and
its powerful role in shaping their children into master musicians who both
compose and perform, thus challenging the notion of individual genius.

Knowing and being guided by tradition is clearly central to the integrity
and survival of these masters' music. At the same time, adapting to change
in audience demand is a required skill as well; that skill has taken these
musicians from court and salon patronage to that of concert stage, broadcasting, and film, and from Indian to global audiences. The musicians in

this book form the central source for making a kind of music that has survived and evolved as a valued cultural and social practice in the spatial and temporal universe that is India or, more clinically accurate, South Asia. Their premises are also shared by other Hindustan musicians who may no longer — or never did — have a hereditary family background, and even middle-class musicians aspire to those norms, preferring to learn and gain validation from hereditary masters.

How is music learned and produced under these premises? From the very beginning of a child's life, music is taught and learned at many levels at once, much like language acquisition. Before and while basic units are practiced, named, and reproduced by repeated playing and singing, repeated listening to the family's musical experts gradually imparts larger musical units to the memory of the student. The voice is always close at hand and ready to illustrate and correct what is to be played. Music is an integral whole, a sonic environment without boundaries between singing and instruments. And all playing at home is a performance before expert listeners. A vocabulary of idioms specific to sound and musical production is shared to circumscribe and correct, providing a parallel track to direct musical demonstration. Above all, musical knowledge is built on a foundation of memory: an ocean in a cup.

Together, the book's master musicians of India have affirmed the presence of tradition, of heritage cherished and transmitted with care across the generations. What they have also taught us is an unexpected degree of flexibility toward applying this heritage in changing times. The portability of their knowledge, and their flexible orientation toward applying it is clearly predisposed to the global expansion of today, starting with Hamid Husain's jazz improvisation and Sabri Khan's early success in playing with Yehudi Menuhin. Today, however, global participation—without alienation from the local—requires more formal schooling and fluency in English, and compressing the training period for music accordingly. As it is, the model for global roaming is already in place; hereditary musicians have long been following opportunities elsewhere while the family stayed at home, raising and training the children—to assure their future, but also their parents' support in old age.

Opportunities vary between cities, however, and between musicians within a city, as the musicians in this book have taught us. Bombay and particularly Delhi—with access to government and foreign missions—are hubs for national and global touring and for a broad spectrum of patronage generally. In contrast, musicians in Lucknow and Benares cannot gain access to this circuit from home, so that government institutions remain the primary patron there. With the decline in staff artist positions in government radio and TV, and with the rapid de-indigenizing of popular music, hereditary musicians in provincial towns will be less and less able to survive on their art or provide opportunities for their children.

At the same time, a core development is taking place that has the potential of moving sarangi playing from an endangered practice to an incipient revival, thanks to the growing numbers of sons and grandsons being trained by the masters in this book. Having long ago moved out of their hometowns to Delhi and Bombay, they are now building their young disciples' careers with the help of Indian and foreign concerts to display their artistic lineage.

I am as aware as anyone can be of the contradictions, pitfalls, and shortcomings of this book project. I undertook it nevertheless because I simply had to acknowledge and showcase the masters who have given me so much. My heartfelt and undying gratitude goes to all the authors of this book; all royalties are theirs. Further information about these artists will be available on a Web site.

When I started on this book the mood in the sarangi community was entirely pessimistic, and leading institutions had held conferences to address the decline of the sarangi. Ten years later the scene has changed, and now that brilliant assembly of sarangi players will not die out. Hamid Husain, the Mahmud lineage, Bahadur Khan, and Hanuman Mishra have left us, but with Aruna, Kamal, Santosh, Archana, and now Suhail, Harsh, Sabir, and many others, the assembly is shining and will shine more, especially with women beginning to embrace the sarangi.

I conclude with an evocative *ghazal* verse of Lucknow poet Majaz that richly summarizes this renewal, including my own heady memory of drinking from the cup of music in the exalted company of masters who offered it generously:

> The splendor of Spring is all around! Oh Cupbearer, what is your worry? Your inspired assembly is not deserted: some have left, but others have come.

> Yeh rang-e-bahar-e alam hai, kya fikr hai tujh ko, ai saqi,
> Mahfil to teri suni na hui, kuchh uth bhi gaye, kuch a bhi gaye.

Glossary

A

achkan — a fitted coat buttoned in front, knee length or longer, traditionally worn in princely courts and at formal occasions

aib — seriously flawed

alankar — literally "embellishment, ornament"; ornamental pitches and clusters of pitches that distinguish one raga from another; such clusters are also practiced to increase technical fluidity

alap — the expository section in the performance of a raga, which explores the raga's distinctive melodic and phrasing parameters; alap is performed unaccompanied and unmetered; vocal styles such as khayal tend to have short alaps, while "heavier" styles like dhrupad may feature very long, extended alaps

Allah ki meherbani — with God's grace

alif be pe — the first three letters of the Urdu (Arabic Persian) alphabet, "ABC"

andaz — approach; style

ang — literally "limb"; a branch of knowledge; a style of playing or singing

angarkha — a long tunic or coat tied on one side, formal dress of 19th-century provenance

anna — a coin equal to 1/16th of a rupee (obsolete since 1975)

antara — the second half of a khayal composition, which usually moves up to sa in the upper pitch register; the *b* in an *aba* form

arohi — the ascending form of a raga's scale

asharfi — gold coin

Asr — the third of the five Islamic prayers recited in the afternoon
asthayi — the recurring section of a vocal or instrumental composition; the a in an aba form
aulad — child, offspring
avrohi — the descending form of a raga's scale
azan (adhan) — Muslim call to prayer

B

bageshri — a late-evening raga, serious and somewhat melancholy in mood, containing flatted third (ga) and seventh (ni) scale degrees that emphasize the fourth degree (ma)
bahar — a seasonal raga for the spring that shares characteristics of the kanada group of ragas — an emphasized flatted third (ga) that oscillates to its upper neighbor, the fourth degree (ma); the seventh scale degree (ni) that alternates between flatted and natural as it turns on the sixth degree (dha); several skips in scalar progression
bahlave — expansions, sequential patterns
baiji — professional singing and dancing women, many of whom live in matrilineal households and entertain (mostly men) with their music and dance performance, polite conversation, and, sometimes, sexual favors (comparable with Japanese geisha or European courtesans)
bandhan — bond
bap, bapu — (colloquial) father
barhat — literally "growth"; elaborating or expanding the raga or its composition
barkat — blessings
barhna — to expand, elaborate the raga (imperative: barho)
bas — "enough"; "that's it"
besurapan — out of tune playing or singing
bhai, bhayi — brother
bhairav, bhairon — a raga, devotional in mood, meant to be performed between the hours of 4 and 7 a.m.; it is characterized by a heptatonic, relatively stepwise scalar movement with a prominent, flatted second scale degree (re) and a flatted, oscillating sixth degree (dha)
bhairon — see bhairav
bhajan — a Hindu devotional song genre also used as light classical repertoire
bhakti — devotion

bhayya — brother (respectful)

bigha — a land measure equal to about five-eighths of an acre

Bismillah — an invocation made when beginning an important task; literally "I begin in the name of God"

bol — the mnemonic system where each stroke of the drum has a syllable attached to it, and the syllables are synonymous with the stroke itself; the syllables are known as bol

bol banao — literally "decorating the words"; expanding the phrases, words, and syllables of a vocal composition through melodic variations

boltan — in vocal music, melodic runs using the words or fragments of the words of the composition being performed; in instrumental music, articulations mimicking the words

bradri — brotherhood or community of hereditary musicians

buzurg — elder(s), ancestor(s)

C

chacha — father's (younger) brother, paternal uncle

chaiti — folk songs of Uttar Pradesh, sung in the month of Chaitra (March-April)

chandni-kedara — the most common type of the nighttime raga kedar

chandrakauns — a pentatonic raga, consisting of flatted third (ga) and sixth (dha) scale degrees, omitted second (re) and fifth (pa) degrees, and an emphasis on the fourth degree (ma) with passing use of pa in descent

chaudhri — headman of a guild profession or professional caste

chehra — literally "facial or physical features"; a sarangi's fingerboard

chilam — the clay bowl of a water pipe that holds hot coals and tobacco

chiz/cheez — literally "thing"; a vocal composition (also bandish)

chhote mote — small fry

churidar (pajama) — tight trousers gathered at the ankle (churi), worn by both men and women under various styles of upper garments

D

dada — paternal grandfather

dadra — a light classical genre, similar to thumri, but having a more prominent, jaunty rhythmic contour; dadras are usually set to either dadra (six beat) or keherva (eight beat) tala

dahi machhli — literally "yoghurt and fish," something that goes with something else very well; a good omen

dana — literally "grains," "something to be strung, as beads on a necklace"; the technical precision of a vocalist or instrumentalist, wherein each note is clearly articulated when in fast succession

dangal — competition; contest

darbar — court of king or saint

darbari — often referred to as the "king of ragas," a majestic raga of the kafi thata, meant to be played late at night and associated with the royal court (darbar) of Emperor Akbar; its characteristic pathos is brought out in the careful treatment of its ati-komal (extra-flat) third and sixth scale degrees, on which one plays slow andolan (oscillation)

Dassehra — literally the "tenth"; a North Indian Hindu festival observed on the tenth day of the new moon in the autumn month of Aashwin, during which the warrior goddess Durga is worshipped; Dassehra directly follows Navaratri, or "nine nights," the first nine days in this festival period, after which comes Divali, the Hindu Festival of Lights

dastur — custom; usage; ritual

derh-pasli — in the sarangi milieu, a "one-and-a-half rib" sarangi, a rib being the right-side extension holding a row of pegs for a separate set of resonating wire strings

desi ghi — clarified butter

dhaivat — the sixth scale degree

dhamal — also *dhamar*, a vocal genre similar to dhrupad, set to dhamar tala, consisting of 14 beats (5 + 2 + 3 + 4); its song lyrics describe the Hindu festival Holi

dhrupad — an ancient style of vocal music, predating khayal by a number of centuries, characterized by a long alap; a systematic unfolding of the raga being performed, with sparse ornamentation and lively rhythmic interplay with the percussionist

dilruba — literally "heart-ravishing"; a long-necked, square-bodied, skin-covered wooden lute played with a bow on wire strings; unlike the sarangi, the dilruba is fretted

dir dir, dar dar — the syllables denoting the plectrum strokes played on sitar and sarod

Divali — the North Indian Hindu Festival of Lights, honoring Lakshmi, the goddess of wealth and the home; Divali, one of the most important festivals in the region, is the culmination of the autumn festival season beginning with Navaratri, followed by *Dassehra*

dom — the name of a community of North Indian Muslim musicians and dancers; various communities of Hindu makers of ropes, baskets, etc.; workers at cremation places

do-maghza — literally "two-brained"; a large sarangi with an extended top piece holding pegs for extra wire strings for resonance

dhrupadgah — a shrine where dhrupad hymns are performed

drut — fast; a musical composition in fast tempo

dua — blessings; intercessory prayer

durdesha — evil plight; misery; unsteadiness

E

ehteram — respect; reverence

ektal — a Hindustani tala that consists of 12 beats divided as 2 + 2 + 2 + 2 + 2 + 2

esraj — (also israj) a long-necked, slender-waisted, skin-covered wooden lute played with a bow, similar to dilruba; esraj is most popular in the eastern region of India, particularly Bengal

F

Fajr — early predawn morning prayer, the first of the five Islamic prayers

faqir — a Sufi mendicant, sometimes also ascetic

farmaish — request

farsh — soft, sheet-covered floor space with bolsters for making music and socializing

fikr — worry

fuzul ki baten — needless, useless, redundant talk or matter

G

ga, gandhar — the third scale degree

gale ki sangat — vocal accompaniment

gamak — an ornament in performance; tonal embellishment; a technique of ornamentation characterized by a rapid shake on a pitch, whereby it subtly moves toward its adjacent pitch

gana bajana — music making; music

ganewala — a singer

gandha — the raw cotton thread, died red and yellow, used in the gandha-bandhan or shagirdi ceremony

gandha-bandhan — tying the gandha, the ceremony in which a disciple ties the special thread that ritually binds him or her to his/her guru (see also: shagirdi)

Ganga ji — respected River Ganges, a river sacred to the Hindus

Gaur — the word suggests the "land of sugar"; the district of Gaur in Bengal

gaur malhar — a very serious raga of the rainy season, to be performed with much dignity in a slow tempo; one of five types of malhar, with flat third and seventh degrees

gaur/gaud sarang — raga to be performed in the early afternoon, having a scalar progression with many turns and double backs

gawayya — a professional singer

gayaki — vocal style

gaz ka pakarna — holding the bow

gaz ka chalana — drawing the bow

ghar — house; abode; household; family

gharana — a stylistic lineage or tradition in North Indian classical music or dance; each gharana features certain unique characteristics of presentation, technique, and repertoire; many take their names from the place where their founders originated or found patronage

gharanedar — pedigreed; a member of a recognized musical lineage

ghazal — a light classical genre based on a ghazal poem; the predominant form of romantic poetry in Persian or Urdu, consisting of epigrammatic couplets following a stylized poetic meter and rhyme scheme

ghaur — deep thought; reflection; meditation

git, geet — literally "song"; in the Hindustani music context, light, melodically elaborated strophic songs in the Hindi language

gunikhana — abode of artists; performance hall

gur — cane sugar crystals

guru — spiritual, musical, or scholarly mentor

H

hamare samne — in front of us

hamare yahan — in our community

hamir — a raga somewhat similar to kedar in pitch structure but with emphasis on the sixth scale degree, performed at night

Harbhallabh Panjab Sangit Sammelan — a musicians' festival (also conference) held in Jalandhar

harmonium — a portable squeezebox reed organ, also called baja
haziri dena — offer one's respectful presence
hindol — literally "swing"; a seasonal springtime pentatonic raga, usually performed in the morning
hisab — literally "calculation"; method of doing something (e.g., sarangi players' bowing)
Holi — the boisterous Hindu spring festival during which people throw colored powder at each other, commemorating the antics of the cowherd god Krishna, his consort Radha, and their cowherdess friends the Gopis; *Hori* also refers to a lively song genre whose texts describe the same
Hori — see Holi

I

ibadat — devotion, worship
imam — a Muslim religious leader who leads prayer and holds sermons at a mosque
Isha — night after 8:30 p.m.; the prayer said at night
izzat — honor, respect

J

jaijaivanti — a romantic raga for the evening whose alternating natural and flatted seventh (ni) and third (ga) scale degrees, in addition to contrasting wide intervallic leaps and stepwise passages, give it a melancholy languor
jalbhar — a rare form of raga kedar
jankar — knowledgeable (jankari, knowledge)
jelebi — a pretzel-shaped sweet made of flour soaked in syrup and fried
jhala — the free, pulsed, rapid ostinato-based improvisation whose increasing speed reaches a climax in the performance
jhaptal — a Hindustani tala that consists of ten beats divided as 2 + 3 + 2 + 3
jinn — a supernatural spirit, sometimes a demon
jogi — a mendicant devotee
jor — in performance, the section immediately following alap, characterized by the unmetered, unaccompanied exploration of rhythmic patterns

jugalbandi — interactive duel, duet between musicians in Hindustani performance

Juma — Friday, the Muslim day of congregational prayer; the Muslim intergenerational musical competitions held on Friday by hereditary musician communities in North India

K

kafi — a light, popular afternoon raga consisting of a heptatonic pitch collection having flatted third (ga) and seventh (ni) scale degrees, often associated with the spring festival Holi

kajri — a genre of songs sung by women during the monsoon, describing the season

kaj tan — elaborated, improvised runs or passages (see *tan/taan*)

kalavant — artist; a community of hereditary performing artists in North India

karam — beneficence

kar ke batana — prove by doing; teach by doing

kasbi — one who earns or gains, specifically, a prostitute

kasht — caste, professional community

kaunsi chiz zyada mangi jati hai — the song type in greatest demand

kedar, kedara — one of the most important ragas of the kalyan thata, characterized by an emphasis on the fourth scale degree (ma), with its natural and sharp form (shudh/tivra ma) and a natural and sharp seventh degree (Ni); romantic in mood, ragas belonging to the kedar group are played at night

khanqah — a Sufi residential establishment or monastery, which includes a shrine

khatarnak — dangerous

khayal — the most common genre of North Indian classical vocal music, characterized by considerable ornamentation and, in most gharanas, a rather subdued expression of rhythm; a performance of khayal begins with a very short alap, usually followed by a bara khayal ("big" or slow composition) and, subsequently, a chhota khayal ("small" or fast composition). Much of the performance is improvised, with the bandish (compositions) functioning as refrains

kirtan — Hindu devotional chant; a devotional assembly for singing

Kotha — a courtesan's salon

kothi — literally "villa, house"; also the lower part of a sarangi's base

kunba — extended family

L

laddu — a ball-shaped sweet made of chickpea flower, ghee (clarified butter), and sugar; obligatory at weddings and other celebration rituals

lai — see laya

lai phenk di — literally "tossed the rhythm"; landing on an accent while playing

lalit — a raga of the very early morning, employing lowered second and sixth degrees and both a raised and lowered fourth degree

laya/lai — rhythm; also tempo

larant — playing or singing in a "fighting style," in which one musician (often the accompanist) tries to confuse the other in terms of either pitch or rhythm

lehra — melodic cycle played on the sarangi to accompany dance or tabla solos, most famously in raga chrandakauns

M

machhar — mosquito; also a code word for Muslims

madrasa — Muslim school at which the curriculum is primarily focused on study of the Qur'an

madhyam — the fourth scale degree

Maghrib — the west; sunset; the fourth Islamic prayer recited at sunset

mahfil — an intimate musical soirée gathering of an assembly of connoisseurs

maharaj — literally "king"; a term of address for kathak dancers

Maharathi bhavgit — the light classical song form in the Maharathi language (of Maharashtra)

malhar, mallar — literally "to remove the unclean"; a group of ragas belonging to the kafi thata, characterized by an oscillation from the fourth scale degree (Ma) to the second (Re) and performed during the monsoon season, which lasts from the middle of June to the end of September

malkauns — a pentatonic raga to be performed at night in a serious, heroic mood. Its pitch collection omits the second (re) and fifth (pa) scale degrees, while the third (ga), sixth (dha), and seventh (ni) are flatted

maloha kedar — a serious raga with a low tessitura belonging to the kedar family, most commonly performed in the evening, although some musicians consider it to be a morning raga

mamun/mama — mother's brother, maternal uncle

mand — a light raga based on the most popular tune-type of Rajasthan

marubihag — a favorite raga of sarangi players using both raised and lowered fourth degrees in its characteristic phrases

marwa — a very serious raga whose characteristic phrase omits the tonic, with emphasis on the raised fourth and lowered second degrees

Mashallah — by the grace of God

masjid — a mosque

Maula — Lord; Muslim address for God and Ali the Prophet's cousin and son-in-law

mauza — place, village, district; allotment

mian malhar — the most famous of the malhar ragas, using a natural seventh degree in ascent

mir khand — the mathematically calculated system of musical permutation-combination in developing a raga

Mirza — a Persian or Mogul title; when placed after a proper name, it usually means "prince," e.g., *Ibrahim mirza* = Prince Ibrahim; when placed before a proper name, it means "gentleman," e.g., *Mirza Ibrahim* = Mr. Ibrahim

Miyan — mister, placed after a proper name

mohalla — neighborhood; community

Mughal — Moghul, Mogul, the third of four traditional ethnic communities of South Asian Muslims represented by the Mughal dynasty

Muharram — "the sacred month," the first month of the Islamic calendar, when the martyrdom of the Prophet's grandson Husain is commemorated

mujra — a courtesan performance, usually in her salon (kotha)

mukhra — the opening part of a composition's asthayi, the recurring reference point of a composition

mulayim — soft

multani — raga named after the city of Multan, to be performed in the late afternoon; its pitch collection consists of flatted second (re) and sixth (dha) scale degrees, omitted in ascent, and a sharp fourth degree (tivra ma); it conveys a mood of quiet, loving contemplation

muqabila — competition between performers

murki — a quickly applied grace note

N

nana — material grandfather

na't — hymn in praise of Prophet Muhammad

nawab — prince; Muslim ruler of a princely state

nawaz — expert

neem — a common tree known for its bitter fruit and the medicinal and antiseptic properties of its leaves

ni, nishad/nilehat — the seventh scale degree

niyatkar — guiding principles

P

pa, pancham — the fifth scale degree

Padma Bhushan — "Petals of the Lotus"; the third highest award given by the government of India for an individual's contribution to society

Padma Shri — "Beautiful Lotus"; the fourth highest award given by the government of India (see Padma Bhushan)

paggar — turban

palta, palte — exercises that consist of sequential patterns

pakhavaj — the large, tapered barrel drum played to accompany the genres dhrupad and dhamar

pakora — a savory dumpling made of chickpea batter stuffed with potatoes or other vegetables and deep fried

pan — a neatly wrapped betel leaf containing an assortment of dried chopped areca nut, lime paste, a paste of red sap, and flakes of fragrant chewing tobacco

pandit — a highly learned (Hindu) man; honorific title for respectful Hindu male and term of address for a Hindu musician; male teacher, artist, priest

parampara — tradition, lineage

pet — literally "stomach; belly"; the bottom part of a sarangi's sound chamber

pilu — a light, popular, romantic raga generally performed in the evening with both natural and lowered third and seventh degrees; most notes of the chromatic scale can be used

piri-muridi — the Sufi bond between a spiritual guide (*pir*) and disciple (*murid*)

pita, pitaji — respected father (also *walid sahib*)

poth — patterned silk

pranam — salutation of utmost respect and obeisance

pakka — literally "ripe, cooked"; in the case of a building, one made of bricks or concrete instead of mud

puriya — raga with a peaceful but longing mood; to be performed early in the evening; its hexatonic pitch collection omits the fifth scale degree (pa), has a flatted second degree (re), a sharp fourth (tivra ma), and emphasizes the seventh (ni) and third (ga) degrees

R

rabab — a wide-necked, skin-covered, plucked lute found primarily in Afghanistan and Kashmir; the rabab is the precursor to the modern sarod

raga, rag — a generalized form of melodic practice ranging from free form improvisation to formally constrained composition. Based on a vast number of modal scales ragas are individually distinct by pitch collection, tonal centres, characteristic phrases, melodic movement, intonation and ornamentation, as well as by associations with time of day, season, and emotional state

rasm — practice; custom

re, rikhab, rishab — the second scale degree

rishtedari — kinship relation

riyaz — practice (usually musical)

rujhan — inclination

rupak — a Hindustani tala that consists of seven beats divided as 3 + 2 + 2

ryasat — princely state

S

sa, shadja — the first scale degree, tonic

sadhak — a practitioner; a devotee; an ascetic

sadhna — spiritual practice, accomplishment; to accomplish, to practice

sahib — a polite term of address for a man showing respect

salam — greeting; salutation; compliment; or parting salutation

sam — the first/concluding beat of a tala, or rhythmic cycle

sama — a transcendent state of consciousness

samajh logi — literally "you will understand"; from *samajh lena*, to understand

samvadi — the second most important pitch in a raga, usually an intervallic distance of a fourth or fifth from the *vadi*

sanad — testimonial; a certificate

sanchai — third section of a Khayal composition or improvisation

sangit or sangeet — the musical arts, including vocal and instrumental music as well as dance

santur or santoor — the hammered dulcimer of India, a wooden trapezoid-shaped box with metal strings stretched across it, played with delicate wooden sticks

sapat — literally "seven"; an octave-long stepwise musical passage straight up and down the scale

sarang — a raga representing the quiet and tender mood of the midday, to be performed at noon or in the early afternoon; its hexatonic progression omits the third (ga) and sixth (dha) scale degrees and emphasizes the fourth (ma)

sarangi — short-necked, fretless bowed lute with skin-covered body and 37 resonating strings, played by sliding fingernails along three gut strings.

sarangiya — sarangi player

Saraswati — the Hindu goddess of learning and the arts, honored by musicians as well as depicted with a vina

sarod, sarode — plucked lute instrument with a fretless metal fingerboard, its bridge resting on a taut membrane covering the resonator; the sarod has 25 strings, including 15 sympathetic strings and 6 drone strings

sargam — the pronunciation of the note names "sa, re, ga, ma, pa, dha, ni, sa," similar to Western solfège; a simple study composition that illustrates the broad parameters of a raga

sasta — cheap

service — wage employment

shabash — praise; applause

shadi-beah — wedding parties

shagird — disciple or pupil in the Muslim musical tradition

shagirdi — discipleship; the ritual of discipleship; also ustadi shagirdi

shahnai — the North Indian shawn, an oboe-like instrument

shakar dori — literally "sugar, thread"; refers to the opening recitation for the gandha-bandhan or shagirdi ceremony

shamamat-ul-amber — a famed Indian perfume

shanti — peace; quiescence

shishya — disciple or pupil in Hindu hereditary musical milieu

shri — an important raga performed in late afternoon, using a lowered second and sixth degree and a raised fourth

shubh — auspicious

shudh-kedar — the pure, original form of raga kedar

silsila — chain; series; sequence; also a Sufi lineage

sina — literally "chest"; the top part of a sarangi's sound chamber

sitar — long-necked, fretted, plucked lute with a gourd resonator

Subhan Allah — praise be to God

sukhi — content; happy
sur, swar — note; tone
sur chhorna — cutoff (of a scale or note)
sut mind — a fast portamento

T

tabla — paired set of skin-covered hand drums—one a bass drum, the other pitched
tala/tal — the rhythmic structures or patterns used in Indian music; metric cycles; tal literally means "clap"
talim — musical training, education
ta'alluqdar — in feudal India, a large landholder or owner of an estate
tan — an improvised phrase or run, often performed in fast tempo passage work, that leads back to the refrain of a piece
tang ana — to become distressed, troubled, fed up
tanpura, tambura — a long-necked lute with four to six strings that are strummed continuously in performance to provide a drone in Hindustani (and Karnatak) music
Tansen — legendary court musician of Mughal Emperor Akbar the Great
tantrakari — instrument specific
tapasya — ascetic fervor or practice
tappa — semiclassical vocal form developed in Punjab that has evolved into an intricate style characterized by quick, rhythmically accentuated melodic embellishments that generally do not move more than two steps away from the pitch they embellish
tarana — a lively song genre characterized by vocables derived from Persian and Arabic phonemes
tar gahan — string holder for a sarangi
tasir — effective
tawaif — courtesan singers and dancers (see *baiji*)
taya/tau — father's older brother, also "elder father," paternal uncle
tayyar — literally "ready"; used to describe a performer in "top shape"
that — the ten heptatonic scalar-pitch collections used as a basis for the classification of ragas: kalyan, bilval, khamaj, bhairav, purvi, marva, kafi, asavari, bhairavi, and todi.
thumri — a light classical style characterized by its somewhat looser adherence to the grammar of raga and tala, with more emphasis on emotively nuanced expression of the text
tihai/tiya — a triple cadence often played or sung to end a phrase and bring it to either the beginning of the rhythmic cycle or of the composition

tilwara tala — a rhythmic cycle of 16 beats, variant of tintal
tintal — a Hindustani tala that consists of 16 beats divided as 4 + 4 + 4 + 4
tip par atakti hai — gets stuck at the upper tonic
tivrata — intensity; ardor; excess
top — a cannon; colloquially, a "big shot"

U

Urs mela — celebration held on the death anniversary/feast day of a particular Sufi saint at his shrine
ustad — a teacher or learned man in the Muslim cultural milieu
ustadi shagirdi — see shagirdi

V

vadi — the most important pitch in a raga, tonal center
vichitra vina — Hindustani plucked stick zither, with a gourd at each end, unfretted and played by sliding a glass ball over the strings

W

Walid, walid sahib — respected father
wazan — weight; scansion

Y

yak-maghza — literally "single-brained"; in the sarangi milieu, a small sarangi lacking the extra top piece and the pegs for extra resonance strings
yaman — a raga associated with early evening and a peaceful, settled feel, using a raised fourth degree; first raga taught to beginners, usually along with raga bhairav

Z

zaban — tongue; language
zamzama — rapid oscillation of pitch
Zohr — midday prayer; the second of the five Islamic prayers

References

Abu-Lughod, L., Writing against culture, in *Recapturing Anthropology: Working in the Present*, Fox, R.G., Ed., School of American Research Press, Santa Fe, NM, 1991, pp. 137–162.

Agawu, K., The invention of "African rhythm," *J. Am. Musicological Soc.*, 48: 380–396, 1995.

Appadurai, A., *Modernity at Large: Cultural Dimensions of Globalization*, University of Minnesota Press, Minneapolis, 1996.

Asch, M., Indigenous self-determination and applied anthropology in Canada: finding a place to stand, *Anthropologica*, 43: 201–207, 2001.

Bauman, R. and Sherzer, J., Introduction, in *Explorations in the Ethnography of Speaking*, 2nd ed., Bauman, R. and Sherzer, J., Eds., Cambridge University Press, New York, 1989, pp. 6–14.

Berliner, P.F., *Thinking in Jazz: the Infinite Art of Improvisation*, University of Chicago Press, Chicago, 1993.

Bharat Bhavan, *Ayojit Rashtriya Sarangi Mela*. Bhopal: Government of Madhya Pradesh, 1989

Blum, S., Bohlman, P.V., and Neuman, D.M., *Ethnomusicology and Modern Music History*, University of Illinois Press, Urbana, 1991.

Boas, F., *Kwakiutl Ethnography*, Codere, H., Ed., University of Chicago Press, Chicago, 1966.

Bor, Joep, F. Delvoye, J. Harvey and E. te Nijenhuis, eds. *Essays on the history of North Indian music*. New Delhi: Manohar, 2007.

Bor, J., Keynote address, presented at Seminar on Sarangi (conference proceedings), Sangeet Research Academy, Bombay, 1994.

Bor, J., The Voice of the Sarangi: An Illustrated History of Bowing in India, *National Centre for Performing Arts Quarterly Journal*, 15/3, 15/4, and 16/1, 1986–1987.

Brown, R.E., The Mrdanga: a Study of Drumming in South India, Ph.D. dissertation, University of California, Los Angeles, 1965.

Buber, M., *I and Thou*, Smith, R.G., trans., Scribner, New York, 1958.

Clifford, J., On ethnographic authority, *Representations*, 1: 118–146, 1983.

Crapanzano, V., *Tuhami: Portrait of a Moroccan*, University of Chicago Press, Chicago, 1980.

Darnell, R., The shaping of artistic structures in performance: introduction, in *Explorations in the Ethnography of Speaking*, 2nd ed., Bauman, R. and Sherzer, J., Eds., Cambridge University Press, New York, 1989, pp. 311–314.

Dasasarma, A., *Musicians of India: Past and Present Gharanas of Hindustani Music and Genealogies*, Naya Prokash, Calcutta, 1993.

Dumont, J.-P., *The Headman and I: Ambiguity and Ambivalence in the Fieldworking Experience*, University of Texas Press, Austin, 1978.

Fabian, J., *Time and the Other: How Anthropology Makes Its Object*, Columbia University Press, New York, 1983.

Frisbie, C. and McAllester, D.P., *Navaho Blessingway Singer: the Autobiography of Frank Mitchell 1881–1967*, University of Arizona Press, Tucson, 1978.

Geertz, C., Epilogue, in *The Anthropology of Experience*, Turner, V.W. and Bruner, E.M., Eds., University of Illinois Press, Urbana, 1986, pp. 373–383.

Ghosh, Nikhil, *Fundamentals of Raga and Tala, with a New System of Notation*, Bombaj: Popular Prakashan, 1978.

Gitler, I., *Swing to Bop: an Oral History of the Transition of Jazz in the 1940's*, Oxford University Press, New York, 1985.

Griaule, M., *Conversations with Ogotemmeli: an Introduction to Dogon Religious Ideas*, Oxford University Press, London, 1965.

Hand, S., *The Levinas Reader*, Blackwell, Oxford, U.K., 1989.

Kippen, J., *The Tabla of Lucknow: a Cultural Analysis of a Musical Tradition*, Cambridge University Press, Cambridge, U.K., 1988.

Kumar, N., *The Artisans of Banaras: Popular Culture and Identity 1880–1986*, University of California Press, Berkeley, 1988.

Lortat-Jacob, B., *Sardinian Chronicles*, Fagan, T.L., trans., University of Chicago Press, Chicago, 1995.

Luthra, H.R., *Indian Broadcasting*, Publications Division, New Delhi, 1986.

Misra, Susheela. *Music Makers of the Bhatkhande College of Hindustani Music*. Calcutta: Sangeet Research Academy, 1985.

Nayar, S., *Bhatkhande's Contribution to Music: a Historical Perspective*, Popular Prakashan, Bombay, 1989.

Nettl, B. and Bohlman, P.V., *Comparative Musicology and the Anthropology of Music: Essays on the History of Ethnomusicology*, University of Chicago Press, Chicago, 1991.

Neuman, D.M., *The Life of Music in North India*, Wayne State University Press, Detroit, 1990.

Neuman, Daniel. "City Musicians and their Country Cousins," in *Eight urban musical cultures : tradition and change* edited by Bruno Nettl. Urbana : University of Illinois Press, 1978.

Parikh, Arvind, ed. *Seminar on Sarangi*: Conference Proceedings. Bombay, 1994.

Platts, J.T.A., *A Dictionary of Urdu, Classical Hindi and English*, Oxford University Press, London, 1930; reprint, 1970.

Powers, H.S., The Background of the South Indian Raga-System, Ph.D. dissertation, Princeton University, Princeton, NJ, 1959.

Qureshi, R.B., *Sufi Music of India and Pakistan: Sound, Context, and Meaning in Qawwali*, University of Chicago Press, Chicago, 1995.

Qureshi, R.B., Music, the state and Islam, in *South Asia: the Indian Subcontinent*, Arnold, A., Ed., Garland Encyclopedia of World Music, Vol. 5, Garland, New York, 2000, pp. 744–750.

Qureshi, R.B., "Confronting the Social: Mode of Production and the Sublime in (Indian) Art Music, " *Ethnomusicology* 44(1): 15-38, 2000.

Qureshi, R.B., *Music and Marx: Ideas, Practice, Politics*, Routledge, New York, 2002.

Rabinow, P., *Reflections on Field Work in Morocco*, University of California Press, Berkeley, 1977.

Rai, S.V., *Sarangi*, Uttar Pradesh Sangeet Natak Akademi, Lucknow, 1983.

Rice, T., *May It Fill Your Soul: Experiencing Bulgarian Music*, University of Chicago Press, Chicago, 1994.

Sahlins, M., *Islands of History*, University of Chicago Press, Chicago, 1985.

Sharar, Abdul Halim. Lucknow: *The Last Phase of an Oriental Culture*, Translated and edited by E.S. Harcourt and Fakhir Hussain. London: Paul Elek.

Shostak, M., *Nisa: the Life and Words of a Kung Woman*, Vintage, New York, 1983.

Singer, Milton *When a Great Tradition Modernizes: An anthropological approach to Indian civilization*. New York: Praeger, 1980 [1972].

Somerville, M., Life history writing: the relationship between talk and text, *Hecate*, 17: 95–109, 1991.

Sorrell, N. and Narayan, P.R., *Indian Music in Performance: a Practical Introduction*, Manchester University Press, Manchester, U.K., 1980.

Slawek, S., The classical master-disciple tradition, in *South Asia: the Indian Subcontinent*, Arnold, A., Ed., Garland Encyclopedia of World Music, Vol. 5, Garland, New York, 2000, pp. 457–467.

Spivak, G., Can the subaltern speak? in *Marxism and the Interpretation of Culture*, Nelson, C. and Grossberg, L., Eds., University of Illinois Press, Urbana, 1988, pp. 271–313.

Tedlock, D. and Mannheim, B., *The Dialogic Emergence of Culture*, University of Illinois Press, Urbana, 1995.

Tomlinson, G., The web of culture: a context for musicology, *19th-Century Music*, 7: 350–362, 1984.

Vander, J., *Songprints: the Musical Experience of Five Shoshone Women*, University of Illinois Press, Urbana, 1988.

Willard, N. Augustus, "A Treatise on the Music of India," in William Jones and N. Augustus Willard, *Music of India*, New Delhi, Vishvabharti, 2006: 1-87.

Notes

Introduction

1. Or by another senior relative; see, e.g., Ch. 1, Sabri K.; Ch. 7, Yaqub H.; Ch. 8, Bahadur K.; Ch.9, Santosh M.
2. Children can include nephews or children of other relatives.
3. For an enduringly excellent exposé on hereditary Hindustani musicians, see Neuman (1990).
4. Jazz, a third global music, differs in fundamental ways from the art music model shared by both Western and Indian musical systems, even though it shares its improvisational character with Indian music, a relationship that is yet to be further explored.
5. See Chapter 3, Sabri Khan.
6. See chapters on Hamid Husain (Chapter 11), Ram Narayan (Chapter 4), Sabri Khan (Chapters 1 to 3), Sultan Khan (Chapter 6), and Dhruba Ghosh (Chapter 5).
7. The most renowned and perhaps earliest example is the magnum opus of V.N. Bhatkhande, whose musical content was extracted from (often unacknowledged) teachers, with the aim of separating music normatively from oral tradition by creating a normative textbook version of music accessible to all (Nayar 1989; see also Chapter 7, the Mahmud Ali lineage).
8. For an overview of this issue, see Qureshi (1995); for anthropology and history, see Tomlinson (1984) and Sahlins (1985); for ethnomusicology and musicology, see Nettl and Bohlman (1991) and Blum, Bohlman, and Neuman (1991).
9. A term introduced to denote scholars whose perspective arises from being "half" from the culture they study by way of one parent or here, by way of a spouse.
10. An allusion to the universally known Indian saying: "No one sees a peacock who dances in the jungle."

11. Bhatkhande College in Lucknow is an exception, but the only known student was hereditary (see Chapter 7, Mahmud Ali lineage). Benares Hindu University has also recently created a post for a sarangi player (see Chapter 9, Bhagvan Das).
12. Sarangi players and other hereditary musicians traditionally include only men. Courtesan singers are the exception; they are not related to male musicians, nor are they acceptable marriage partners.
13. For case studies and discussion, see Neuman (1990), Kumar (1988), and Qureshi (1995).
14. This inclusiveness is reflected in Urdu/Hindi kinship terms of address: the term "father" (*abba, bap, pitaji*) may designate a father's elder brother or a father's father, often with the prefix "senior" (*bade*, e.g., *bade bap, bade abba*).
15. The contradiction between high cultural status and low social status is explored more systematically in Qureshi (2000).

Chapter 1: Sabri Khan: My Guru, a Complete Musician

1. Significantly, this constellation of an acculturated discipleship was also something already familiar to Sabri Khan, given his ongoing and far older relationship with Daniel Neuman and his wife Arundhati Sen.
2. Sabri Khan's music room, Mohalla Nyariyan, Old Delhi, August 25, 1984.
3. Wrestling was an artful sport among Muslims, with its roots in Iran.
4. In Urdu/Hindi, the eldest brother is singled out by a special term (*taya*); he traditionally takes on the leadership of the families of all brothers.
5. A polite reference to Ahmad Jan Thirakwa, the most famous mid-century tabla player who also hailed from Muradabad but taught at Bhatkhande College for many years.
6. All India Radio had a national orchestra made up of all the standard instruments of classical music, playing composed pieces essentially in unison. Ravi Shankar was its director (composer-conductor) for some years.
7. Indian notation uses letters or syllables to denote scale degrees (much like Western solfège). Each of the languages mentioned uses a different script, which Sabri Khan had to know to read the written compositions that were used in the radio orchestra.
8. Minto Road was renamed GB Road after India achieved independence.
9. A remarkable expression of the way in which musical knowledge was considered the property of its oral holder until properly bestowed upon his disciple.
10. These regional styles originated at regional courts but are today disseminated widely through individual teaching lineages. Italian court styles, or French, German, and English instrumental styles of the Baroque are perhaps appropriate analogues.
11. These are the so-called light genres.
12. Excerpt from Sabri Khan, Delhi, November 11, 1992.
13. Sabri Khan implies that studio composing, even in the radio, was a Western-style process; whether other Western instruments were involved is yet to be explored.
14. Afaq Husain was the doyen of the Lucknow *gharana* (musical lineage) of tabla playing.